Douglas Gray

Canadian

HOME BUYING

MADE EASY

The Streetsmart Guide for First-Time Home Buyers

2ND EDITION

McGraw-Hill Ryerson

Toronto   Montréal   New York   Auckland   Bogotá   Caracas
Lisbon   London   Madrid   Mexico   Milan   New Delhi   San Juan
Singapore   Sydney   Tokyo

McGraw-Hill
Ryerson Limited

A Subsidiary of The McGraw·Hill Companies

300 Water Street, Whitby, Ontario L1N 9B6
http://www.mcgrawhill.ca

CANADIAN HOME BUYING MADE EASY

ISBN: 0-07-552900-9

3 4 5 6 7 8 9 0   BBM   6 5 4 3 2 1 0 9

Printed and bound in Canada.

Care has been taken to trace ownership of copyright material contained in this text; however, the publisher will welcome any information that enables them to rectify any reference or credit for subsequent editions.

Canadian Cataloguing in Publication Data
Gray, Douglas A.
    Canadian home buying made easy

2nd ed.
Previously published under title: Home buying made easy.
Includes index.
ISBN 0-07-552900-9

1. House buying — Canada. I. Title. II. Title: Canadian Home buying made easy.

HD1379.G74 1997   643'.12'0971   C97-930242-0

Publisher: **Joan Homewood**
Editor: **Erin Moore**
Production Coordinator: **Jennifer Burnell**
Editorial Services: **Ron Edwards**
Cover Design: **Jack Steiner**
Interior Design/Composition: **Dianna Little/Bookman Typesetting Co.**
Printer: **Best Book Manufacturers**

REVIEWER PRAISE FOR BOOKS BY DOUGLAS GRAY

Making Money in Real Estate; Mortgages Made Easy; Home Buying Made Easy; Condo Buying Made Easy

"... Gray delivers the goods. It is all-Canadian, and not a retread book full of tips that are worthless north of the U.S. border. It's chock full of practical streetsmart strategies and advice, pitfalls to avoid, samples, what-to-look-out-for checklists and information sources ... the information that Gray passes along is invaluable, thorough and eminently usable ... the book has an easy style to it that is almost conversational ..."

Business in Vancouver

The Complete Canadian Small Business Guide (with Diana Gray)

"... This guide is truly a gold mine ... an admirable job ... taps into the author's extensive expertise ..."

Profit Magazine

"... I can say with absolute certainty that this guide is *the best* ... It is well organized, written in a very informative way and at the right level of detail ... The samples, checklists, glossary, and sources of other information can best be described as exemplary. Just a great piece of work ... recommended to everyone I deal with ..."

Steve Guerin, Former Project Manager, Office of Research and Innovation, Ryerson Polytechnical University, Toronto

"... Detailed, very informative, scrupulously objective as well as being written in a style that is refreshingly clear of jargon ... This one is a 'must buy' ..."

B.C. Business

Home Inc.: The Canadian Home-Based Business Guide (with Diana Gray)

"... Should be required reading for all potential home-basers ... authoritative, current and comprehensive ..."

Edmonton Journal

"... An absolute necessity for your bookshelf ... crammed with useful information ... will pay for itself in short order ..."

Victoria Times-Colonist

The Complete Canadian Franchise Guide (with Norman Friend)

"... This book tells it like it is, a realistic look at franchising and what it takes to be successful. The information provided is clear, concise, practical and easy to apply ..."

Richard B. Cunningham
President, Canadian Franchise Association and
Co-Chair, World Franchise Council

Raising Money: The Canadian Guide to Successful Business Financing (with Brian Nattrass)

"... The authors have combined their formidable talents to produce what may be *the* definitive work on raising money in the Canadian marketplace ... written in plain language, with a user-friendly question and answer format, and contains invaluable checklists, appendices and information sources ... a definite keeper for potential and practising entrepreneurs alike ..."

Canadian Business Franchise

The Canadian Snowbird Guide

"... an invaluable guide to worry-free part-time living in the U.S. ... by one of Canada's bestselling authors of business and personal finance books ..."

Globe & Mail

"... I hate to sound like a cheerleader for Gray and his *Canadian Snowbird Guide*, but RAH! RAH! RAH! regardless ... the book is a complete how-to written in his characteristically thorough style ... Gray delivers the goods right where the Snowbirds live. If you or someone close to you winters in the U.S., you should have this book ..."

Business in Vancouver

"... Gray has written a reference book, thoughtful and complete, and prepared with the authoritative research skills and knowledge of a fastidious solicitor. To this end, the *Snowbird Guide* is as practical as a sunhat on a Tampa afternoon, and that alone warrants it a place on every southbound RV's bookshelf ..."

Quill & Quire

Risk-Free Retirement: The Complete Canadian Planning Guide
(with Graham Cunningham, Tom Delaney, Les Solomon, and Dr. Des Dwyer)

"... This book is a classic ... will be invaluable for years to come ... it is arguably the most comprehensive guide to retirement planning in Canada today ..."

Vancouver Sun

BESTSELLING BOOKS AND SOFTWARE PROGRAMS BY DOUGLAS GRAY

Small Business Titles
- *Start and Run a Profitable Consulting Business*, 5th edition
- *Have You Got What It Takes?: The Entrepreneur's Complete Self-Assessment Guide*, 3rd edition
- *Marketing Your Product* (with Donald Cyr), 2nd edition
- *The Complete Canadian Small Business Guide* (with Diana Gray), 2nd edition
- *Home Inc.: The Canadian Home-Based Business Guide* (with Diana Gray), 2nd edition
- *Raising Money: The Canadian Guide to Successful Business Financing* (with Brian F. Nattrass)
- *The Complete Canadian Franchise Guide* (with Norm Friend)

Real Estate Titles
- *Making Money in Real Estate: The Canadian Residential Investment Guide*
- *Mortgages Made Easy: The Canadian Guide to Home Financing*
- *Canadian Home Buying Made Easy: The Streetsmart Guide for First-Time Home Buyers*
- *Condo Buying Made Easy: The Canadian Guide to Apartment and Townhouse Condos, Co-ops and Timeshares*, 2nd editon
- *Mortgage Payment Tables Made Easy*

Personal Finance/Retirement Planning Titles
- *Risk-Free Retirement: The Complete Canadian Planning Guide* (with Tom Delaney, Graham Cunningham, Les Solomon and Dr. Des Dwyer)
- *The Canadian Snowbird Guide: Everything You Need to Know about Living Part-time in the U.S.A. and Mexico*, 2nd edition

Software Programs (Disk/Manual/Book Albums)
- *Making Money in Real Estate* (Jointly developed by Douglas Gray, Phoenix Accrual Corporation and McGraw-Hill Ryerson Limited)

TABLE OF CONTENTS

PREFACE TO THE SECOND EDITION

It's the Canadian Dream to many, that is, owning their own home. Millions of people do. And unless they inherited the home or built it themselves, all of them went through the challenging process of finding, evaluating, deciding on, and paying for their new home.

For many people, their first home may also be their only home. But for most people, the home buying process will be repeated a number of times during the course of their lives. The vast majority of buyers are not knowledgeable experts in the field of real estate, so it is understandable that many of these transactions are accompanied by considerable anxiety and emotion.

The intended goal of this book is to replace stress and uncertainty with knowledge and confidence. Knowledge breeds confidence. In order to develop confidence, it is necessary to broaden one's knowledge and understanding of the complexities of buying residential real estate, as well as effectively dealing with the underlying emotions that are so often involved.

In the pages that follow, we'll go through the process step-by-step. You'll learn the ins and outs of finding the right home and getting the best deal. You'll also learn the secrets known by the experts and develop some insight into some of the things to look for — and look out for — when shopping for a home.

This book deals primarily with buying a house or townhouse or apartment condominium. It assumes that you are buying a home to live in, not for investment purposes as such, although your home will normally be a good investment, over time. Investment real estate involves additional concerns that are beyond the scope of this book. If you become interested in that latter aspect, refer to my book, *Making Money in Real Estate*.

There is a great deal of information in this book, but do not feel intimidated. There is always the risk of information overload. Take it one step at a time. Some technical material has been included for your information, to give you an idea of the various processes involved. However, the book has been written specifically with your needs in mind — that is, the first-time home buyer.

Canadian Home Buying Made Easy is divided into 14 chapters. Each chapter is self-contained but, of course, most are interrelated. The Table of Contents and Index have been made to be comprehensive to act as a roadmap for you. Take a look at the detailed Table of Contents before you start the book to get a flavour of what to expect.

Examples are given throughout the book to illustrate and highlight key concepts, tips or formulas. As well, there are numerous samples, checklists and tables to refer to and apply. There is a glossary to help you comprehend the jargon, as well as an Appendix with sources of further information.

In the four years since the first edition was released, there have been many changes in the real estate industry. This expanded edition, which is also completely updated and revised, includes many new topic areas to assist you. For example, using the Internet, the moving process, taking care of your home, in addition to the buyer/broker relationship, buying pre-sales and how to deduct home office expenses.

This book is written in a practical and candid fashion to maximize the benefit to you and accelerate your learning curve. It is written from the perspective of a lawyer who has practised extensively in the area of real estate for many years, personal involvement in real estate for over 30 years and feedback from readers of my columns, and questions from students in real estate seminars given nationally. As well, insights from other experts were obtained. In other words, the content is an eclectic mix of combined insights and "streetsmart" experience.

By the time you complete this guide, you will have a realistic understanding of the market, know how to save money, avoid the pitfalls, and enjoy the challenge. Once you have purchased your home, you will also have the satisfaction of knowing that you made the right decisions and negotiated the best deal.

Good luck and best wishes.

DOUGLAS GRAY
Vancouver, B.C.
July, 1997

ACKNOWLEDGEMENTS

I am grateful for the kind assistance given me by many parties, including the Canadian Real Estate Association and the Appraisal Institute of Canada. I would particularly like to thank GE Capital Mortgage Insurance Canada and Canada Mortgage and Housing Corporation for their generous assistance with information.

Many thanks to Steve Reed, C.A., of Manning Jamison, Chartered Accountants, Vancouver, British Columbia, for his review of the chapter pertaining to tax. Also, thanks to Barry Gordon of Gordon Auctioneers Realty, Kingston, Ontario, for his assistance on buying by auction.

I would like to thank the following organizations and companies for their kind assistance in providing information and educational insights from their helpful consumer publications. Much appreciation to Royal LePage, United Van Lines, Allied Van Lines, Mayflower Van Lines and North American Van Lines, the U.S. Interstate Commerce Commission Office of Compliance and Consumer Assistance, the Canadian Alarm and Security Association, the Royal Canadian Mounted Police, Amerispec Home Inspection Services, and Revenue Canada.

Thanks to the Royal Insurance Company of Canada for their kind permission to utilize material, with modifications and additions, from their excellent consumer publication developed for Canadians, called "Taking the Mystery Out of Insurance: Your Guide to Understanding Property Insurance." Also, thanks to Paul Green, corporate marketing director for his time and constructive feedback on the insurance chapter.

Last, but not least, I would also like to express my appreciation to the staff at McGraw-Hill Ryerson Limited for their patience, encouragement and insightful suggestions.

Chapter 1

WHY BUY?

The current low interest rates, the lowest in over 30 years, provide you with the opportunity to carry a mortgage for about the same rent as you are probably paying now. However, a home is not only a financial investment, but an emotional one as well. There is excitement and thrill in buying your first home, but also added responsibilities. Home ownership is not necessarily suited for everyone.

As you have just read the preface, you have a bit of an overview of what to expect from this book. This chapter will discuss wanting the dream, the advantages and disadvantages of renting vs buying and making the dream a reality.

WANTING THE DREAM

Many people have the dream of owning their own home. The psychological aspects are very strong and persuasive. A home evokes a feeling of security, pride, safety, freedom and a sense of cohesiveness. Also a sense of retreat, a sanctuary. Basically, your own castle, no matter how small that castle may be. A home also makes people feel that by entering the real estate market, they have started the first step in wealth creation and over time will enjoy an increase in value in their purchase.

A home also represents a financial challenge — to save for a downpayment and pay for the mortgage payments and other expenses that home ownership involves. However, for most people, they are willing to make the financial sacrifices that may be required to reach their dream.

There are many reasons why people want to own. Their parents owned, they are tired of an unresponsive landlord, annoyed with unfriendly or noisy neighbours or frustrated at paying rent without anything to show for it in terms of equity. Some people just want to make their own statement about their living environment and lifestyle.

Apart from the financial realities, the prospect of buying your first home should be exciting and the search for that dream home should be fun.

It would probably be helpful at this point, to cover some of the pros and cons of renting and buying to place the whole matter in perspective. Then we will cover how you can make the home buying dream a reality.

ADVANTAGES AND DISADVANTAGES OF RENTING

To assist you in making your rent vs buy decision, let's take a hard look at renting. There are several advantages:

- your monthly payments are usually somewhat lower than buying. However, in the current low interest rate environment, mortgage payments can be lower or the same as what you are paying in rent now.
- your only initial "down payment" could be a security deposit, which could be equal to 1/2 monthly rent or more, and in some cases the last month's rent. If you left the rental suite in good condition (clean and without damage, other than normal wear and tear), than you should get your security deposit back in full when you leave.
- your heat and utilities (water, electricity, etc.) costs are included in your rent in most cases. Therefore, you would not have to be concerned about costs of increased energy use (electrical heating or fuel (oil or gas)) if you had a particularly cold winter or hot summer. However, the landlord could attempt to increase your rent the following year to compensate for their extra and unexpected expenses and provide a buffer for future variable expenses.
- you don't usually have to pay for repair and maintenance costs e.g., electrical, plumbing, appliances, leaky roof or other problems. Naturally, if the problem, e.g., a broken window, was caused by your own actions, than you would be responsible for that. In actual fact, your tenant insurance would probably cover that, after you pay the deductible.

- you only need to give your landlord one clear month's notice, in most cases, or wait until the term of your lease expires. Even then, depending on your lease terms, you might need to give your landlord one month's notice that you do not intend to re-new your lease, so that the landlord can find someone to move in after you move out.

In other words, there is little financial risk involved in renting, short-term commitment on how long you decide to live there, and relative freedom from unexpected expenses.

However, there are some considerable disadvantages to renting, especially when compared to buying:

- your rent can be increased every year. There may or may not be a limit on the amount of the increase, depending on the province you live in. Some provinces have rent control legislation, others do not. In the case of mortgage payments, the amount of monthly payments stays fixed for the duration of the term of the mortgage. For example, you could select a term from six months to 10 years.
- you have nothing to show for your monthly rent payments, other than your cancelled cheques. However, for the same amount of monthly outlay or slightly more, you could be building equity (additional debt-free value) in your own home. A portion of your mortgage payments goes to reduce the principal amount of your mortgage, the rest goes towards interest. In addition, you could be increasing your equity through appreciation of the market value of your property.
- you could have an unresponsive or disagreeable landlord. For example, you could have hassles in getting things repaired in a timely fashion or at all. With your own home, you are your own landlord.
- you are a temporary resident in someone else's "home." You don't have the pride of ownership and freedom of choice to change the home to meet your tastes, needs and wants e.g., renovation, interior decorating such as wallpaper, paint, carpet, etc.

ADVANTAGES AND DISADVANTAGES OF BUYING

Now that we have covered the rental aspects, let's take an objective look at the pros and cons of buying a home. First the good news:

- **equity build-up.** Basically, the longer you own the home, the greater the equity that you build, that is, the more of the home that you actually own, after you take the mortgage debt off. As mentioned earlier, this is because a portion of all your mortgage payments goes to reducing the original amount of your mortgage debt. In realistic terms, your actual equity is what you would net upon sale, after the real estate commission and closing costs are taken into account. Lenders realize this as well, which is why they want to see that you have put some of your own money into buying the house, in terms of down payment, to reduce the lender's potential risk.

- **historically real estate has been a sound financial investment.** Over the past 20 years, the average increase in residential property values on a national basis has been approximately 10% a year. However, that figure includes the normal cyclic peaks and valleys of the real estate market.There are other factors that affect prices, such as the geographic location, condition of home, economy and interest rates, etc. These are discussed in more detail in Chapter 8. Naturally if your timing is off, that is you buy at the top of the real estate cycle and sell at the bottom, within a short time period, you are not going to realize the benefits of a long-term hold of your property. Timing is everything. However, normally your home's value will increase over time, or at least retain its value. Of course there are no guarantees. It also depends on what type of home you have. A single-family house (because it is sitting on its own land) generally appreciates higher than a townhouse condominium, which generally appreciates higher than an apartment condominium. It is the land that appreciates or goes up in value. Buildings depreciate or go down in value. However, by taking the time to read this book, you have greatly increased your chances of making the right purchase decision.

- **inflation hedge.** You are probably very aware of the concept of inflation. As a review, inflation means the increasing cost of buying a product or service. In other words, it is the decrease in your purchasing power. For example, something that cost you $5 five years ago might now be priced at $10. People on fixed incomes which are not indexed (increased) for inflation are very aware of the eroding purchasing power of the dollar. The inflation rate in Canada varies at different times and in different regions of the country, based on various factors. At

one time Canada had double-digit inflation, but currently
Canada enjoys low single-digit inflation, e.g., less than 2%.
The economic policy of the federal government is to attempt
to keep inflation at that low level.

Naturally, the appreciation of the value of property over
time includes an inflation factor. Historically, land appreciation value for residential homes has been 3 to 4% greater than
the inflation rate. However, as mentioned earlier, this can vary,
depending on a number of variables.

- **low down payment.** You can get into the real estate market
by paying as little as 5% down. The balance would be financed
through a mortgage, using the property as security. This is
called "high-ratio" financing, that is the ratio between your
debt (95%) relative to your equity (5%) is high. So if you are
buying a $100,000 home, you would have to come up with
$5,000 down payment. You would need some more money for
closing costs, as discussed later in this book.

- **leverage.** This simply means that a small amount of money
can control a much larger asset. For example, putting in a low
down payment and borrowing the rest. You would therefore
be "levering" the inherent value in the home to give as security to the mortgage company in exchange for money. This has
the added value of getting a higher return on your original
financial outlay. For example, if you put $5,000 down and bor-
row the rest and the property increased in value over 10 years
by $50,000, than you have increased your original "invest-
ment" by 10, in other words, a 1000% return on that $5,000
over that 10 year period! The interest portion of your mortgage payments would presumably be about the same as you
would be paying anyway to a landlord for rent.

- **tax advantage.** If your home goes up in value over time, from
your original purchase price, that extra value or gain is referred to as a "capital gain." In other words, a gain over your
original (capital) cost. In Canada, the government has exempted
anyone who owns a principal residence (home) from tax on
that gain. So any increase you make is tax-free. This could
create a considerable increase in your personal net worth or
wealth accumulation, as illustrated in the previous example.

- **more stable neighbourhood.** If you buy in a neighbourhood
in which most of your neighbours are also owners, this tends
to create a more stable environment, rather than the more

transient environment of a neighbourhood comprised primarily of renters. Overall, the neighbourhood will probably be cleaner, quieter, safer and friendlier.

- **increased borrowing powers.** Homeowners tend to be viewed by lenders as less risky than non-homeowners. That is because of the primary asset being the home and the financial responsibility required to maintain payments on the mortgage. As long as you regularly pay your mortgage on time, it is would be much easier to borrow money if you wanted to, on the equity in your home, as homeowners represent a safer financial risk.
- **increased freedom.** One of the key benefits of buying a home, is the psychological one. That is the feeling of freedom that you don't have as a renter. For example, the feeling of increased privacy, the ability to live the way you want and the freedom to make personal choices about many aspects of your home. Naturally, if you buy a condo, there are certain restrictions that could apply to your activities. These can vary depending on the condominium policy. This issue is discussed in more detail in Chapter 4.

Of course, there are some disadvantages to be aware of.

- you can't sell your home quickly to get the cash out. How quickly you could sell your home depends on a lot of outside variables, such as the current demand in the marketplace for homes like yours, the economy, interest rates, and where home prices are in the real estate cycle at the time. If you need cash quickly, however, you should be able to borrow against the equity in the home.
- you will need to save up enough money for a down payment. However, this can be as low as 5% for a first-time homebuyer.
- you could find that you have extra financial expenses that you had not anticipated or budgeted for. For example, unexpected or emergency repair and maintenance costs, increase in property taxes, utility costs and insurance.
- you can't move as quickly from a home as from the place that you are renting. Depending on a number of factors, it could take from two to nine months or longer to list, market, negotiate, sell, transfer title and receive your money.
- a house can require a lot of work that you were not expecting. For example, painting, mowing the lawn, fixing leaky pipes,

planting and maintaining a garden and numerous other responsibilities to maintain the house. Some people really enjoy this type of activity, others do not. If you don't, you may want to consider the advantages of starting out with a town-house or apartment condominium, as the maintenance and repair of all external matters is included in your monthly condominium maintenance fee.

As you can see, the advantages of buying a home are considerable and far outweigh the disadvantages. However, in the end, whether you buy or not is a highly personal decision which has as much to do with dreams and desire as reality. Having considered all the above, you may determine that your financial situation at this point in your life does not really justify buying. However, the pleasure you would get out of being your own landlord would more than compensate for any extra financial outlay that you might incur.

MAKING THE DREAM A REALITY

You can make your dream of buying a home a reality. Your decision to read this guide is a first pro-active step to attaining that goal.

Your first home will probably be a starter home, that is, to get into the real estate market at an affordable cost.

There are many ownership possibilities to consider. Depending on what your needs are, they dictate your search approach. For example, if you cannot afford very much down payment, you may prefer to buy a small condo. A condo could also be your choice if you don't like gardening or maintenance. If you love gardening, then you might prefer to move to the country with more land. If you dislike commuting, you may prefer to buy a house or condo near your work. If you have children or expecting to start a family, you may prefer to find a house with lots of room with a rec room and a back yard near a school, and possibly with a "mortgage helper" in a basement suite. As you can see, the reasons for people's choices in buying a home are endless and as individual as the people involved.

You want to plan each and every move you make carefully. With the information packed into this book, you should develop the self-assurance that comes from knowing what to expect and knowing that you are making the right decisions. That will make the process of attaining your home-buying dream more enjoyable. As suggested in the preface, you should review the detailed table of contents to see what topics will be covered throughout the book.

There are various criteria that should be present in deciding on the proper home purchase. You should like it and it should fulfil your present needs. You should be able to afford the home without financial stress. And the purchase of your home should make sense in terms of being a good investment. That is, getting good value for the money, with the prospect of at least keeping up with inflation, if not exceeding it considerably.

Now let's get into some home buying preliminary stages, such as determining your current financial status and budget needs, assessing your future personal needs and planning your purchase strategies. You should also do a list of personal pros and cons of buying a home at this point in time. Also, how long you intend to live in home and how you like to spend your personal time. This will all help in defining your next purchase steps.

Chapter 2
HOME-BUYING STRATEGIES AND TIPS

To buy the home that you want with a minimum of risk and frustration, you need to have clearly defined goals and objectives, and a plan for achieving them. There are various steps in the process of determining your plan. Step one is to determine your current financial status. Assessing your future personal needs is step two. And step three is planning your purchase strategies.

DETERMINING YOUR CURRENT FINANCIAL STATUS

It is important to review your financial health to establish whether you can afford to buy a home. To do this, complete Sample 2-1, "Personal Cost of Living Budget," (page 12) and Sample 2-2, "Personal Net Worth Statement." (page 14) Then complete Samples 2-3 (page 19) and 2-4 (page 20), which involves calculating your Gross Debt Service Ratio and Total Debt Service Ratio respectively. Talk to your bank. They can help you determine if you can afford to buy. Samples 2-3 and 2-4 will give you some guidelines in terms of mortgage eligibility. Keep in mind that these are guidelines only. There are exceptions, and there are other creative ways of accomplishing your financial objectives. How to determine your mortgage eligibility is discussed in detail in Chapter 6.

DETERMINING YOUR FUTURE PERSONAL NEEDS

It is important to project what your needs will be, as that will largely dictate the nature and location of your purchase. For example: How close is your home to your work? Will you need more space in the future for a growing family? What about proximity to schools, parks, or other lifestyle amenities? If you intend to have a full-time or part-time business at home, do you have space for it?

Checklist 3-1 at page 36 covers the various issues you need to consider when projecting your future real estate housing needs.

PLANNING YOUR PURCHASE STRATEGIES

There are many issues and tips to keep in mind in order to meet your goals. Here is a highlight of some key ones.

- Make sure that you can afford to buy.
- Determine the amount of mortgage you are able to carry.
- Use professionals at all times before making a commitment. Tap into their expertise for your peace of mind. This includes carefully selecting a realtor, lawyer, accountant, home inspector, appraiser and contractor, if you plan any renovations. Professionals will also help you in realistic projections.
- Get a second opinion from someone you trust who knows you personally.
- Never pay more than "fair market value."
- Always view and inspect before you buy.
- Verify all financial information.
- Don't buy largely for emotional reasons. Attempt to be as objective as possible.
- Short list the possible places you might want to purchase. Use the same comparative criteria. Refer to Checklist 3-1, " Real Estate Assessment Checklist."
- Don't rush into a purchase. Take your time. Determine your needs, goals, and resources.
- Determine whether you are going to buy with someone else and the advantages and disadvantages of that.

ADDITIONAL TIPS

In addition to the strategies above, here are some additional tips. By being aware of these tips at the outset, it should help you place the rest of the book in context. In most cases, people who avoid problems generally **do** the following:

- Have a clear understanding of their personal and financial needs.

- Have a clear focus and a realistic purchase plan, with strategies and priorities.
- Do thorough market research and comparison shopping before making the purchase.
- Select the right property considering specific personal needs, the potential risks, and money involved.
- Do financial calculations beforehand.
- Buy at a fair market price.
- Buy real estate at the right time in the market.
- Have an understanding of how the real estate market works.
- Buy within their financial debt servicing capacity, comfort zone, and skill level.
- Understand the financing game thoroughly, and comparison shop, and get the best rates, terms, and right type of mortgage.
- Make a decision based on an objective assessment but not just an emotional one.
- Determine the real reason the vendor is selling.
- Have the property inspected by a home inspector before purchase.
- Select an experienced realtor with expertise in the type of real estate and geographic location you are considering.
- Select an experienced real estate lawyer and obtain advice beforehand.
- Negotiate effectively.
- Put the appropriate conditions or "subject clauses" in the offer.
- Verify independently all financial information beforehand.
- Obtain and review all the necessary documentation appropriate for a given property (e.g. condo) before making a final decision to buy.
- Detail precisely what chattels (fridge and stove, drapes, etc.) are included in the purchase price.

* * *

You've done your financial calculations and looked at other factors, and have decided that you're ready to buy your first home. You're now ready to get started on your home-buying adventure.

SAMPLE 2-1

PERSONAL COST OF LIVING BUDGET (MONTHLY)

I. Income (Average monthly income)

Salary, bonuses, and commissions	$
Dividends	$
Interest income	$
Pension income	$
Other: _____	$
_____	$
TOTAL MONTHLY INCOME (A)	$ _34000⁰⁰_

II. Expenses

(i) Regular Monthly Payments:

Rent	$ _300_
Automobile(s)	$ _100_
Appliances/TV	$
Credit card payments (not covered elsewhere)	$
Personal loan(s)	$
Medical plan	$
Instalment and other loans	$
Life insurance premiums	$
House insurance	$
Other insurance premiums (auto, extended medical, etc.)	$
RRSP deductions	$ _200_
Pension fund (employer)	$
Investment plan(s)	$
Miscellaneous	$
Other: _GAS_	$ _175_
BILLS	$ _100_
TOTAL REGULAR MONTHLY PAYMENTS	$ _775_

(ii) Household Operating Expenses:

Telephone	$ _____
Gas and electricity	$ _____
Heat	$ _____
Water and garbage	$ _____
Other household expenses (repairs, maintenance, etc.)	$ _____
Other: _____	$ _100_
_____	$ _____

TOTAL HOUSEHOLD OPERATING EXPENSES $ _100_

(iii) Food Expenses:

At home	$ _____
Away from home	$ _____
TOTAL FOOD EXPENSES	$ _300_

(iv) Personal Expenses:

Clothing, cleaning, laundry	$ _300_
Drugs	$ _____
Transportation (other than auto)	$ _____
Medical/dental	$ _____
Day care	$ _____
Education (self)	$ _____
Education (children)	$ _____
Dues/professional fees	$ _____
Gifts, donations and dues	$ _____
Travel	$ _____
Recreation	$ _300_
Newspapers, magazines, books	$ _____
Automobile maintenance, gas and parking	$ _____
Spending money, allowances	$ _____
Other: _____	$ _____
_____	$ _____

TOTAL PERSONAL EXPENSES $ _600_

(v) Tax Expenses $ _____

III. Summary of Expenses

Regular monthly payments (i) $ _745,000_

Household operating expenses (ii) $ _100_

Food expenses (iii) $ _300_

Personal expenses (iv) $ _600_

Tax expenses (v) $ _____

TOTAL MONTHLY EXPENSES   (B) $ _1800_

TOTAL MONTHLY DISPOSABLE INCOME
AVAILABLE (A–B) $ _1600_
(subtract total monthly expenses from total
monthly income)

SAMPLE 2-2
Personal Net Worth Statement
(Format Commonly Requested by Lenders)
(Not all sections may be applicable)

Name   Date of Birth   Social Insurance Number

Street Address   City/Province/Postal Code

Home Phone   Residence   How long at address?
( ) _____   ___ Own ___ Rent ___ Other   ___ Years ___ Months

Occupation   Currently employed with   How long with employer?
     ___ Years ___ Months

Employer's Phone   ___ Married ___ Unmarried ___ Separated
( ) _____   ___ Number of dependants

Your principal financial institution and address

Personal Data on Your Spouse

Spouse's Name   Spouse's Occupation

Spouse currently   Spouse's work phone   How long with employer?
employed by   ( ) _____   ___ Years ___ Months

Financial Information
As at _____ day of _____ month, 19___.

Assets   Value
(List and describe all assets)

Total of chequing accounts $ _____
Total of savings accounts $ _____
Life insurance cash surrender value $ _____
Automobile: Make _____ Year ____ $ _____
Stocks and bonds (see Schedule
    A attached) $ _____
Accounts/notes receivable (please itemize):
    _____ $ _____
    _____ $ _____
    _____ $ _____
Term deposits (cashable) $ _____
Real estate (see Schedule B attached) $ _____
Retirement plans:
    _____ RRSP $ _____
    _____ Employment pension plan $ _____
    _____ Other $ _____

Other assets (household goods, etc.) $ _____
_____ Art $ _____
_____ Jewellery $ _____
_____ Antiques $ _____
_____ Other $ _____

TOTAL ASSETS(A) $ _____

Liabilities	Balance Owing	Monthly Payments
(list credit cards, open lines of credit, and other liabilities including alimony and child support)		
Bank loans	$ _____	$ _____
Mortgages on any other real estate owned (see Schedule B attached)	$ _____	$ _____
Monthly rent payment (if applicable)	$ _____	$ _____
Credit cards (please itemize):		
_____	$ _____	$ _____
_____	$ _____	$ _____
_____	$ _____	$ _____
_____	$ _____	$ _____
_____	$ _____	$ _____
Money borrowed from life insurance policy	$ _____	$ _____
Margin accounts	$ _____	$ _____
Current income tax owing	$ _____	$ _____
Other obligations (please itemize):		
_____	$ _____	$ _____
_____	$ _____	$ _____
_____	$ _____	$ _____

TOTAL MONTHLY PAYMENTS/LIABILITIES(B) $ _____
NET WORTH (A-B) $ _____

Income Sources

Income from alimony, child support, or separate maintenance does not have to be stated unless you want it considered.

Your gross monthly salary	$ _____
Your spouse's gross monthly salary	$ _____
Net monthly rental (from Schedule B attached)	$ _____
Other income (itemize):	
_____	$ _____
_____	$ _____
_____	$ _____
TOTAL	$ _____

Sundry Personal Obligations

Please provide details below if you answer yes to the following question:

Are you providing your personal support for obligations not listed above (i.e., co-signer, endorser, guarantor)?

Yes _____ No _____

Details of any of the above:

_____

_____

_____

_____

Schedule A:
Stocks, Bonds and Other Investments

Quantity	Description	Where Quoted	Market Value	Pledged as Collateral? Yes	No

TOTAL _____

Schedule B:
Real Estate Owned

Please provide information on your share only of real estate owned.

Property address (primary residence)	Legal description	

Street	City	Province

Type of property	Present market value	Amount of mortgage liens
	$	$1st $2nd

Gross monthly rental income	Monthly mortgage payments $1st $2nd

Monthly taxes, insurance, maintenance and miscellaneous $	Net monthly rental income $

Name of mortgage holder(s)	First mortgage	Second mortgage

Percentage ownership %	Month/year acquired	Purchase price $

General Information

Please provide details if you answer yes to any of the following questions:

Have you ever had an asset repossessed? Yes ____ No ____
Are you party to any claims or lawsuits? Yes ____ No ____
Have you ever declared bankruptcy? Yes ____ No ____
Do you owe any taxes prior to the current year? Yes ____ No ____

Details:

_____

_____

The undersigned declare(s) that the statements made herein are for the purpose of obtaining mortgage financing and are to the best of my/our knowledge true and correct. The applicant(s) consent(s) to the Bank making any enquiries it deems necessary to reach a decision on this application, and consent(s) to the disclosure at any time of any credit information about me/us to any credit reporting agency or to anyone with whom I/we have financial relations.

_____   _____

Date   Signature of applicant(s) above

SAMPLE 2-3
Calculating Your Gross Debt Service (GDS) Ratio

Your GDS Ratio is calculated by adding the total of your monthly mortgage principal, interest and taxes (PIT) together and dividing that figure by your monthly income. Guidelines have been set that allow a maximum of 27% to 30%, depending on the financial institution, of your gross income to be used for the mortgage PIT.

$$GDS\ Ratio = \frac{Monthly\ Principal\ Interest\ Taxes\ (PIT)}{Monthly\ Income}\ 340^0$$

Gross (pre-tax) **monthly** income of purchaser(s) $ _6000_

Other forms of income (e.g., annual) averaged to
monthly $ _____

TOTAL MONTHLY INCOME $ _____

1. To estimate the **maximum** monthly mortgage
   payment **plus** property taxes you could carry
   (monthly PIT), calculate 30% of the total
   monthly income:
   30% of $_____ $ _____

2. Estimate **monthly** property tax on home
   (net after any provincial homeowner's grant
   is taken into consideration, if applicable) $ _____

3. To estimate the **maximum** monthly mortgage payment, not including taxes (PI), that you could carry, subtract the monthly tax amount (2) from the monthly PIT (1):

Monthly PIT (1)	$ _____
Less: Monthly property tax (2)	$ _____
MAXIMUM MONTHLY MORTGAGE PAYMENT (1 – 2 =) 3	$ _____

Use Chart 2-1 to determine the maximum mortgage (not including taxes) for which you qualify under your GDS Ratio guidelines, based on your maximum monthly mortgage payment.

Maximum mortgage available under GDS Ratio guidelines	$ _____

SAMPLE 2-4
Calculating Your Total Debt Service (TDS) Ratio

Most lenders require that an applicant meet a TDS Ratio, in addition to looking at the GDS Ratio. The TDS Ratio is a maximum of 35% to 40% of gross income, although actual rules may vary between financial institutions. The TDS Ratio is calculated in much the same way as the GDS Ratio, but takes into consideration all other debts and loans you may have.

$$\text{TDS Ratio} = \frac{\text{Monthly Principal Interest Taxes (PIT) \& Other Monthly Payments}}{\text{Monthly Income}}$$

Gross (pre-tax) **monthly** income of purchaser(s)	$ _____
Other forms of income averaged to monthly	$ _____
TOTAL MONTHLY INCOME	$ _____
Other monthly payments:	
Credit cards	$ _____
Other mortgages	$ _____
Car loan(s)	$ _____
Other loans	$ _____
Alimony/child support	$ _____

Other debts (list):

_____ $ _____

_____ $ _____

_____ $ _____

_____ $ _____

TOTAL OTHER MONTHLY PAYMENTS $ _____

To calculate your TDS Ratio, take 40% of $_____ (total monthly income) = $_____ available for monthly principal + interest + taxes + other payments (PIT Other).

To estimate the **maximum monthly mortgage payment** you could carry within your allowable TDS Ratio:

Monthly PIT Other $ _____
Less: Other monthly payments $ _____
SUBTOTAL $ _____
Less: Estimated property taxes $ _____
MAXIMUM MONTHLY MORTGAGE PAYMENT $ _____

Use Chart 2-1 to determine the maximum mortgage for which you qualify under the TDS Ratio guidelines, based on your maximum monthly mortgage payment.

Maximum mortgage available under TDS
Ratio guidelines $ _____

CHART 2-1
Monthly Mortgage Payments for Principal Plus Interest

The table gives the monthly payments for principal and interest (not including taxes) for each $1,000 of the amount of the mortgage. To estimate your monthly payment, find the figure under the mortgage rate (%) that corresponds to the number of years you want to pay off the loan.

For example: if your interest rate is 7% and the length of the mortgage is 25 years, then the number you need is 7.01. To figure your monthly payment: 7.01 × mortgage amount, divided by 1,000 = monthly payment. For example, if your mortgage is $100,000, your monthly payment is $701. Please note: the monthly payments have been rounded to two decimal points from five decimal points. The figures are therefore approximate.

Interest Rate (%)

Amortization Period (length of mortgage)	5.75	6.00	6.25	6.50	6.75	7.00	7.25
1 Yr	85.93	86.04	86.15	86.26	86.37	86.49	86.60
3 Yrs	30.28	30.39	30.50	30.61	30.73	30.84	30.95
5 Yrs	19.19	19.30	19.42	19.53	19.64	19.78	19.87
10 Yrs	10.95	11.07	11.19	11.32	11.44	11.56	11.69
15 Yrs	8.27	8.40	8.54	8.67	8.80	8.94	9.07
20 Yrs	6.99	7.13	7.27	7.41	7.55	7.70	7.84
25 Yrs	6.25	6.40	6.55	6.70	6.86	7.01	7.16
30 Yrs	5.80	5.95	6.11	6.27	6.43	6.59	6.75
35 Yrs	5.50	5.66	5.82	5.99	6.15	6.32	6.49

Amortization Period (length of mortgage)	7.50	7.75	8.00	8.25	8.50	8.75	9.00
1 Yr	86.71	86.62	86.93	87.05	87.16	87.27	87.38
3 Yrs	31.06	31.17	31.28	31.39	31.60	31.62	31.73
5 Yrs	19.00	20.10	20.22	20.33	20.45	20.57	20.58
10 Yrs	11.82	11.94	12.07	12.20	12.33	12.45	12.58
15 Yrs	9.21	9.35	9.49	9.63	9.77	9.91	10.05
20 Yrs	7.99	8.14	8.29	8.44	8.59	8.74	8.90
25 Yrs	7.32	7.48	7.64	7.80	7.96	8.12	8.28
30 Yrs	6.92	7.08	7.25	7.42	7.59	7.76	7.93
35 Yrs	6.67	6.84	7.01	7.19	7.37	7.54	7.72

Amortization Period (length of mortgage)	9.25	9.50	9.75	10.00	10.25	10.50	10.75
1 Yr	87.49	87.60	87.72	87.83	87.94	88.05	88.16
3 Yrs	31.84	31.95	32.06	32.18	32.29	32.40	32.52
5 Yrs	20.80	20.92	21.04	21.15	21.27	21.39	21.51
10 Yrs	12.71	12.84	12.98	13.11	13.24	13.37	13.51
15 yrs	10.19	10.34	10.48	10.63	10.77	10.92	11.07
20 Yrs	9.05	9.21	9.36	9.52	9.68	9.84	10.00
25 Yrs	8.45	8.62	8.78	8.95	9.12	9.29	9.46
30 Yrs	8.11	8.28	8.46	8.63	8.81	8.99	9.17
35 Yrs	7.90	8.08	8.26	8.45	8.63	8.81	9.00

Amortization Period (length of mortgage)	11.00	11.25	11.50	11.75	12.00	12.25	12.50
1 Yr	88.27	88.38	88.50	88.61	88.72	88.83	88.94
3 Yrs	32.63	32.74	32.85	32.97	33.08	33.19	33.31
5 Yrs	21.63	21.74	21.96	21.98	22.10	22.22	22.34
10 Yrs	13.64	13.78	13.91	14.05	14.19	14.32	14.46
15 Yrs	11.22	11.37	11.52	11.67	11.82	11.97	12.13
20 Yrs	10.16	10.32	10.49	10.66	10.81	10.98	11.15
25 Yrs	9.63	9.80	9.98	10.15	10.32	10.50	10.68
30 Yrs	9.34	9.62	9.71	9.89	10.07	10.25	10.43
35 Yrs	9.18	9.37	9.56	9.74	9.93	10.12	10.31

Chapter 3

GETTING STARTED

A major aspect in buying a home is being very organized. Set up a home buying file and follow a step by step process. This will help you tremendously and make the whole process less confusing and intimidating.

Buying your first home is very exciting! It is an extremely important step in your life and it is a very emotional one as well. But don't let your heart rule your head. You want to look at the property with an eye to avoiding expensive maintenance and repairs. You also want to make money when you resell in the future.

Ideally, you want to buy low, sell high, and minimize stress and inconvenience. If you follow the guidelines outlined here, there is a good chance you will be able to do that.

This chapter will explain how to get started, where to get helpful information, the main factors to consider, and tips when selecting a property.

FACTORS TO CONSIDER WHEN SELECTING A HOME

There are many factors to consider when selecting a home. In general, not one but a combination of factors will determine your decision to buy in a particular area. It is important to make a final assessment based on an objective review, taking into account the various factors. This section discusses where to get general and specific real estate information. Refer to Checklist 3-1 for an outline of many of the things you should consider when comparing the various properties that interest you.

Where to Get General Information

Part of your initial research is to obtain a general overview of trends and economic factors that might have an impact on your choice of location. There are many sources of information to seek out, depending on your available time, personal priorities, and the degree of effort you are willing to expend. The saying that "knowledge is power" is appropriate. The more information you have, the better chance you will have to make the right judgments and be aware of suitable opportunities. However, if you do not have the time or inclination to do all the research yourself, you can obtain much of this information from experts you hire, such as your real estate agent (see Chapter 5).

Here are some sources of general economic and real estate information you may wish to consider. Remember, each market is unique, so general trends may or may not have a direct bearing, but they will give indications. Other factors in your specific geographic area will influence demand and prices.

Bank Economic Reports. Most of these are free for the asking. Contact the public affairs or marketing department of the banks' closest regional office and ask to be placed on the mailing list. They are also available on the institution's Internet site, in most cases.

- Bank of Montreal
  Business Review (quarterly)

- Bank of Nova Scotia
  Global Economic Outlook (three times a year)
  Provincial Pulse (three times a year)
  North American Real Estate Report (two times a year)

- Canada Trust
  Signpost (monthly)

- Canadian Imperial Bank of Commerce
  CIBC Leading Indicators (monthly)
  Interest Rate and Currency Outlook (monthly)

- Hong Kong Bank of Canada
  Quarterly Economic Letter
  Economic Bulletin (bi-weekly)

- Royal Bank of Canada
  Econoscope (monthly)
  Provincial Economic Service (quarterly)

- Toronto Dominion Bank
  Quarterly Economic Report

National Newspapers. There are two publications that deal with financial and economic issues and trends, and have regular features and reports on real estate. Consider subscribing to the *Globe and Mail* and *The Financial Post*.

Regional and Local Business or Real Estate Publications. Check with your local newsstand or public library to find out what publications are available that may be relevant to your needs. Some publications are free.

Courses and Seminars. There are courses on real estate as well as general business management offered by school boards and college adult-education programs. Also, check with your local real estate board for any seminars offered for first-time buyers.

Where to Get Specific Information

The following sources will provide helpful assistance or more specific research steps. (See also Chapter 8.)

Statistics Canada. This federal government department can provide you with invaluable information relating to population movements, general trends, census data, socioeconomic profiles and other demographic data. Your local library will have Statistics Canada research data and analysis, or contact Statistics Canada directly. Look in the Blue Pages of your telephone directory under "Government of Canada."

Canada Mortgage and Housing Corporation (CMHC). This federal Crown corporation compiles historical data, and analyses of housing trends and projections, among other things. Most of the publications are free upon request. They also have some market and trend publications available for a fee, that are not listed here. You may want to contact CMHC and request that you be put on the mailing list. Contact the CMHC branch office nearest you, or write to CMHC at the address listed under "Sources of Further Information." The main CMHC publications include the following:

- *Canadian Housing Markets* (quarterly)
- *Mortgage Market Trends* (quarterly)
- *Real Estate Forecasts* for all major metropolitan areas (semi-annual)
- *Builders' Forecasts* for all major metropolitan areas (semi-annual)
- *Rental Market Survey Reports* for all major metropolitan areas (semi-annual)

- *Local Market Housing Reports* (monthly)
- *National Housing Outlook* (quarterly).

Real Estate Survey of House Prices. Royal LePage publishes a quarterly *Survey of Canadian House Prices*. It is free of charge and can be picked up at your local Royal LePage office. This survey is invaluable and provides information on current (as of survey) estimated "fair market value" house prices, prices three months earlier and one year earlier, and percentage change over the year. Estimated average taxes and average monthly rentals are also indicated. Four different categories of single-family housing are surveyed along with three different categories of condominiums. Each housing type and its amenities are specifically described, permitting comparisons of value across the country. The survey will also give you an idea of price and rental trends in a particular location. Naturally, the quality of location has a major influence on real estate values.

Real Estate Boards. Most boards keep statistics on historical prices in the geographic area covered by the board. A real estate agent can provide you with helpful data. If the real estate board operates on a Multiple Listing Service system (MLS), there is even more data available through a member realtor.

Real Estate Agents. Agents are a vital source of information about housing in the market you are considering. How to select and effectively use an agent will be covered in Chapter 5 "Professionals and Other Experts." If the real estate board operates an MLS system, the real estate agent can locate a great deal of information such as price comparisons, current % difference between listing and selling prices, historical data and trends, listing profile of property, etc.

Municipal Planning Department. This department should be able to advise you as to whether there is a development planned in the area in which you are interested. This, for example, could include apartment buildings, condominium complexes, shopping centres or highway expansions. You could also enquire if there is any planned rezoning that might affect the purchase you are considering. Check to see if there have been any natural disasters that could affect your property, such as flooding or mud slides. Also check building permits issued. What areas have the greatest activity in new construction or renovation? If you are interested in applying for rezoning, building a new house, or renovating an old one, ask for the following material as your circumstances dictate:

zoning maps, zoning regulations, building codes, building permit application forms and instructions, municipal codes, regional master plans, etc.

Economic Development Department. This department is normally associated with the municipality or regional district. Its function is to stimulate economic activity and employment in the area. The staff should be able to tell you about long-term growth plans that will have a positive economic impact on the community. Purchasing a residential property near the future growth area could increase the value of your home, but may have negative impacts as well — more traffic and congestion, overcrowding etc. Always enquire about any development plans for rapid transit, subways, shopping malls, or offices.

Municipal Tax Department. Find out how property taxes are calculated. Perhaps the municipality which you have targeted has a high commercial tax base, which helps keep residential taxes down. Perhaps the municipality is growing rapidly and is becoming, in effect, a bedroom community characterized by young families. If the supply of schools and teachers in the municipality is low and the demand is increasing, then property taxes could go up to pay for more schools and teachers. Check to see if there are any major property tax increases planned in general and for the property you are considering, specifically. The costs of things such as a new drain system, sidewalks, or street paving could be passed on directly to you, the property owner.

Local Newspapers. These can be an excellent source of information on issues affecting the community in general or a specific location in particular. You can pick up back issues for the past few months from the newspaper office or the local library.

Local Home Builders' Association. The community you are considering may have a Home Builders' Association. Check in the Yellow Pages or contact the Home Builders' Association in your province, and make enquiries as to local associations. Provincial Home Builders' Associations are listed under "Sources of Further Information." The Home Builders' Association should have members who could tell you which areas of the community have high growth and the trends that indicate future high growth.

Remodelling Contractors. Look in the phone book for contractors who specialize in remodelling. Call at least three and ask what areas of the community appear to have a high percentage of remodelled homes. Naturally these types of homes can add value to the property you purchase, because they improve the overall attractiveness of the neighbourhood.

Home Inspectors. Check the Yellow Pages for local private home inspectors. Ask them which areas of the community are expanding; which areas have had a lot of remodelling done; which areas have problems such as drainage, insects, and the like; which areas have resale homes in excellent condition.

Neighbours. Don't forget to ask the people in the area you are considering how they enjoy the neighbourhood. Would they buy there again? What specific features about the neighbourhood do they like or dislike? What is the ratio of owners to renters? Look for feedback that gives you some feeling for the quality and stability of the community.

TIPS WHEN LOOKING FOR A HOME

Certain factors may be more or less important, depending on your situation. This section is broken into three parts for greater clarity: general tips when looking for a home; tips when selecting a neighbourhood; and tips when selecting a street location. Tips when choosing a specific home will be covered in Chapter 11, "Finding the Right Home."

General Tips When Looking for a Home

Location. One of the prime considerations is the location. How close is the property to your place of work, schools, cultural attractions, shopping centres, recreational facilities, community and religious facilities, and transportation? How attractive is the present and future development of the area surrounding the property? You could buy a home and six months later a high-rise complex could be built across from you, creating congestion, blocking your view, and decreasing the value of your property. The location should have ample access to parking and other features. Check on the amount of traffic on the streets in your area. Heavy traffic can be a noise nuisance as well as a hazard for young children and pets. As there are many factors to consider when deciding on location, be thorough in reviewing all aspects of location.

Pricing and Affordability. The pricing of the property you are considering should be competitive with that of other, similar offerings. This can be difficult unless you are comparing identical homes in a subdivision or condos in the same complex. Your realtor can obtain accurate information on comparative pricing. How properties are evaluated and calculating your mortgage eligibility are discussed in Chapter 6.

Zoning By-Laws. Many people don't give much thought to zoning by-laws when buying a house, but since these can change, it is important to verify with the municipality if there are any proposed or pending changes to the current zoning by-laws in the area you are considering. Also attempt to find out if there are any specific developments planned that would affect the character of the area. Some of the larger municipalities or regional districts have a proposed land use plan policy for each community, although these are subject to change. Make your enquiries regarding degree of density, height of buildings, and property uses (residential or commercial) before you commit yourself to a binding agreement of purchase and sale.

If you are considering using part of your home for a home-based business, check on the permitted use and then speak with your lawyer, if necessary. A home occupation business license may also be required. Generally, city hall is concerned about irritants such as noise, pollution, and traffic congestion, but since about 80% of people who operate home businesses do not have clients or customers coming to their home, this generally is not a problem. Therefore, in most cases, the quality of the residential environment is still maintained without giving neighbours a cause of complaint. (For further information, refer to my book, *Home Inc.: The Canadian Home-Based Business Guide.*)

Be particularly careful if you are buying an older home and it is classified as "a legal non-conforming use." What this means is that it no longer conforms to current zoning by-laws. For example, the house could be set too far back or be too large for the property, by current standards. You can still continue using the property, but if you wish to renovate it, make additions, or rebuild, you would normally be required to comply with existing by-law standards for the complete house. If this is an important issue for you, check it out with city hall and your lawyer before you buy.

Thoroughly Scrutinize the Home and Neighbourhood. Surveys have shown that the average home buyer spends 17 minutes looking at the home before making the decision to purchase. And in many cases that decision is made entirely on an emotional basis. You don't want to suffer from buyer's remorse. Do not make a hasty decision after a superficial look. You want to look at the property on several occasions to obtain a fresh perspective. Look at it in the day and evening, and preferably in rainy and sunny weather. Make up a list of questions for the agent to ask of the vendor. Look at the house when the owner is not present so you can examine it thoroughly and at a leisurely pace. Bring a friend or relative with you. If you are serious about buying the place, take pictures outside and inside to help you remember. Make sure you drive around the neighbourhood to get a feeling for the appearance and conditions of other homes in the vicinity. If adjacent streets appear run-down, that could affect the desirability of your home. (See Chapter 11 for more information.)

If you wish to place an offer, remember to make it conditional on inspection by a professional home inspector. How to select an inspector is covered in Chapter 5. The issue of a vendor signing a "property condition disclosure statement" is referred to later in this chapter. Refer to Checklist 3-1 at page 36 as an objective basis for evaluating and comparing the property.

Reasons for Sale. It is important to determine why the property is for sale. Maybe the vendor knows something you don't, which will have a bearing on your further interest. On the other hand, maybe it is simply due to a desire to move up to a larger home or down to a smaller one. Other reasons include separation or divorce, loss of employment, job relocation, or serious illness or disability. A more detailed discussion of vendor's motives is covered in Chapter 12, "Negotiating."

Tips When Selecting a Neighbourhood

Property Taxes. Compare the costs of property taxes in the area that you are considering with those of other areas you find equally attractive. Different municipalities have different tax rates and there could be a considerable cost saving or expense. Also enquire whether there is any anticipated tax increase and why. For example, if the area is relatively new, there could be future property taxes or special levies to establish schools or other community support services, while older neighbourhoods may need repairs and upgrading to important services.

Local Zoning Restrictions and Opportunities. Check to see what restrictions on use and other matters may exist. For example, is there a community plan? What type of by-law zoning is there, and is it changing? Is there a rezoning potential for different use? Is there a land use contract? What about non-conforming use of older buildings? (Other considerations dealing with zoning were covered above in the section on general tips when looking for a home.)

Transportation. How close are you to your work? If you drive a car, how heavy is the traffic and how long would the commute take, at various times of the day? Is public transportation conveniently available? How reliable and frequent is it? Whether it is a bus, subway, rapid transit, freeway, ferry, or other mode of transportation, the quality of transportation will have a bearing on your enjoyment as well as the resale price of your home.

Crime Rate. Naturally this is an important issue. Check with the local police department, as well as neighbours on your street. Ask if there is a "block watch" or "neighbourhood watch" program in the area.

Services in Community. Different services available in the community will attract different types of tenants or purchasers, depending on their needs. A community will often be characterized by the local services. This is discussed in the next few points.

Support Services

Is there adequate police, fire, and ambulance protection? Is there a hospital in the area? Are there doctors and dentists located in the vicinity? How often is garbage collected, streets maintained, and snow removed? Is mail delivered to your door or to a central mailbox location on the street or in your neighbourhood?

Schools

Are preschools, elementary, or secondary schools convenient and safe to walk to? Is there convenient transportation available otherwise? Are special school programs available such as French immersion, English as a Second Language (ESL), or adult continuing education?

Community Activities

If you wish to join an organization or club, are they conveniently close?

Recreation Facilities

Are there community centres, libraries, or public parks nearby? Are there sports leagues for children and adults?

Religious Facilities

Is there a place of worship of your faith in your neighbourhood?

Shopping

If there is a commercial development nearby, are noise and traffic a problem? What types of businesses, stores, or services are in the area?

Stage of Development. An area will typically go through a series of stages, phases, and plateaus over time. For example, the normal stages are development (growth), stabilization (maturing, plateau), conversions (such as apartment to condos), improvements of existing properties, decline of improvements (deterioration), and redevelopment (tearing down of older buildings and new construction, more efficient use of space).

Image of Area. What image does the media or the public in general have about a certain area? Is it positive or negative, and why? The perception people have about the area may affect decisions to buy there. But remember, don't believe everything you read in the paper. Always do your own research.

Economic Climate. This is a major factor to consider. What is stimulating the economy, not only in terms of renters but actual home-buyers? Is development such as shopping centres, house and condo construction, office buildings, franchise outlets, and other commercial activity growing? Is the provincial or federal government going to construct or move offices to the community? Or is a major single industry employer the main cause of economic activity in the area? In the latter case, you can appreciate the risk involved if the main employer has problems and downsizes or closes down. There could be a lot of houses put on the market causing a loss of property value.

Employment. This factor is of course related to the previous one, economic climate. The closer the tenant lives to work, the lower the turnover. The closer the work to the employee, the higher the demand will be when the time comes to sell your property. Because of this, many companies are moving their operations to suburbs, where the commuting, rent, and cost of land is cheaper, and finding employees who can afford to live in the area is easier.

Rental Situation in Area. If you plan to rent out part of your home, look for an area that enjoys a high rental demand. You want to minimize the risk of having a vacancy. Check with the Royal

LePage *Survey of Canadian House Prices,* referred to earlier, to obtain average house rentals in the area. On the other hand, you don't want too high a number of rental houses, as that will increase competition, decrease long term stability, and possibly reduce the overall desirability of the neighbourhood.

Population Trends. Look for the trends in the community you are considering. Are people moving in or out, and why? What is the average age? Type of employment? Income level? Family size? Many of these demographic statistics can be obtained from Statistics Canada or from your provincial or municipal government. If the population is increasing, it will generally create more demand for housing which will drive up prices, but allow you to sell more easily when the time comes. Conversely, if it is decreasing, the opposite will occur. House prices may be lower but you will also have more difficulty reselling your home. If the population is aging, people may prefer downsizing to condominiums rather than buying smaller houses. There are many variables to consider.

Unattractive Features. Look for factors that will have a negative influence on a prospective tenant or purchaser. For example, unpleasant odours from an industrial plant, poor lighting because of too many trees, inadequate municipal services such as a lack of street lighting, sewer facilities, poor roads, open drainage ditches, etc. Awareness of these negative factors will also assist you in your decision-making negotiating approach. (This is covered in more detail in Chapter 12, "Negotiating.")

Neighbours. Look at the surrounding neighbourhood and make an assessment about whether the value of the residences in the neighbourhood will affect the value of your property. For example, are the homes in the area well maintained? What are the demographics of the neighbourhood? Is the neighbourhood characterized by single adults, young couples (with or without children), or older retired people? Are there children in the same age group as your own children?

Climate. The issue of climate is important. Certain areas of your community may have more rain, snow, and higher winds than others, depending on historical climate patterns.

Tips When Selecting a Street Location

Parking and Traffic. Is parking outdoors, in a garage, open carport, or underground? Do you feel there is sufficient lighting for security protection? Is it a long walk from the parking spot to your home? Is there parking space available for a boat, trailer, recreational vehicle, or second car? Is there ample parking for visitors on the lot or on the street? Is there a private driveway or back lane connected to the garage or carport? Is street parking restricted in any fashion (e.g., residents' parking only)? Is it enforced? Do you need to buy a permit? Is the street relatively free of traffic? Is it quiet? Or is there heavy traffic flow and noise?

Servicing. Is the property fully serviced with water, gas, hydro, and sewers? Are the telephone wires or hydro poles unsightly? Do public utilities have rights-of-way or easements over the lot which they could build on in the future? Do street lamps shine directly into the house at night?

Topography. The layout of the land is an important consideration. If the property is at the foot of a hill, it could cause drainage problems. Water collecting around the base of the house can cause settling, resulting in cracks in the plaster, sticking windows and uneven doors. Maintaining the property, such as cutting the grass, could be more difficult if it is irregular, and not level. Is the property surrounding the house useable, and for what purpose? These are just some of the questions to consider.

Drainage. This was referred to in the previous point. Do neighbouring houses drain onto your lot? Is there adequate run-off from your property in that event? Does the land slope away from the house so that there is adequate drainage?

Corner Lots. These can be a benefit or drawback. If the lot reduces privacy and security and has increased taxes because of the frontage, it could be a negative. On the other hand, if it creates a more spacious environment and permits the construction of a larger house, it could be an advantage.

Road Allowance. Find out if the property extends to the edge of the road. Does the municipality reserve some footage to expand the road, and if so, how much? Is there a public sidewalk existing or planned? If the lot is a corner lot, has the municipality put restrictions on the height of fences, shrubbery, or trees on the lot to ensure that drivers can see any oncoming traffic? Can you live with those restrictions?

Exposure. Many people prefer to have a home that has a sunny southern exposure for their backyard. Check to see which direction the back and front of the house faces.

Size and Shape of Lot. Is the lot oddly shaped or rectangular? How deep and wide is the property? The size and shape of the lot is relevant if you are building a new house or if you intend to renovate and expand the existing home. It will also affect how close you are to houses on adjacent lots. Large lots could provide enhanced enjoyment and greater potential for resale, but they also carry higher taxes and require more maintenance.

View. "Desirable view" lots are more expensive, but they increase the market value of the property when the time comes to resell. If there is a view, check to make sure that the sight line from the property is protected by municipal by-laws; in other words, that there are height restrictions for adjacent lots on the street. Also, make sure that there are no plans for buildings that could obstruct your view.

* * *

We have examined the many factors you must consider when buying your first home. Now that we are comfortable with this information, let us move on to examine the different types of homes available.

CHECKLIST 3-1

Real Estate Assessment Checklist

1. This assessment checklist has most of the essential features to look for in a house or condominium.
2. Not all the categories are necessarily applicable in your individual case. Terminology in some instances can vary from province to province.
3. Indicate on the line provided your rating of the listed factor as: excellent, good, poor, available, not available, not applicable, further information required, etc.

A. General Information

Location of property

Condition of neighbourhood

Zoning of surrounding areas

Prospect for future increase in value

Prospect for future change of zoning

Proximity of:
- Public transportation _____
- Shopping _____
- Schools _____
- Churches _____
- Recreation _____
- Entertainment _____
- Parks _____
- Children's playgrounds _____
- Highways _____
- Hospital _____
- Emergency services (police, fire, ambulance) _____

Traffic density _____

Garbage removal (+ recycling program) _____

Sewage system _____

Quality of water _____

Taxes:
- Provincial _____
- Municipal _____

Easements _____

Maintenance fees/assessments (condo) _____

Quietness of:
- Neighbourhood _____
- House _____
- Condo complex _____
- Individual condominium unit _____

Percentage of units that are owner-occupied (condominium) _____

If next to commercial centre, is access to residential section well-controlled? _____

Is adjacent commercial development being planned? _____

Size of development related to your needs (small, medium, large) _____

Does project seem to be compatible with your lifestyle? _____

Style of development (adult-oriented, children, retirees, etc.)   _____

Age of development (new, moderate, old)   _____

B. Exterior Factors

Privacy   _____

Roadway (public street, private street, safety for children)   _____

Sidewalks (adequacy of drainage)   _____

Driveway (public, private, semi-private)   _____

Garage:

- Reserved space (one or two cars)   _____
- Security   _____
- Automatic garage doors   _____
- Direct access to house   _____
- Adequate visitor parking   _____

Construction material (brick, wood, stone)   _____

Siding (aluminum, other)   _____

Condition of paint   _____

Roof:

- Type of material   _____
- Age   _____
- Condition   _____

Balcony or patios:

- Location (view, etc.)   _____
- Privacy   _____
- Size   _____
- Open or enclosed   _____

Landscaping:

- Trees   _____
- Shrubbery, flowers   _____
- Lawns   _____
- Automatic sprinklers   _____

Condition and upkeep of exterior   _____

C. Interior Factors

Intercom system   _____

Medical alert system _____

Fire safety system (fire alarms, smoke
detectors, sprinklers) _____

Burglar alarm system _____

General safety:

- TV surveillance _____

- Controlled access _____

Pre-wired for television and telephone cable _____

Lobby:

- Cleanliness _____

- Decor _____

- Security guard _____

Public corridors:

- Material used _____

- Condition _____

- Plaster (free of cracks, stains) _____

- Decor _____

Stairs:

- General accessibility _____

- Number of stairwells _____

Elevators _____

Wheelchair accessibility _____

Storage facilities:

- Location _____

- Size _____

Insulation: (The R factor is the measure of
heating and cooling efficiency; the higher
the R factor, the more efficient) _____

- R rating in walls (minimum of R-19,
depends on geographic location) _____

- R rating in ceiling (minimum of R-30,
depends on geographic location) _____

- Heat pumps _____

- Windows (insulated, storm, screen) _____

Temperature controls:

- Individually controlled _____

- Convenient location _____

Plumbing:
- Functions well   _____
- Convenient fixtures   _____
- Quietness of plumbing   _____

Suitable water pressure   _____

Heating and air conditioning (gas, electric,
hot water, oil)   _____

Utility costs:
- Gas   _____
- Electric   _____
- Other   _____

Laundry facilities   _____

Soundproofing features   _____

D. Management (if condominium)

Apartment management company   _____

Condominium management company   _____

Owner-managed   _____

Resident manager   _____

Management personnel:
- Front desk   _____
- Maintenance   _____
- Gardener   _____
- Trash removal   _____
- Snow removal   _____
- Security (number of guards, hours,
  location, patrol)   _____

E. Condominium Corporation

Experience of directors of corporation   _____

Average age of other owners   _____

F. Recreation Facilities (if condominium)

Clubhouse   _____
- Club membership fees (included, not
  included)   _____

Sports:

- Courts (tennis, squash, racquetball, handball, basketball)
- Games room (ping pong, billiards)
- Exercise room
- Bicycle path/jogging track
- Organized sports and activities

Children's playground:

- Location (accessibility)
- Noise factor
- Organized sports and activities (supervised)

Swimming pool:

- Location (outdoor, indoor)
- Children's pool
- Noise factor

Visitors' accommodation

G. Individual Unit (if condominium) or House

Location in complex

Size of unit

Is the floor plan and layout suitable?

Will your furnishings fit in?

Is the unit exposed to the sunlight?

Does the unit have a scenic view?

Is the unit in a quiet location (away from garbage unit, elevator noise, playgrounds, etc.)?

Accessibility (stairs, elevators, fire exits)

Closets:

- Number
- Location

Carpet:

- Colour
- Quality/texture
- Hardwood floors

Living room:
- Size/shape _____
- Windows/view _____
- Sunlight (morning, afternoon) _____
- Fireplace _____
- Privacy (from outside, from rest of condo) _____

Dining room:
- Size _____
- Accessibility to kitchen _____
- Windows/view _____

Den or family room:
- Size/shape _____
- Windows/view (morning or afternoon sunlight) _____
- Fireplace _____
- Privacy (from outside, from rest of condo) _____

Laundry room:
- Work space available _____
- Washer and dryer _____
- Size/capacity _____
- Warranty coverage _____

Kitchen:
- Size _____
- Eating facility (table, nook, no seating) _____
- Floors (linoleum, tile, wood) _____
- Exhaust system _____
- Counter-top built in _____
- Counter-top material _____
- Work space _____
- Kitchen cabinets (number, accessibility) _____
- Cabinet material _____
- Sink (size, single, double) _____
- Sink material _____
- Built-in cutting boards _____
- Oven (single, double, self-cleaning) _____

- Gas or electric oven
- Age of oven
- Microwave (size)
- Age of microwave
- Refrigerator/freezer (size/capacity)
- Refrigerator (frost-free, icemaker, single/double door)
- Age of refrigerator
- Dishwasher (age)
- Trash compactor/garbage disposal
- Pantry or storage area
- Is there warranty coverage on all appliances?
- Number of bedrooms

Master bedroom:
- Size/shape
- Privacy (from outside, from rest of condo)
- Closets/storage space
- Fireplace
- Floor and wall covering
- Master bathroom (en suite):
- Size
- Bathtub
- Whirlpool tub/jacuzzi
- Shower
- Steam room
- Vanity
- Sink (single, double, integrated sink bowls)
- Medicine cabinet
- Number of bathrooms
- Complete, or sink and toilet only?
- Overall condition of condo or house
- Overall appearance and decor of condo or house

H. Legal and Financial Matters

- Project documents (e.g., disclosure/ declaration) received and read (if new condominium) _____
- By-laws received and read (if condominium) _____
- Rules and regulations and condominium council minutes from past 12 months, received and read (if condominium) _____
- Financial statements received and read (if condominium) _____
- Other documents (list):

_____

_____

_____

_____

- All above documentation (as applicable) reviewed by your lawyer _____
- Financial statements reviewed by your accountant _____
- All assessments, maintenance fees, and taxes detailed _____
- Condominium corporation insurance coverage adequate _____
- Condominium restrictions acceptable (e.g., pets, renting of unit, number of people living in suite, children, etc.) _____
- All verbal promises or representations of sales representative or vendor's agent that you are relying on written into the offer to purchase _____
- Other

_____

_____

_____

Chapter 4

TYPES OF HOMES

There are many types of residential real estate and deciding on which type to buy depends on many things such as your budget and financial resources; the degree of risk involved; whether you are buying with others; and your personal needs and goals.

There are also some general advantages and disadvantages to different types of real estate that are discussed below. This chapter provides an overview of the most common residential real estate options available to you, and provides tips and warns you of the pitfalls. The following discussion will cover single-family houses (including resale houses, houses for renovation, new houses, buying a lot and building a house, and raw land) and condominiums. See Chapter 11 "Finding the Right Home," for a further discussion of different home styles and features.

SINGLE-FAMILY HOUSE

A single-family house is the most common form of home ownership. There is generally a wide selection of houses to select from and various single-family house choices: buying a resale house, buying a new house, buying a lot and building a house yourself or with a builder, or assembling a prefabricated house. There are advantages and disadvantages to each option.

The terms "builder" and "contractor" are essentially interchangeable in practical terms. If buying a newly built home, the term "builder" is frequently used. When contracting for someone to build a house for you on a lot you have purchased, the term "contractor" is commonly used.

Resale Houses

Many people prefer to buy a resale house. Here are some of the advantages and disadvantages involved in buying a resale house rather than a new house. Like any guidelines, they are general in nature and do not necessarily apply in each case.

Advantages

- Generally less expensive than a new house.
- Has character or a "lived-in feeling."
- Utilizes architectural styles that are unique and no longer in common use.
- Problems in house design or construction are discernible by a competent professional home inspector, due to the aging of the house (e.g., settling, cracks in the walls, etc.).
- Landscaping is in place.
- Neighbourhood is established and has developed its own character.
- Community services are available.
- Often located in and near the centre of the city.
- May include extras not normally included in new home, such as customized features that previous owners have built or installed.
- No GST.
- Very often will have larger lots than new subdivisions.

Disadvantages

- May not have been built according to existing building standards, therefore could be deficient on matters dealing with electrical or insulation codes (e.g., aluminum rather than copper wiring, lead rather than copper pipes, inefficient insulation or UFFI (urea formaldehyde foam insulation), etc.).
- Defects in the house construction may not be visible or identifiable unless a thorough inspection is done in advance by a professional home inspector. Buyers of new homes may be protected by a New Home Warranty Plan.
- If a resale house is in a metropolitan area, the price could be higher because of the higher value of land, whereas a new house in a suburban area could be less expensive due to lower cost of land and smaller lots.

- An older home may have been renovated by the owner or a handyman without a local building permit and inspection; therefore the safety or functional aspects of the house could be deficient.
- Some older homes do not have an attractive or functional design (e.g., rooms too small or poor layout), have low basements that make that area less functional for comfortable use or rental suite, are poorly located on the property (e.g., set back too close or too far from front of property line), have small or old-fashioned bathrooms and kitchens, etc. Renovating an older house can be expensive and time-consuming. (See Chapter 14.)
- The equipment (e.g., heating system) may be outdated and need repair, and appliances could be older and perhaps worn and lack modern features.

Resale Home Warranty Plan. This is a relatively new concept in Canada and is used primarily for resale homes, although new homes could also be covered. It has been offered in the U.S. for about 15 years. Basically the plan involves warranty protection for one year to cover repairs required, under normal operating conditions, for the mechanical systems, including the plumbing and heating, as well as the major appliances. Warranties against structural problems on resale homes are offered in the U.S., but in most cases either the premiums are prohibitively high or there are too many loopholes in the coverage for that type of warranty to be available in Canada.

The approximate cost of the Home Warranty Plan is about $350 plus taxes, with a $50 deductible on each service call. Naturally, these prices could vary over time. In some cases, the coverage extends to two years beyond the usual manufacturer's warranty on new appliances. Coverage for the following items is normally included: refrigerator, range, washer, dryer, hot water heater, built-in microwave, furnace, heating system, central vacuum, plumbing system, built-in dishwasher, electrical system, air-conditioning system, ceiling fans, sump pump, water softener, trash compactor, garage door opener, well pump, range hood fan, and garbage disposal. For an additional fee, optional coverage could include a swimming pool and spa equipment.

Coverage can be purchased by either the vendor or buyer through a participating real estate agent or through GE Capital. A new owner can buy the coverage or attempt to negotiate it as a condition of purchase. Coverage takes effect on the possession date. For the seller, this coverage will increase the value of his home, provide a marketing edge in a competitive real estate market, and lead to a potentially faster sale. For the prospective buyer, the coverage will provide peace of mind from unexpected costly expenses and limit any potential after sale problems.

Houses for Renovation

There are many types of residential properties that could make suitable homes through renovation. Generally, single-family houses and multi-unit dwellings are the most common choices.

Considerations. When selecting a property for renovation, there are some specific factors to consider.

- Look for a neighbourhood that has property renovation already occurring. This factor alone creates a positive image that rejuvenation is taking place.
- The property should be readily accessible by various forms of transportation, including public.
- The neighbourhood should be an attractive one, well kept, that reflects pride of ownership. Assess the area's crime rate.
- The property to be renovated should be in a neighbourhood that is not yet in high demand.
- New residential construction implies that others have viewed the neighbourhood as a growing one.
- Existing or newly constructed commercial areas (such as a shopping centre) nearby is a positive sign.
- The property should ideally have some character, quality construction, and craftsmanship.
- The property should be ideally close to other attractive draws that enhance the general area, such as rapid transit, schools, parks, libraries, waterfront.
- The property should have the potential for renovation without problems from city hall (e.g., a "non-conforming use" problem).
- If the neighbourhood has a community organization that is striving to improve the quality of the area, that is a positive sign in terms of pride and initiative.

Tips. Before you buy a property that you are considering for renovation, review the following:

- Make sure that you have some familiarity with the renovation process. If you are not, take courses, read books and magazines, and get expert advice.
- Be realistic and focused on the types of renovations you are considering. Certain types of renovations get a better return on your investment in terms of price and general saleability. The highest return generally comes from renovating the kitchen and bathrooms. (See Chapter 14.)
- Compare various properties and shortlist down to two or three. That way you can negotiate with more leverage because you are not interested in just one property.
- Consider having an architect view the property and give you ideas on how the property can be improved. Look in the Yellow Pages under "Architects."
- Have a professional appraiser give you an idea of the current market value. Look in the Yellow Pages under "Appraisers."
- Have a professional home inspector give you a report on the physical aspects of the building, internally and externally, including what potential changes would be possible. Refer to Chapter 5 "Professionals and Other Experts" for tips on how to select a home inspector.
- Have several contractors, ideally a minimum of three, give you written quotes on the cost of the renovations. Refer to the next sections on "New Houses" and "Buying a Lot and Building a House" to get tips on selecting a contractor. Also, refer to Chapter 14, "Taking Care of Your Home."

New Houses

These are some of the advantages and disadvantages of buying a new house over an older resale house.

Advantages

- Tends to be better designed in terms of room layout (e.g., larger kitchen, bathrooms, en suites), functional purpose (e.g., higher ceilings in basement, patios, family room), and brighter atmosphere (e.g., skylights).
- Frequently a builder has several different models to choose from and you can generally select certain features to cus-

tomize the house to your needs, if you contact the builder before the house is fully completed. Features you may be able to select could include items such as carpet colour and fabric, kitchen appliance colours, kitchen and bathroom floor coverings, paint colours, etc.

- Has been constructed in compliance with current building code standards (e.g., plumbing, electrical, heating, insulation, etc.).
- Looks clean, modern, fresh, and smells new.
- First occupant in the house, which to some people is a psychological plus because you can personalize the house to meet your needs rather than having to redo the previous owner's changes.
- Market evaluation of the house is easier because of similar comparables built in the same area.
- Price of house could be lower or house could be larger, compared to a similar resale house, if the new house is built in a suburb with lower land costs.
- Many new homes are built by builders who are registered with the New Home Warranty Program (NHWP) in their province. Therefore, if problems occur after the sale is completed, the builder or the NHWP will correct them if the specific problems are covered by the program. You can check with your provincial New Home Warranty Program. Some reputable and experienced builders have their own warranty program in addition to the NHWP. Refer to "Sources of Further Information" (in the Appendix) for further information and addresses.

Disadvantages

- The builder may not be registered with the NHWP, thereby creating a potentially high risk to the purchaser if problems occur.
- Due to land availability and cost, many builders construct new houses a considerable distance from the city core, which may increase commuting time and cost. Also you may not be able to get all the services available in more established metropolitan areas.
- It is not uncommon to have construction delays (e.g., paving of driveways, landscaping, finishing touches) and defects, which may cause frustration and additional expense.

- Many new houses are purchased before construction begins and are selected based on an artist's sketch or various model plans. Frequently a model home is not constructed at this stage and it can be difficult to conceptualize how the final house will feel.
- Purchase documents prepared by the builder tend to be more complex and detailed compared to resale house contracts. This is discussed shortly.
- Pay GST. (A substantially renovated house could be deemed to be a new home for the purpose of GST.) However, a partial rebate could be available. Check with the builder, your lawyer and local GST office. Refer to Chapter 10 for more discussion on a GST rebate.
- The deposit funds you pay to the company could be lost if the builder goes out of business. In some provinces there is consumer protection legislation that protects these funds. Unless you put the funds in a lawyer's or realtor's trust account, though, you could lose your deposit.

New Home Warranty Program. The NHWP in each province have similarities but there are also some differences. The builder adds the fee for NHWP coverage on to the house price or builds it into the price. NHWP coverage generally includes buyer protection for the deposit, incomplete work, warranty protection up to a year, basement protection for two years, and major structural defect protection for five years. Although the NHWP was designed to protect purchasers of newly constructed houses (condominiums can also be covered) against defects in construction, there are limits to the coverage. These limitations and exclusions could cost you a lot of money. That is why you need to check out the NHWP and the builder thoroughly. As mentioned earlier, refer to the "Sources of Further Information" in the Appendix for NHWP contact numbers and addresses.

Evaluating the Builder. It is particularly important that you check on the builder's reputation by obtaining information on the contractor from the following:

- New Home Warranty Program. If the builder is registered with the New Home Warranty Program, in some provinces the deposit funds are partially protected. If the builder is not registered with NHWP be very cautious, and don't pay any money or sign a builder's contract without your lawyer's advice.

- Local or provincial Home Builders' Association should have information on the builder (see "Sources of Further Information" for addresses).
- Local Better Business Bureau for any complaints against the contractor.
- Ask the contractor for the names of past customers as references and for names and locations of previous development projects. You can then knock on doors and ask the owners their candid opinion on the quality of the house and responsiveness of the builder in correcting any problems. Ask if they got what they bargained for. A key question to ask is would they buy from the same builder again; why or why not?
- Local (municipal) business licensing office to verify that the contractor is licensed.
- Local planning department to make sure that there are no outstanding work orders, and that all inspections and approvals have been obtained.

If the contractor has no previous history or record in the industry, be very cautious. The contractor could have been operating under another name but went bankrupt. Alternatively, the contractor could be a first-timer and be learning at your expense. Take the time to check out the contractor. It will save you time, frustration, and money later on.

Building Contract. Make sure to take the contract supplied by the house builder to your lawyer before you sign it. Builders' contracts tend to be customized primarily for the benefit of the builder. Sometimes you can negotiate changes to the contract, other times you cannot. It depends on the builder, the changes, and the market. Occasionally the builder will be flexible if an experienced lawyer for the purchaser finds certain clauses in the contract unfair.

You should have your lawyer advise you in general about the contract, as well as specifically on issues such as the following:

Deposit Money

Is the deposit money going to be held in trust, and where? Is interest going to be paid on the deposit to the credit of the purchaser? There is high risk if the money is going directly to the builder and not being held in trust by a lawyer or real estate company.

Financing

Is the builder going to arrange financing at a fixed rate through a lender or carry the financing himself? Make sure the payment terms are clearly spelled out. Check to make sure the rates and terms are competitive and that the financing package is attractive. For example, the builder could arrange for a discounted interest rate for a year. The rate could be below the prevailing market rate, to attract buyers. But what if interest rates go up at the end of the year when you have to refinance? Can you handle the increased monthly payments?

Assigning or Selling

Does the builder's contract have a restriction in it preventing you from assigning your interest in the contract to someone else before the closing date, or selling your property to someone else after closing, within a certain period of time? Some builders will not want you to assign before closing so that you make a potential profit in a "hot" market. Other builders will not want you to resell your property after closing and before they have sold out the rest of the project, otherwise they could lose a potential sale, or you could offer your house for sale at a lower price, thereby affecting their pricing structure.

Closing Date

What if the builder does not close on the agreed date? Consider adding clauses reducing the house price by an agreed sum for each day late, or giving you the option to back out of the contract and get the deposit money back, plus accrued interest (although you might not want to exercise this option with a fixed sale price in an escalating market). You may want to add your own penalty clause outlining what the builder must pay you if the building is not completed on time.

Depending on your needs and objectives, you should ask your lawyer to advise you. Attempt to negotiate a better deal yourself or through your lawyer. If you are not satisfied with the outcome, consider buying from a different builder.

Buying a Lot and Building a House

Some people prefer buying a lot, hiring a contractor to build the house, build it themselves or buy a pre-fab house.

If you plan to build your own house, make certain that you know what you are doing, otherwise it could be massively time-consuming, frustrating, and expensive. An alternative is to take a course on house building to familiarize yourself with the process and then hire a contractor you trust on an hourly basis to advise you. Check with your municipal planning department on the building codes, permits, and inspections required. There are many regulations involved. Read consumer books on the topic. You could save money and obtain personal satisfaction by doing it yourself, but don't overestimate your abilities or the amount of time you have available. Do-it-yourself construction almost always turns out to be more complicated and time-consuming than you expect.

Many of the problems that owners have in their dealings with contractors are due to misunderstanding of the rights, responsibilities, and functions of the various people who are involved in the work.

Homeowner's Responsibilities. Homeowner's responsibilities generally include the following:

- Deciding what is to be done. Write a description of the work to be done, with as much detail as possible.
- Obtaining blueprints from an architect or "stock" blueprint plan.
- Deciding all the contents of the house in detail.
- Making arrangements with a lender for construction financing.
- Selecting a contractor.
- Making sure the written contract describes the job completely, thoroughly and correctly.
- Obtaining zoning approval and building permits, as required.
- Providing the space and freedom the workers need to do their work.
- Informing the contractor about deficiencies or mistakes as quickly as possible, preferably confirmed in writing so there is a dated record and no misunderstanding.
- Paying for the work as required by the contract, holding back a portion to comply with provincial builder's lien legislation (normally 10%).
- Making the final decision on whether or not the job has been done satisfactorily.
- Releasing the builder's lien holdback when satisfied.

Contractor's Responsibilities. Contractor's responsibilities generally include the following:

- Carrying out the work described in the contract.
- Following the details in the blueprint.
- Not doing any work not covered in the contract without written authorization from owner for the changes.
- Maintaining public liability and property damage insurance, and workers' compensation coverage for workers. Ensuring the subcontractors carry the same for their workers.
- Obtaining any permits, licences, and certificates required by the municipality, unless there is a written agreement that the homeowner is responsible for this.
- Adhering to all building codes (federal, provincial, and municipal) and other government construction regulations.
- Supervising the quality of all work carried out by the contractor, including work done by subcontractors.
- Paying all workers, suppliers, and contractors.
- Removal of construction debris upon completion of the job.
- Warranties on all work and materials (in addition to manufacturers' warranties) for a period of at least one year if possible.

Selecting a Contractor. It is important to be clearly focused on what your needs are before you commit yourself. You should attempt to have at least three competitive bids (written fixed price quotes) from contractors before selecting the one you want. There are various ways of finding names of contractors:

- Check with friends or neighbours for recommendations.
- Check with local building material suppliers or hardware stores.
- Check with local or provincial home builder associations. (See "Sources of Further Information" for provincial associations.)
- Check with provincial New Home Warranty Program offices for names of contractors registered with them. (See "Sources of Further Information" for provincial offices.)
- Check in the Yellow Pages under "Contractors, Building."

Before finalizing your decision, check on the reputation and past performance of the contractor, using the cautions listed in the previous section on "New Houses." This is very important. Also, consider the advantages of hiring a contractor who is registered with the New Home Warranty Program. You will pay extra for this coverage protection, but the benefits are obvious. Refer to the earlier discussion of the NHWP. Ask the contractor who his insurance company is and ask for written verification that he has adequate public liability and property damage insurance. Verify with the insurance company if you have any doubts or concerns.

If you are having the contractor do a remodelling job, rather than the whole house, ask the contractor for the following:

• Plans and/or sketches of the work to be done.
• Samples and literature showing different products that could be used.
• Photographs of previous work completed.

Contract. As mentioned earlier, it is essential that you have a written contract with the contractor. Many homebuilder associations have sample contracts available that you can use, so check with them. Make sure you have your lawyer look at the contract, and have your lawyer involved in the release of any monetary payments that are made to the contractor as the work progresses. Depending on the nature of the house construction, there could be from three to five different payments at various stages of construction. At each stage verify that the work is complete, and ideally that the subtrades, suppliers, etc., have been paid, and that there is nothing outstanding from the previous stage. It is not uncommon for contractors to pay for services performed by subtrades or supplies purchased from suppliers from each progress draw. Frequently, lien searches are done by your lawyer to ensure that no liens have been filed before the payment is made.

Your lender will normally require that progress draws are made. This is the usual custom. You can see the problem that could occur if you give too much money to the builder without the work being done. The contractor could go out of business or just not do the work and you could lose the money advanced.

The normal contents of a construction contract include the following:

• Date of agreement.
• Complete correct address of the property where the work will be done.
• Your name and address.

- Contractor's name, address and telephone number. If a company name is used, the name of their on-site representative should be indicated.
- Detailed description of the work, sketches, and list of materials to be used.
- The type of work that will be subcontracted.
- The right to retain a builder's lien holdback as specified under provincial law.
- A clause stating that work will conform to the requirements of all applicable federal, provincial, or municipal building codes.
- Start and completion dates.
- The contracted price and payment schedule (remember the lien holdback is normally 10%).
- An agreement on who is responsible for obtaining all necessary permits, licences, and certificates.
- A clause setting out the procedures for confirming in writing any "extras" to the contract requested by the owner.
- Signatures of the parties to the contract.

Raw Land

Possibly you are buying raw (bare) land for the purpose of building a house. If so, you have to take into account many factors, including the cost of servicing the land in order to prepare it for construction, assuming the land is not already in a subdivision.

If you are buying raw land with no building on it at a price that is reasonable and you can afford (preferably with cash or a large down payment), with plans to build your house on it, then a raw land purchase might be an appropriate option to consider. In addition, if the land is a large enough area and has good soil, you may be able to generate some revenue by leasing it out to a farmer, until you build.

Here are some of the advantages and disadvantages of raw land:

Advantages
- Relatively low cost.
- High potential gain if re-zoned, subdivided, or developed, or if an increase in value occurs for other reasons such as roads, a highway, rapid transit, or sewers being built near the property.

Disadvantages

- No income being generated, therefore negative cash flow. You have to subsidize the debt servicing of expenses such as mortgage, interest, and property taxes yourself, unless you paid cash.
- If land cannot be converted to a better use or your assumptions don't materialize, you could lose money.
- Expansion of community to utilize the raw land may not materialize.
- Municipality may place zoning or environmental restrictions on use of land (e.g., agricultural use only).
- Municipality may potentially expropriate the land for highway expansion, designate the land as green space, or request a right of way over part of the land.
- Financing from banks and other lending institutions to purchase the land is difficult to obtain because of the speculative nature of raw land and the lack of income to service the debt.

CONDOMINIUMS

What Is a Condominium?

Condominium living may not be right for everyone, as it involves individual ownership in a unit and shared ownership in other property, as well as adherence to rules and regulations. On the other hand, many people prefer condominium living over other alternatives. At present, there are over one million condominiums in Canada.

The word condominium does not imply a specific structural form, but a legal form. Condominiums may be detached, semi-detached, row-houses, stack townhouses, duplexes, apartments, building lots, subdivisions, or mobile home parks. Whatever the style, a residential unit is specified and is owned by an individual in a freehold (also referred to as "fee simple") or leasehold format. In summary though, freehold means you own title to the condominium you live in plus a portion of the common property. Leasehold means you do not own title to any property, but have a lease on the property for a period of time, e.g., 99 years. These formats are described in more detail in Chapter 9 "The Legal Aspects." The rest of the property, including land, which is called the common elements in most provinces, is owned or leased in common with the other owners. For example, if there are 50 condominium owners, then each would own 1/50 of the common elements as tenants in common. The legislation of each province can vary, but it is always designed to provide the legal and structural framework for the efficient management and administration of each condominium project. Once the condominium project documents are registered, the project is brought into legal being.

The part of the condominium that you will own outright is referred to as the unit in most provinces. You will have full and clear title to this unit when you purchase it (assuming you are buying a freehold, not a leasehold, property), which will be legally registered in your name in the local land registry office. The precise description of the common elements, and exactly what you own as part of your unit, may differ from development to development, but in any event it will be provided for in the documents prepared and registered for each condominium. Common elements generally include walkways, driveways, lawns and gardens, lobbies, elevators, parking areas, recreational facilities, storage areas, laundry rooms, stairways, plumbing, electrical systems and portions of walls, ceilings and floors, and other items. Part of the common elements may be designated for the exclusive use of one or more of the individual unit owners, in which case these are called limited common elements. In other words, they are limited for the use only of specific owners. Examples would include parking spaces, storage lockers, roof gardens, balconies, patios, and front and back yards.

Condominiums can be built on freehold or leasehold properties. A condominium can also be in a stratified format, where a legal description for the unit is allocated in a vertical dimension. So that, if you live in a condominium apartment on the 30th floor, there is a precise legal description in the land registry office for that specific unit in the complex. Another form is a bare land condominium. This would be similar to a building lot subdivision with individual units owned by the unit holders, although the units would appear as detached homes. The rest of the land would be considered common elements.

A condominium development is administered by various legal structures set out in provincial legislation.

Types of Condominiums

There are numerous types of condominium formats for residential and recreational or resort purposes. Here is an overview of the most common options.

Residential Condominiums. Residential condominiums can be found in either a metropolitan or a suburban setting. In a metropolitan setting the most common types are:

- A high-rise apartment building.
- A three- to five-story new mid-rise building.
- A converted older building that formerly consisted of rental apartments.
- A building where the street level floor is owned jointly by the condominium corporation members (the unit owners) and is rented out to retailers to help offset the common maintenance fees of the residential condominiums in the rest of the building.
- Same format as the previous one, except that the retail space is sold as condominiums.

Suburban condominiums tend to be of a different format and are most often found in the following form:

- Cluster housing consisting of multi-unit structures, using housing of two or four units apiece, each with its own private entranceway.
- Townhouse-type single-family homes distributed in rows.
- Garden apartments consisting of a group of apartment buildings surrounding a common green, frequently with each of the floors held by separate condominium owners.
- A series of detached single-family homes in a subdivision, all utilizing the same land and parking areas.
- Duplexes, triplexes, or fourplexes.

The suburban condominium format tends to make maximum use of the land while creating attractive views, private driveways, and common recreational facilities, such as swimming pools, tennis courts, saunas, playgrounds, etc.

Many residential condominium developments, with the conveniences and amenities being offered, have created a complete lifestyle experience. The purpose of these separate developments such as restaurants, shopping centres, recreational and entertainment facilities, and care facilities for seniors is to make the condominium community a very distinct and self-contained environment for many people.

Recreational/Resort Condominiums. Recreational condominiums can take various forms, including mobile home parks where the "pad" with utility hookups is owned in fee simple with a share in the common property of the rest of the park. Alternatively, it could be in a leasehold format. These terms were explained on previous page 58. Another option is a bare land condominium in rural, wilderness, or waterfront areas. In these examples, an owner could build a cabin with fee simple ownership to the land underneath the building but own only a partial interest in the common elements. The common elements could include a marine, beach, farm, or forest. Common recreational facilities could include a playground or community centre, and assets could include boats or farm animals.

The development of condominiums in resort areas is extensive, and they are frequently built on lakeshores, sea coasts, or island resorts, or in ski country. There are two main types of resort condominiums: those developed for warmer climates and those developed for winter climates.

The warmer-climate type is generally built around a common recreational facility that can be enjoyed throughout the year by the owners; one that includes such facilities as a seashore, lake, marina, or golf course. The buildings range from high-rise apartments to cluster housing.

Winter resort areas tend to be built near popular ski resorts. Many provide recreational facilities for the summer season as well, such as golf courses, tennis courts, and swimming pools, so that it is a year-round resort. The buildings are often in the form of cluster housing, modular housing, or attached townhouses.

People who purchase a recreational or resort condominium tend to:

- Own it outright and use it throughout the year.
- Own it outright and when not using it, rent it out themselves, or through the condominium corporation, management company, or a real estate agent.
- Own a portion of the condominium as a timeshare and use it for one week or more a year; normally each one-week block purchased is equivalent to approximately 1/50 ownership in the condominium.

Additional Expenses Relating to Condominium Ownership

Once you have completed the purchase and are now an owner of a condominium unit, there are ongoing monthly or annual expenses and potential expenses that you have to plan for. People frequently don't take these extra expenses into consideration. Some of the most common additional expenses that you should be aware of, other than mortgage payments, are:

Property Taxes. Each individual condominium unit is assessed by the municipality and therefore the owner has to pay property taxes. If you have a mortgage, the lender may have included extra monthly payments along with your mortgage. These are held in a property tax account so that the lender can pay for your annual property taxes. However, if you did not make this arrangement, or if you do not have a mortgage, you will have to pay the property tax separately. The common elements have a property tax as well, but that tax is covered in your monthly maintenance payments.

Maintenance Payments. Maintenance payments or "assessments for common expenses" cover all of the operating costs of the common elements and are adjusted accordingly for any increase or decrease in expenses. You are responsible for a portion of the development's total operating costs. The formula for determining your portion is discussed below.

Unit entitlement is the basis on which the owner's contribution to the common expenses or maintenance fees of the condominium corporation are calculated. Various methods are used for the calculation. In some developments the percentage calculated for the unit's share is determined by the original purchase price of each unit in relation to the value of the total property. Another way is to apportion costs on the basis of the number of units in equal proportion, regardless of unit size. But the most common formula is to calculate the unit entitlement by dividing the number of square feet in an owner's unit by the total square footage for all of the units. For example, let's say a condominium development contains 15 units and the total square feet is 15,680. Your individual unit is 784 square feet, and the annual cost to maintain the common elements and other related expenses is $40,000. To calculate your monthly financial commitment you would go through the following steps:

- Calculate the unit entitlement (15,680 divided by 784 = 1/20 share in the common property).
- Calculate the annual share of maintenance costs ($40,000 × 1/20 = $2,000 per year).

- Calculate the monthly share of maintenance costs ($2,000 ×
1/12 = $166.66 per month).

The payments for common expenses are made directly to the
condominium corporation and generally cover the following
items:

Maintenance and Repair of Common Property
This includes costs for maintenance and repairs, landscaping,
recreational facilities, equipment, and other expenses.

Operating and Service Costs
This includes expenses relating to garbage removal, heat, hydro,
and electricity.

Contingency Reserve Fund
This is a fund for unforeseen problems and expenses (e.g.,
replacing the roof or repairing the swimming pool or heating system). This fund is for expenses not included in the annual budgeted expense calculations for the common property and other
assets of the condominium corporation. Owners contribute
monthly to this fund on the basis of a portion of the monthly maintenance fee. The condominium legislation in most provinces
requires a minimum amount to be contributed to the contingency
reserve fund (e.g., 10% of annual budget). Check to see what percentage of the monthly payments is being allocated to this fund,
especially if you are buying an older condominium, which has a
greater risk of needing to use this money. In older buildings, the
fund should be 25% or more, depending on the circumstances. In
most cases you are not entitled to a refund of your contribution to
the reserve fund when you sell your unit.

Management Costs
These are the costs associated with hiring private individuals or
professional management firms to administer all or part of the
daily functions of the condominium development.

Insurance
Condominium legislation requires that the development carry
sufficient insurance to replace the common property in the event
of fire or other damage. Condominium corporations generally
also have insurance to cover other payables and liabilities. The
insurance does not cover the damage to the interior of individual units.

Special Assessment. There could be situations in which condominium members wish to raise funds for special purposes not covered by the contingency reserve fund or the regular monthly assessments. For example, they might want to build a swimming pool or tennis courts, or to pay for repairs beyond the contingency reserve fund. Once the decision has been properly approved, you cannot refuse to pay the special assessment, even though you might not agree with it.

Condominium Owner Insurance. As mentioned earlier, the condominium's insurance does not include the interior of your unit. Therefore, you will need to get separate insurance to cover the contents as well as the walls, windows, and doors inside your unit. There are several types of insurance, including replacement cost, all-risk comprehensive, and personal liability. It is also prudent to get insurance to cover deficiencies in the condominium corporation's insurance coverage so that any damage to your unit could be required in full; otherwise, the unit owners would have to pay on a proportional basis any deficiency by means of a special assessment. Many insurance companies have developed a specialized program referred to as condominium home owner's package insurance. If you do not have an insurance broker, check in the Yellow Pages under "Insurance Brokers" and compare coverages and costs.

Lease Payments. If you have a leasehold condominium, you will be required to make monthly lease payments in addition to the other costs outlined in this section.

Utilities. You are responsible for paying for the utilities that you use in your unit, including hydro, water, heat, etc. The common area utility expenses, for items such as heat and light for hallways and stairs, etc. are included in your monthly common area maintenance fee. In apartment condominiums these expenses are usually included in the maintenance fee, whereas townhouse and other similar types of condominiums tend to be separately metered and you are billed directly by the utility companies.

Unit Repair and Maintenance Costs. You will have to allocate a certain amount of your financial budget for repair and maintenance inside your unit. Your monthly assessment fee would cover common elements outside your unit only.

Advantages and Disadvantages of Condominium Ownership

In any situation of shared ownership and community living there are advantages and disadvantages.

Advantages

- Ready availability of financing as a single-family home.
- Range of prices, locations, types of structures, sizes, and architectural features available.
- Availability of amenities such as swimming pool, tennis courts, health clubs, community centre, saunas, hot tubs, exercise rooms, sun decks, etc.
- Benefits of home ownership in terms of participation in the real estate market and potential growth in equity.
- Individual ownership of living units.
- Pride in home ownership.
- Enables people of moderate income to own their own home.
- Freedom to decorate interior of unit to suit personal tastes.
- Enhancement of security by permanence of neighbours and, in many cases, controlled entrances.
- Enhancement of social activities and sense of neighbourhood community by relative permanence of residents.
- Elimination of many of the problems of upkeep and maintenance often associated with home ownership, since maintenance is usually the management's responsibility.
- Often considerably cheaper than a free-standing single-family home because of more efficient use of land and economy of scale.
- Potential for appreciation in value if selected carefully.
- Good transitional type of home between rental apartments and single-family houses for growing families, singles or couples; it is also a good transition for "empty nesters" who wish to give up their larger family house.
- Reduction of costs because responsibilities for repair and maintenance are shared.
- Elected council that is responsible for many business and management decisions.
- Participation of owners in the operation of the development, which involves playing a role in budget-setting and approval,

decision making, determination of rules, regulations and by-laws, and other matters affecting the democratic operation of the condominium community.

Disadvantages

- Real estate appreciation is generally not as high as it is for a single-family house, due to the common ownership of land. (It is land, more than the buildings, that goes up in value.)
- May be difficult to accurately assess the quality of construction of the project.
- Unacceptable loss of freedom may be experienced through restrictions contained in the rules and by-laws (e.g., restrictions on things such as the right to rent, pets, the minimum age of owners, having children in the complex, etc.).
- People live closer together, creating potential problems; frequent areas of conflict include the "Five P's": pets, parking, personality, parties, and people.
- Flexibility may be affected if circumstances require that the condominium be sold quickly, because condos may sell more slowly than single-family houses.
- One could be paying for the maintenance and operation of amenities that you do not use.
- Management of the condominium council is by volunteers, who may or may not have the appropriate abilities and skills.
- Possible apathy of owners, so that the same people continually serve on council.
- Some elected councils behave in an autocratic fashion.

* * *

Now that you are aware of the types of homes available and the advantages and disadvantages of each, it is time to take the next step. Let us examine the "Professionals and Other Experts" who can make your home buying easier.

Chapter 5
PROFESSIONALS AND OTHER EXPERTS

When buying a home, it is important to select a team of experts and professionals to assist you in achieving your goals and protecting your interests.

This chapter deals with the seven main categories of expertise you should consider:

- lender
- mortgage broker
- realtor
- lawyer
- home inspector
- insurance broker
- accountant.

Common selection criteria will be covered first, followed by specific selection criteria.

COMMON SELECTION CRITERIA

You should be very selective in your screening process. The right selection will enhance your prospects for a safe purchase and increase in value; the wrong selection will be costly in terms of time, money, and stress. Do not make a decision as to which advisor to use without first checking around. It is a good rule of thumb to see a minimum of three experts before choosing the right one. The more exacting you are in your selection criteria, the better the match, and the more beneficial that advisor will be. It is a competitive market, and you can afford to be extremely selective when choosing professionals to complement your home-buying team.

There are many factors you should consider when selecting experts:

- qualifications
- experience
- compatible personality
- confidence
- fees.

It is helpful to prepare a list of questions and pose these to each of the prospective advisors. Some people may feel awkward discussing fees and qualifications with a lawyer, for instance, but it is important to establish these matters at the outset before you make a decision to use that person's services.

Qualifications

Before you entrust an advisor with your work, you will want to know that he has the appropriate qualifications, such as a professional degree or some other professional training or qualifications relative to the area of work.

Experience

It is very important to look at the advisor's experience in real estate. Such factors as the degree of expertise, years of experience, and the percentage of time spent offering a service in real estate are critically important since you will be relying heavily on their advice and insights. For example, a lawyer who has been practising law for 10 years may have spent only 10% of his time in the area of real estate. A real estate agent may only have two years' part-time experience, and in another province. Inquire about the degree of expertise and length of experience. If you don't ask, you won't be given the answer that may make the difference between inadequate and in-depth advice.

Compatible Personality

When deciding on an advisor, make certain that you feel comfortable with his personality: the degree of communication, attitude, approach, candor, and commitment to your interests. A healthy respect and rapport will put you more at ease and enhance your further understanding.

Confidence

You must have confidence in your professional if you are going to rely on his advice. After considering the person's qualifications, experience, and personality, you may feel a strong degree of confidence in the individual. If you do not, don't use the person because there is a very good chance that you will not use him as extensively as you should. This could have a serious negative impact on your decision-making.

Fees

At the outset, ask about the estimated fee. It is important to feel comfortable with the fee and payment terms. Are they fair and competitive? Can you afford them? Be certain the rate is within your budget, or you may not fully use the advisor effectively because of the expense. Not using available professional advice when you need it is poor management. Are the fees commensurate with the person's qualifications and experience? For instance, if you need a good tax accountant to advise you on minimizing taxes, you may have to pay a higher hourly rate for the quality of advice that will save you several thousands of dollars.

LENDER

When deciding which bank, credit union, or trust company to deal with for your mortgage needs, you may want to start with your own financial institution since they already know you. However, it is advisable to shop around. You will find that service, attitude, and mortgage lending flexibility can vary among branches of the same lending institution. It is helpful to have a lender who has had experience in the area of real estate. As a lender's loan approval limit will vary from branch to branch, you will ideally want a lender who has a loan approval level greater than the amount of money that you need to borrow. See Chapter 6 for more information on dealing with lenders.

MORTGAGE BROKER

Since mortgage lending has become very complex, with constantly changing rates, terms, and conditions, you may decide to hire a mortgage broker to help you obtain a mortgage. Mortgage brokers make it their business to know all the various plans and lending policies, as well as the lender's attitude toward various aspects of mortgages. A mortgage broker is, in effect, a match-maker, attempting to introduce the appropriate lender to the borrower.

Mortgage brokers have access to numerous sources of funds, including the following:

- conventional lenders such as banks and trust companies
- Canada Mortgage and Housing Corporation (CMHC)
- private pension funds
- union pension funds
- real estate syndication funds
- foreign bank subsidiaries
- insurance companies
- private lenders.

Since the broker knows the lender's objectives, the broker is therefore capable of matching the applicant with the appropriate plan and lender. The broker can also provide a series of mortgage plans from which the borrower may select the best one.

There are two main types of mortgage brokers: traditional and franchise/chain-type.

1. Traditional Mortgage Broker

This is an independent mortgage broker, normally with one location, who represents a wide variety of institutional, syndicated, and private lenders. The normal procedure is for you to complete an application form supplied by the mortgage broker, provide a copy of the agreement of purchase and sale, proof of employment, length of time employed, and annual salary. A letter from your employer is frequently required.

If you are self-employed, you are normally required to provide the last three years of your businesses's financial statements and/or copies of the last three income tax returns.

If required, you pay the mortgage broker the cost of obtaining an appraisal of your property. The broker also does a credit bureau search. The broker then attempts to find a lender who will lend you money based on your financial needs, the terms you require, and the information that you have supplied.

2. Franchise/Chain-Type Mortgage Broker

This type of broker is usually a company with a chain of representatives/offices across the country which are company owned or independent brokers licensed to represent the company.

The company arranges with a number of financial institutions, both national and local, to "bid" on your request for mortgage financing. The broker has you complete an application form, provide a copy of the agreement of purchase and sale, and then "packages" a summary of the other information you have supplied, along with the appraisal and credit bureau report, and forwards it by fax to the lenders who are associated with the company "mortgage lender program." The lenders normally have a one- or two-day deadline to reply. You are then given a summary of the lenders who are prepared to finance you, along with the amount, terms, and conditions.

Types of Services

Mortgage brokers basically offer two types of services:

1. They arrange a *simple mortgage* that will generally get automatic approval in your particular circumstance. As a consequence, this saves you a lot of time searching. The broker generally receives a commission directly from the lender, as a "finder's" or "referral" fee. Lenders do this because the mortgage market is so competitive. Ask for the best deals from at least three lenders so you can compare. For this type of service, **you do not have to pay a fee to the mortgage broker**.

2. They arrange a more *complex mortgage* that would not be automatically approved. This takes more time, skill, and persuasion to source out a lender or lenders who will provide the funds you need. For example, if you did not have the normal amount of down payment required, had a negative credit rating, were highly leveraged already, or did not have the normal income required, you would probably be turned down by a conventional lender such as a bank, credit union, or trust company. In this case, if a mortgage broker succeeds in arranging your financing, you would pay a commission. The commission could be between 1% and 5% of the amount of the mortgage arranged, depending on the degree of difficulty, the urgency of the need for funds, etc. Mortgage brokers are regulated by provincial legislation, and in some provinces, there is legislation that prohibits

a mortgage broker from charging an advance fee (application fee) if the mortgage amount is below a certain figure.

To find a mortgage broker, look in the Yellow Pages of your telephone directory, ask your real estate lawyer, or your realtor. Remember to comparison shop before deciding who to deal with.

REALTOR

There are distinct advantages to having a realtor acting for you in buying a home. As in any profession, there is a range of competence among the over 75,000 licensed real estate agents throughout Canada, but you can minimize the risks and benefits greatly by choosing a knowledgeable, experienced, and sincere realtor. (The terms agent, broker, and realtor are often used interchangeably.) You do not pay a commission fee to a realtor for assisting your purchase. Only the vendor pays the commission.

How To Select a Realtor

There are a number of approaches to finding a good real estate agent:

- Friends, neighbours, and relatives can give you the names of agents with whom they have dealt, and tell you why they recommend them.
- Open houses provide an opportunity to meet realtors.
- Newspaper ads list the names and phone numbers of agents who are active in your area.
- "For Sale" signs provide an agent's name and phone number.
- Real estate firms in your area can be contacted.

After you have met several agents, there are a number of guidelines to assist you with your selection:

- Choose an agent familiar with the neighbourhood you are interested in. Such an agent will be on top of the available listings, will know comparable market prices, and can target the types of homes that meet your needs.
- Choose an agent who is particularly familiar with the buying and selling of residential properties.
- Choose an agent who is experienced and knowledgeable in the real estate industry.

- Look for an agent who is prepared to prescreen properties so that you are concerned only with those that conform to your guidelines for viewing purposes.
- Look for an agent who is familiar with the various conventional and creative methods of financing, including the effective use of mortgage brokers.
- Choose an agent who is thorough on properties you are keen on, in terms of background information such as length of time on the market, reason for sale, and price comparisons among similar properties. An agent who is familiar with the Multiple Listing System (MLS) computer can find a lot of information in a short time, assuming the property is listed on the MLS.
- Choose an agent who will be candid with you in suggesting an offer and explaining the reasons for the recommendation.
- Look for an agent who has effective negotiating skills to ensure that your wishes are presented as clearly and persuasively as possible.
- Look for an agent who is working full-time.
- Look for an agent who attempts to upgrade professional skills and expertise.
- Look for an agent who is familiar with financial calculations.

Because of the time expenditure by the agent, you should give the agent your exclusive business if you have confidence in him. Keep the agent informed of any open houses in which you are interested. Advise any other agents that you have one working for you. Focus clearly on your needs and provide your agent with an outline of your specific criteria to assist in shortlisting potential prospects. If for any reason you are dissatisfied with your agent, find another one as quickly as possible.

Benefits to the Purchaser

There are obvious benefits to the buyer of using a realtor as outlined above. One of the main benefits is that the realtor can act as an intermediary between you and the listing broker. The listing broker will probably never meet you and therefore cannot exert any influence on you, or make an assessment of you that could compromise your negotiating position with the vendor. This "arm's length" negotiating position is an important strategic tactic that will benefit you.

However, if your agent is also the listing broker (e.g., the agent for the vendor), confusion may arise. (See next section Buyer-Broker.)

Another advantage to a buyer is the opportunity for the realtor to access the MLS computer which can provide instant, thorough, and accurate information on properties that might interest you. Without an agent searching for you, you seriously minimize your range of selection and the prospect of concluding the deal at a price that is attractive to you.

Another benefit is that realtors can refer you to a lender, mortgage broker, or other professionals to assist you in your home buying.

Buyer-Broker

As of January 1, 1995, there is a new structure for the relationship between real estate agents and home buyers and sellers across Canada. It is referred to sometimes as agency disclosure, and replaces the old system of sub-agency. The reason for this change had to do with public confusion as to the respective roles of a realtor "representing" the buyer and the realtor representing the vendor. Many people assumed that if they found a realtor and the house was listed on the MLS system for example, that that realtor would represent their interests exclusively when an offer was presented and candid financial and negotiating information was shared by the buyer to "their" realtor.

The law, however, took a different view. It had to do with the issue of principal and agent. The agent (e.g. realtor) owed a fiduciary duty to the seller, that is a duty of trust. This took the form, legally, of being completely loyal to the seller, not disclosing any information to the prospective purchaser that could compromise the seller's interests, confidentiality, reasonable care in the actions of the realtor required, etc. Any sub-agent, e.g. another realtor involved, was considered to be bound completely to the seller by an extension of the principal/agent law. Hence the confusion. As might be expected, various litigation issues could result because of this confusion, by either the buyer or the seller against the selling or listing realtor.

The new system spells out the respective roles and responsibilities of each realtor involved. Here is how the system works. The seller still pays the real estate commission, which is shared with any other realtor involved. All disclosures of who is acting for whom is spelled out in the agreement of purchase and sale. In some cases, an agent working with the buyer may also enter into a Buyer Agency Contract. In other words, each realtor is acting exclusively for the benefit of the buyer or seller. There is no confusing perceived overlap. However, if the listing realtor is also the selling realtor (double-end deal), that is, wears both hats, the agent has to enter into a Limited Dual Agency Agreement. This is agreed upon and signed by both the buyer and the seller. The agent modifies his or her exclusive obligations to both the buyer and the seller by limiting it primarily to confidentiality as to each parties' motivation and personal information.

You can get more information from any real estate agent, real estate company, or your local real estate board.

LAWYER

With any real estate transaction, it is important that you have a lawyer to represent your interests. The agreement for purchase and sale and related documents are complex. To most people the purchase of a home is the largest investment of their life, and the agreement for purchase and sale is the most important legal contract they will ever sign. As you will realize by the time you have completed this book, there are many potential legal pitfalls for the unwary when buying a home.

The Selection Process

There are a number of ways to select the right lawyer for your needs:

- Ask friends who have purchased real estate whom they used, whether they were satisfied with the lawyer, and why.
- Contact the lawyer referral service in your community. Under this service, sponsored by the provincial law society or a provincial division of the Canadian Bar Association, you can consult with a lawyer for a half-hour for free or for a nominal fee (usually $10). Make sure you emphasize that you want a lawyer who specializes in real estate. Many provinces also have a "dial-a-law" service, which provides toll-free taped information over the phone on various legal topics relating to real estate and other issues. Contact the Law Society in your province for further information.

- Look in the Yellow Pages under "Lawyers" and check the box ads which outline the areas of expertise.
- When obtaining a mortgage, speak to the lawyer who is preparing the mortgage documents on behalf of the lender. You could save on some duplicated disbursement costs and negotiate a package price. Be cautious, though, to avoid conflict; you want to make certain that the lawyer provides you with a full explanation of the mortgage terms and conditions that might affect your interests. Keep in mind that the mortgage is being prepared on behalf of the bank, but at your expense. If you have any concerns in this area, obtain a separate lawyer to do the non-mortgage legal work and explain the contents of the mortgage to you.

Have all your questions and concerns prepared in writing so that you don't forget any. If you wish to make an offer to purchase, bring your offer-to-purchase document with you, and the details about the home you are considering. Ask about anticipated fee and disbursement costs. If you are not pleased with the outcome of the interview for any reason, select another lawyer.

Understanding Fees, Disbursements, and Costs

Generally, for transferring ownership of property, plus preparing and filing a mortgage, the lawyer charges either a flat rate, or a sliding scale, based on the purchase price or mortgage amount. Some lawyers have a reduced rate for certain lenders and some lenders contribute up to a certain amount toward legal costs as a marketing incentive. Ask. In addition, there are disbursement expenses.

As in any other business relationship, in order to maintain an effective rapport with your legal advisor, good communication is essential. Misunderstandings over fees or other matters should be immediately cleared up to avoid having them escalate into serious problems. If the relationship does not appear to be a beneficial one, you may decide to use the services of another lawyer and have the working file transferred to the new lawyer. If you seriously question a lawyer's invoice, you can have it "taxed" (reviewed) by a court registrar. This is an informal procedure and results in the fee being upheld or reduced. Your local court office will be able to provide further information on the procedure.

In summary, make sure that you select a lawyer, and consult that lawyer before you commit yourself to any final agreement for purchase and sale.

HOME INSPECTOR

One of the most important aspects of purchasing your home is to know in advance the condition of the property. That way you can decide if you want to buy the property at all, or at the price that you were considering. You don't want to have problems after you buy that will cost you money to repair. It is therefore wise to hire a professional home inspector to protect your interests.

Services Provided

A home inspector is an objective expert who examines the home and gives you a written opinion of its condition and ideally, the approximate range of costs to repair the problems. Home inspectors look at all the key parts of the building, such as condition of the roof, siding, foundation, basement, flooring, walls, windows, doors, garage, drainage, electrical, heating, cooling, ventilation, plumbing, insulation and so on. They should also look for signs of wood rot, mould and insects.

The older the building the more potential problems, but new buildings can have serious problems as well. If the new building is covered by the New Home Warranty program, than you have some protection. However, that program does have some exclusions, and you don't need the hassle of having to have a problem rectified. If a new home is not covered by the New Home Warranty program, you definitely want a home inspection, otherwise, you could be out all the money to repair the problem if the builder refuses to do so, or goes out of business. You can have an inspection done of a house, townhouse or apartment condominium.

Older homes present a more challenging inspection process, for example, to check for aluminum wiring, asbestos, urea formaldehyde foam insulation (UFFI), lead paint and termites or carpenter ants.

Quite apart from avoiding expensive surprises, using a home inspector has another potential benefit. If the report shows problems with a quantifiable cost to rectify them, you could use that information to attempt to negotiate a reduction in the home price to reflect the estimated cost of repair. You may not want the home, even if problems can be rectified. At least the report gives some objective professional outside opinion on the condition of the home to discuss with the vendor.

You want to make sure that you put a condition in your offer that says "subject to purchaser obtaining a home inspection satisfactory to the purchaser within X days of acceptance of the offer." This way it is totally to your discretion as to whether you want to complete the deal or not. In addition to the need for a home inspection, you might also be able to obtain a "vendor's disclosure statement." Real estate boards in some provinces have prepared such a form for vendors to sign, disclosing any known problems with the home. As this is a voluntary program in many cases, you want to ask for the reasons for a vendor's refusal to complete the form. You want to have a professional home inspection done anyway, for obvious reasons. The owner may honestly not be aware of serious problems with the home that are not visible or obvious.

The Selection Process

It is important to obtain a qualified and independent inspector. Avoid someone who has a contractor business on the side and may hope to get the repair business from you. Their advice could be self-serving and biased. Apply the same selection criteria discussed earlier in this chapter. Look in the Yellow Pages of your telephone directory under "Building Inspection Services." You can also ask friends, relatives, neighbours or your real estate agent for names of inspection companies they know and recommend. Call several inspectors in your area and interview them. Check with your local Better Business Bureau to see if there has been any complaints against the company that you are considering. Make sure you comparison shop and check out at least three different firms. You need that comparison to start making selection decisions. Ask for references and check out the references.

Home inspection fees range from approximately $200 to $400+ depending on the expertise required and nature of the inspection, size of home, age and condition, your geographic area, nature of inspection services requested and other variables. It normally takes a minimum of three hours to do a thorough inspection.

Here are the questions that you should ask in deciding which inspection company to select:

- How long has the inspector been in the business as a home inspection firm and what type of business was the inspector doing before inspecting homes?
- Is the inspector specifically experienced in residential construction?
- What does the inspection include? Inspections should include the areas previously discussed under "Services Provided." In addition, there are extra services you may wish such as radon testing, a pest infestation survey or inspection of the septic sys-

tem or wells. Always make sure that you are going to get a written report and ask for a sample of what it looks like and what is covered.

- How much will it cost? Determine the fees upfront. The range of fees was discussed earlier.
- How long will the inspection take? This was discussed earlier.
- Does the inspector encourage the client to attend the inspection? This is a valuable educational opportunity. It will give you the ability to see the problems firsthand and become more familiar with your new home. You will also learn various helpful maintenance tips. If an inspector refuses to have you attend for the inspection, this should raise a red flag.
- What and where was the inspector's training? Does the inspector participate in continuing education programs to keep his expertise up to date?
- Does the company offer to do any repairs or improvements based on its inspection? This might cause a conflict of interest.
- Does the inspector carry any errors and omission insurance? This means that if they make a mistake in their inspection and you have to pay to rectify the problem, their insurance will cover it. How much do they have and are there any restrictions or exceptions and will they confirm all that in writing before you make a decision to have them do the inspection?
- Does the inspector belong to an association that will investigate any consumer complaint? This is an important point. Ask what association they belong to, if any, and if not, why not? One of the main associations in Canada is the Canadian Association of Home Inspectors (CAHI), with various provincial chapters. In Ontario and B.C., the association can grant the exclusive designation called a "Registered Home Inspector" or "RHI."

To become a member of CAHI, an inspector must meet various professional and educational requirements, successfully complete a training course and write exams, and practice professionally for a trial period before being considered by the association. In addition, there are annual continuing education requirements.

INSURANCE BROKER

Any home you purchase needs insurance. Insurance is frequently required by creditors such as a mortgage lender. Ask an insurance broker for brochures describing the main type of insurance and an explanation of each. A broker is not committed to any particular insurance company and therefore can compare and contrast the different policies, coverage, and premiums from a wide range of companies. Refer to Chapter 14 for a detailed discussion.

It is important to have confidence in the broker in terms of his expertise and experience. If you already have an insurance broker, speak to him about your needs or you can find an insurance broker by looking in the Yellow Pages under "Insurance Brokers" or through friends, business associates, accountant, or lawyer. Attempt to use the same broker for all your policies as you may be able to negotiate better rates.

The main categories and types of insurance that you should consider and discuss with your insurance broker are mentioned below.

Property Insurance

Property insurance covers destruction or damage to the insured property caused by fire, flood, earthquake, burglary, etc. You want to make sure that you obtain replacement cost coverage. Property insurance also covers property items such as glass (from breakage) and automobiles (from collision, theft, fire, and vandalism).

Liability Insurance

Liability insurance covers any area in which the owners or their agents might be held liable for negligence, or some other act or omission. The most common type of liability insurance is general liability, which covers negligence causing injury to tenants, guests, and the general public. For example, if one of your dinner guests happened to trip on your carpet and was seriously injured, your liability insurance would protect you if the guest sued you.

Home-Based Business Insurance

If you decide to operate a business from your home, this could present certain areas of risk exposure. It is important to recognize these types of insurance policies available for protection against them. Talk to your broker.

Life Insurance

There are various forms of life insurance used by those buying a home, including term life purchased through an insurance broker, and bank loan or mortgage insurance purchased through the lender. In the latter case, the balance of the mortgage would be paid out in the event of your death.

Disability Insurance

This covers loss of income due to accident or illness. If you take this coverage out with your mortgage lender, it covers up to 100% of your monthly mortgage payment up to a maximum amount, and for a set period of time.

ACCOUNTANT

If you are buying a home simply as a dwelling for yourself and your family, you probably will not require an accountant. However, if you intend to rent out a suite in your home or operate a business out of your home, you will want to receive tax advice. An accountant's chief concern is to monitor your finances and reduce the subsequent risks and tax payable. Along with your lawyer, your accountant will complement your "real estate team" to ensure that your real estate or business decisions are based on sound advice and good planning, by providing the following services:

- Setting up a manual or computerized bookkeeping system.
- Setting up systems for the control of cash and the handling of funds.
- Preparing or evaluating budgets, forecasts, and investment plans.
- Assessing your break-even point and improving your profitability.
- Preparing and interpreting financial statements.
- Providing tax and financial planning advice.
- Preparing corporate and individual tax returns.

Qualifications

In Canada, anyone can call himself an accountant or "public accountant" without any qualifications, experience, regulations, or accountability to a professional association. That is why you have to be very careful when selecting the appropriate accountant for your needs. There are three main designations of qualified professional accountants governed by provincial statutes: Chartered Accountant (CA), Certified General Accountant (CGA), and Certified Management Accountant (CMA). The conduct, professional standards, training, qualifications, professional development, and discipline of these professionals are regulated by their respective institutes or associations.

How to Find an Accountant

Referrals. Often a banker, lawyer, or other business associate will be pleased to recommend an accountant. Such referrals are valuable since these individuals are probably aware of your area of interest and would recommend an accountant only if they felt he was well qualified and had a good track record.

Professional Associations. The professional institute that governs CAs, CGAs, and CMAs may be a source of leads. You can telephone or write the institute or association with a request for the names of three accountants who provide public accounting services within your geographic area. It is not uncommon for an initial consultation to be free of charge.

The Yellow Pages. In the Yellow Pages, under the heading "Accountants," you will find listings under the categories "Chartered," "Registered," "Certified General," and "Management."

Preparing for the Meeting

Prior to a meeting with your accountant, make a written list of your questions and concerns in order of priority. Ask the accountant what his range of experience is in relation to your need. Ask about fees, how they are determined, how accounts are rendered, and what retainer may be required. Ask who will be working on your file — the accountant, junior accountant, or a bookkeeper. It is common for accountants to delegate routine work to junior staff and keep the more intricate matters for their own review.

As with your lawyer, a good level of rapport and communication with your accountant will enhance the quality of advice and the effectiveness of your use of that advice. Openly discuss your concerns and questions with your accountant. You may from time to time wish to seek a second opinion. This is not an uncommon occurrence. However, your new accountant may ask you to sign a confirmation letter written to the previous accountant acknowledging that you no longer are using his services.

* * *

Remember, when it is time to select your professional real estate and business advisors, speak to at least three in each area. This will provide you with an objective basis for comparison and selection, and in the long run, make your home buying easier and more beneficial.

You have your team of professional advisors in place but before proceeding, you have to stop and examine the unfamiliar and sometimes confusing world of mortgages.

Chapter 6

FINANCING YOUR HOME

If you have been considering purchasing a home, you probably have some savings already set aside for a down payment. In order to be realistic in your search and to provide you with a price range for your new home, it is important to know the amount of mortgage for which you are eligible. However, before becoming serious about home buying, it is wise to speak to your lender about whether you will be able to obtain a mortgage.

This chapter covers what a mortgage is, the different types available, the sources of mortgage financing, selecting a mortgage, factors that affect mortgage interest rates, and defaulting on your mortgage. Also discussed is how to use your RRSPs and how to deduct home office expenses if you have a business.

USING YOUR RRSP TO BUY YOUR FIRST HOME

The Home Buyers' Plan (HBP) began on February 25, 1992, and was renewed annually until February 22, 1994 when the Federal government announced that it would be extended indefinitely. Since the program began, almost half a million people have used it to obtain a total of $4.5 billion in financing. The program is run by Canada Mortgage and Housing Corporation (CMHC) a Federal Government Crown Corporation. The plan has been tightened up recently, by requiring a buyer to have a minimum of 5% of the purchase price in accessible financial assets such as mutual funds, outside of an RRSP. This policy is to protect a buyer from over-extending themselves, by having a financial buffer outside of an RRSP.

Overview

The HBP allows you to withdraw up to $20,000 from your RRSPs to buy or build a qualifying home. Two or more joint owners may use the HBP for the purchase of the same residence. Although you generally can participate in HBP only once in your lifetime, you may be able to make more than one withdrawal, as long as the total withdrawal does not exceed $20,000. You do not have to include the withdrawn amounts in your income, and the RRSP issuer will not withhold tax on these amounts.

Under the HBP, you have to repay these withdrawals to your RRSPs within a period of no more than 15 years. Generally, you will have to repay a minimum amount to your RRSPs each year (1/15 of the withdrawn amount) until you have repaid all of the amount you withdrew. If in any year you do not repay the amount you have to repay for that year, the amount you do not repay will be included in your income for that year.

Each year Revenue Canada will send you a statement indicating the amounts you have repaid, and the minimum amount you will have to repay the next year.

If you made contributions to your RRSP or your spouse's (married or common-law) RRSP during the 89-day period immediately before they are withdrawn under the HBP, you may not be able to deduct all or part of those contributions when calculating your income for any year.

Purchase Agreement Required

Another condition you have to meet when you withdraw an amount, is that you have entered into a written agreement to buy or build a qualifying home.

A qualifying home is a housing unit located in Canada. Existing homes and those being constructed are both qualifying homes. Single-family homes, semi-detached homes, townhouses, mobile homes, condominium units, and apartments in duplexes, triplexes, fourplexes, or apartment buildings, are all qualifying homes. A share in a co-operative housing corporation that entitles you to possess, and gives you an equity interest in, a housing unit is also a qualifying home. However, a share that only provides you with a right to tenancy in the housing unit is not considered a qualifying home.

Must be a First-Time Home Buyer

To participate in the HBP, you have to be considered a first-time home buyer when you withdraw an amount from your RRSPs under the HBP.

You are not considered a first-time home buyer if, at any time during the four-year period prior to withdrawal, and ending 31 days before your withdrawal, you owned a home while you occupied it as your principal place of residence.

For the purpose of the HBP, a home is a housing unit, or a share of a co-operative housing corporation (the share must entitle you, the owner, to possess and have an equity interest in a housing unit owned by the cooperative). If you have previously acquired a share that provided you with only a right to tenancy, you may still be considered a first-time home buyer.

If you want to withdraw more than one amount under the HBP, make sure you are considered a first-time home buyer when you withdraw each amount. If you are not considered a first-time when you withdraw an amount, that amount will not qualify under the HBP and you have to include it in your income.

If at the time of your withdrawal you have a spouse (married or common-law), it is possible that only one of you will be considered a first-time home buyer.

Need to Occupy Your Home

When you withdraw an amount from your RRSPs, you have to certify on the application form that you intend to occupy the qualifying home as your principal place of residence no later than one year after buying or building the home. Once you occupy the home, there is no minimum period of time that you have to live there.

Should you Finance Your Home Using Your RRSP?

When looking at your sources of financing, you may wish to look at the benefits of finding other sources of financing (e.g. borrowing money from family), rather than dipping into your RRSP funds. On the other hand, if you don't have access to any other sources of down payment, than you may wish to use as little as possible from your RRSP and pay it back as soon as possible, rather than just paying the minimum amount of 1/15 a year over 15 years. The reason for this suggestion has to do with the massive compounding benefits of tax-free investments in your RRSP, relative to the possible equity increase in your real estate over the same time period.

For example, if you are married and you and your spouse put the maximum amount of $20,000 each into your home down payment from your RRSP funds that would total $40,000 less money growing in your RRSP. If you invested that same money in your RRSP and received a 10% compounded return, the value of your RRSP in 15 years would be $167,080, that is $127,080 more than the $40,000 RRSP base starting point. Given changing demographics, low inflation and other real estate cyclical variables, your home, in realistic terms, may not have increased in value $127,080 during the same time period. That is the issue to consider when looking at borrowing from your RRSP. Chapter 8 discusses the various factors that influence real estate prices. Your increase in home value (e.g. capital gain) over your original purchase price is not taxable for a principal residence. This is explained in more detail in Chapter 10.

WHAT IS A MORTGAGE?

A mortgage is a contract between someone who wants to borrow money and someone who lends money. The "borrower" is also referred to as the "mortgagor," and the "lender," the "mortgagee." The mortgage agreement states that the borrower will provide security to the lender in the form of a mortgage document to be filed against the property in exchange for the money the lender is providing. The term "property" refers to the home you are considering purchasing. The mortgage document specifies the rights that the lender has to the property in the event that the borrower defaults on the terms of the mortgage. The difference between the amount for which the property could be sold and what you still owe on your mortgage is referred to as your "equity."

Mortgages are regulated by federal and provincial law. Although the laws may be different from one province to another, the description of a mortgage outlined in this book applies to most mortgages.

TYPES OF MORTGAGES

There are several kinds of mortgages available from banks, credit unions, trust companies, mortgage companies, private lenders, government, and the seller or vendor. Although most residential property borrowers obtain financing through a conventional mortgage, it is wise to be aware of other alternatives. The following is a very brief discussion of the main types of mortgages. For a detailed discussion of mortgages, see my book *Mortgages Made Easy*.

Conventional Mortgage

The conventional mortgage is the most common type of financing for residential property. It is fairly standard in its terms and conditions, although there can be variations. In this type of mortgage, the loan generally cannot exceed 75% of the appraised value or purchase price of the property, whichever is less. The purchaser is responsible for raising the other 25%, either through a down payment, a second mortgage, or a vendor mortgage. Conventional mortgages are available through most financial institutions including banks, trust companies, and credit unions. Make sure you comparison shop and check rates, terms, and incentives. Some lenders give financial inducements to get your business, depending on the competitive marketplace. For example, up to $1,000 credit toward legal expenses, free property evaluation, etc. See the section later in this chapter on "Factors That Affect Mortgage Interest Rates," to see if you can negotiate a better deal. In most cases, conventional mortgages do not have to be insured, but occasionally a lender may require it. For example, if the building is older or smaller than is normally required by the lender, or if it is located in a rural or run-down area, then the mortgage may have to be insured with the Canada Mortgage and Housing Corporation (CMHC) or GE Capital Mortgage Insurance Canada (GE). CMHC is a federal Crown corporation, and GE is the largest private insurer in Canada. The benefits of a pre-approved mortgage are covered later in this chapter.

High-Ratio/Insured Mortgage

If you are unable to raise the necessary 25% funding then a high-ratio mortgage may be available to you. These are conventional mortgages that exceed the 75% and must be insured. They are available only through CMHC or GE approved lenders, unless the lender self-insures for the extra, as some credit unions will do. They may lend up to 80% financing and charge a high-ratio insurance fee on the total mortgage amount. The purpose of the insurance is to protect, and if required, pay the lender in the event of a mortgage default.

High-ratio mortgages are available for up to 90% of the purchase price or appraisal, whichever is lower, and in some cases 95%. There is a premium for this insurance, generally between 0.5% and 3% of the amount of the mortgage. The higher the debt ratio, the higher the risk, and therefore the higher the premium. You can obtain more information from your realtor, banker, mortgage broker, GE, or CMHC. Also, compare the qualifying requirements between CMHC and GE as they can vary and change from time to time.

Government-Assisted Mortgage

National Housing Act (NHA) mortgages are loans granted under the provisions of this federal act. They are administered through CMHC. You can apply for an NHA loan at any chartered bank, trust company, or credit union. Borrowers must pay an application fee to CMHC that usually includes the cost of a property appraisal and an insurance fee. The latter is usually added to the principal amount of the mortgage, though it may be paid at the time of closing. In addition, some provinces have second mortgage funding or funding guarantees. Contact CMHC or your financial institution for the most current information on borrowing requirements.

Variable Rate Mortgage

This type of mortgage, sometimes referred to as a VRM, is quite different from a fixed payment mortgage, as the interest rate may change during the term of the mortgage. Generally, these mortgages are set up initially like a fixed mortgage, based on the current interest rate. The mortgage interest rates are adjusted at specific intervals based on the market mortgage or prime interest rates.

Therefore, VRM is a popular option when interest rates are stable or going down.

Secondary Financing

Secondary financing generally consists of a second and possibly a third mortgage. You may wish to take out a second mortgage because the existing first mortgage you are assuming has an attractive interest rate or other desirable features, or your down payment is not large enough. You therefore need to obtain extra funds. Conventional lenders will usually provide money for second mortgages if you qualify. You can also obtain second mortgages through mortgage brokers or other sources that could go up as high as 90%.

Builder's Mortgage

If purchasing a new house or building one from scratch, you may be able to assume the builder's mortgage. Make sure that you obtain legal advice to ensure that the provisions in the mortgage are acceptable to you. If you are building the house, the lender may approve a mortgage for the various stages of construction (e.g., foundation, framing, roofing, etc.). It depends on the nature of the construction and the policy of the lender.

Vendor Mortgage

In a vendor mortgage, sometimes referred to as a vendor-back or vendor-take-back mortgage, the vendor or seller encourages the sale of the home by giving the purchaser a loan on the purchase of the property. For example, if the purchaser is able to get 75% conventional financing but does not have sufficient funds for the 25% down payment, the vendor may give, in effect, a second mortgage for 15%, as an example, of the purchase price. Therefore, the purchaser would only need to come up with a 10% down payment. The purchaser would then make mortgage payments to the vendor as if it were a second mortgage held by a normal commercial lender.

Agreement for Sale

An agreement for sale is not actually a mortgage, but it is another way of financing a sale, and should not be confused with an agreement for purchase and sale. An agreement for sale is normally used in a situation where the buyer of the property does not have sufficient funds for down payment and the vendor wishes to dispose of the property.

Agreements for sale are frequently used where the purchaser cannot assume the existing mortgage or obtain a new mortgage; in effect, the purchaser assumes a mortgage that he could not get otherwise. The purchaser pays the vendor and the vendor maintains payments on his original mortgage. The purchaser gets possession and the vendor keeps title until the debt is paid off in full. At that point, title is transferred to the purchaser.

SOURCES OF MORTGAGES

It is important to keep in mind that the competition among institutions to provide mortgage financing is extremely intense. You should therefore do research before deciding on which mortgage lender to use. You will probably want to begin with your own financial institution since you have a history together. This may be more convenient, but you must do some comparison shopping. A comparison of mortgage rates by institution appears in the real estate section of most weekend newspapers. You can also check with mortgage brokers in your community who frequently publish a list of current comparative rates which you can obtain free upon request.

The main sources of mortgage funds for residential purchases are as follows:

- Commercial banks
- Trust companies
- Credit unions
- Government
- Mortgage companies
- Real estate companies
- Mortgage brokers
- The vendor
- Family, friends, or business associates

SELECTING A MORTGAGE

There are many factors you should examine before making your decision about your mortgage, such as:

- amortization
- term of the mortgage
- interest rate
- interest averaging
- open or closed mortgage
- payment schedules
- prepayment privilege
- assumability, and
- portability

Amortization

Amortization is the length of time over which the regular (usually monthly) payments have been calculated on the assumption that the mortgage will be fully paid over that period. The usual amortization period is 25 years, although five-, 10-, 15-, or 20-year periods are also available. Naturally the shorter the amortization period, the more money you save on interest. Refer to my book, *Mortgage Payment Tables Made Easy* for extensive coverage of the topic area including many different mortgage payment options. For monthly interest payments refer to Chart 6-1 at page 93.

Term of the Mortgage

The term of the mortgage is the initial length of time the mortgagee (lender) will lend you the money. Terms may vary from six months to 10 years. Over a 25-year amortization period, you may possibly have 10 to 20 separate mortgage terms before you have completely paid off the loan. However, many people sell their home after five to 10 years, due to changing needs, and buy a new home.

At the end of each term, unless you are able to repay the entire mortgage, you would normally either renew the mortgage with the same lender on the same terms, renegotiate the mortgage, or refinance the mortgage through a different lending institution. The lender is not obliged to renew the mortgage at the end of the term, but will generally do so as long as you have met your payment terms. If you renew with a different mortgage lender, there could be extra administrative charges involved. However, because there is considerable competition among lenders, the other institution frequently will waive administrative fees and may also absorb the legal fees and costs to induce you away from a competitive lender. Naturally, you want to pay off your mortgage as quickly as possible by making annual prepayments, increasing your payments, or paying more frequently, e.g., weekly rather than monthly.

Interest Rate

There are various ways to calculate the interest: the *fixed rate*, which means the interest rate remains fixed for the period of the term of the mortgage; and the *variable rate*, which means that the interest rate varies every month according to the prime interest rate set by the lender. In this latter case, although the actual monthly payments would usually remain the same, the interest portion would vary. Earlier in this chapter, we discussed variable rate mortgages.

How often interest is compounded — the interest charged on interest owing — will determine the total amount of interest that you actually pay on the mortgage. Obviously, the more frequent the compounding, the more interest you will pay. The lender can charge any rate of interest, within the law, and compound that at any frequency desired. That is why it is important for you to check on the nature of the compounding of interest.

Be careful when comparing interest rates. Make sure that the "best rate" is not artificially low because it is based on monthly calculations rather than semi-annual interest calculations. Refer to Chart 6-1 at page 93 for interest payments.

Interest Averaging

If you are considering assuming an existing first mortgage because the rate and term is attractive, but are concerned about the current interest rate of second mortgage financing, do an interest averaging calculation. You might find the average interest rate to be quite acceptable. Here is an example of how you calculate it:

1st Mortgage   – $60,000 \times 7\%$ $= \$4,200$
2nd Mortgage   – $30,000 \times 9\%$ $= \$2,700$
                   $90,000 \times "x"\%$ $= \$6,900$

Average interest rate $"x"\% = \$6,900 / \$90,000 = 7.6\%$

Open or Closed Mortgage

An *open* mortgage allows you to increase the payment on the amount of the principal at any time. You can pay off the mortgage in full at any time before the term is over without any penalty or extra charges. Because of this flexibility, open mortgages cost more than standard closed mortgages, generally about 1/2% more. Open mortgages are generally for a one year maximum period. For this reason, unless you know you are going to have extra funds, you would probably consider a closed over an open mortgage. However, there are various issues to consider.

The more common, *closed* mortgage locks you in for the period of the term of the mortgage. There is usually a penalty for any advance payment. Most closed mortgages have a prepayment feature (see page 94).

Payment Schedules

Normally, mortgage payments are a blend of principal and interest. These have traditionally been amortized assuming a monthly payment basis. However, in terms of payment schedules, there are many options available in the marketplace, including weekly, bi-weekly, semi-monthly, and monthly. Naturally, the more frequent

CHART 6-1
Interest Payments

Interest on each $1,000 of mortgage is based on monthly payments.*

Interest Rate %	Amortization Period		
	15 years	20 years	25 years
3.00	6.90	5.54	4.74
3.25	7.02	5.67	4.87
3.50	7.14	5.79	5.00
3.75	7.26	5.92	5.13
4.00	7.39	6.05	5.27
4.25	7.51	6.18	5.40
4.50	7.63	6.31	5.54
4.75	7.76	6.44	5.68
5.00	7.89	6.58	5.82
5.25	8.01	6.71	5.96
5.50	8.14	6.84	6.10
5.75	8.27	6.98	6.25
6.00	8.40	7.12	6.40
6.25	8.53	7.26	6.55
6.50	8.66	7.41	6.70
6.75	8.80	7.55	6.85
7.00	8.94	7.70	7.01
7.25	9.07	7.84	7.16
7.50	9.21	7.99	7.32
7.75	9.35	8.14	7.48
8.00	9.49	8.29	7.64
8.25	9.63	8.44	7.80
8.50	9.77	8.59	7.96
8.75	9.91	8.74	8.12
9.00	10.05	8.90	8.28
9.25	10.19	9.05	8.45
9.50	10.34	9.21	8.62
9.75	10.48	9.36	8.78
10.00	10.63	9.52	8.95
10.25	10.77	9.68	9.12
10.50	10.92	9.84	9.29

*Interest being compounded semi-annually.

the payments, the lower the interest (see Chart 6-2), and the sooner you will pay off the mortgage. Some lenders give you the option of increasing or doubling the amount of your payments. There are many options available, so do your research.

To ensure that you obtain the maximum benefit, you want to make sure that more of your payments, whatever format you select, will go to reducing the principal, rather than paying the interest. The result is that you could, for example, pay off a mortgage in 17 years or sooner rather than 25 years, and save a large amount of money in interest. Remember to comparison shop to ensure that the lender is reducing your mortgage at the fastest rate available.

Prepayment Privilege

This is a very important feature to have in your mortgage if it is a closed one. Though called a closed mortgage, it is in fact partly open, permitting prepayment at certain stages. For example, you may be permitted to make a prepayment of between 10% and 20% monthly or annually on the principal. This could make an incredible difference in terms of saving on interest and reducing the amortization period (see Chart 6-2). It is wise to take advantage of the prepayment options as often as possible, especially if you know you will have extra money available from various sources. Over time, this will save you a lot of interest.

CHART 6-2
Prepayment or Increased Payment Savings

Based on a $50,000 mortgage at a 10% interest rate.*

	Standard Mortgage 25-Year Amortization	10% Annual Increase In Mortgage Payment	10% Annual Prepayment of Principal
Mortgage repaid in months:	300	119	84
Total interest charged:	$84,172	$34,449	$20,086
Interest savings vs. standard 25-year mortgage:	N/A	$49,723	$64,086

*Interest being compounded semi-annually.

Assumability

Assumability means that the buyer takes over the obligation and payments under the vendor's or seller's mortgage. Most mortgage contracts deal with the issue of assumability very clearly.

Portability

Some lenders have a feature called portability. This means that if you sell one home and buy another during the term of your mortgage, you can transfer the mortgage from one property to the other. Check carefully, though. Some lenders place restrictions on this.

Refer to the Mortgage Checklist 6-1 at page 101.

Factors that Affect Mortgage Interest Rates

There are many factors that impact on the rate of mortgage interest you will eventually pay. Here are the key ones:

Federal Government Policy. The federal government, through the Bank of Canada (Central Bank) sets the prime bank rate. This is the rate that the central bank charges on short-term loans to financial institutions. The rate is set each week at 25 basis points above the average yield (interest return) on three-month treasury bills. The government auctions these bills weekly. 100 basis points represents 1% interest, therefore 25 basis points would represent 0.25% interest. Conventional lenders (banks, trust companies, and credit unions) adjust their prime rates and mortgage rates using the federal bank rate as a guide. The Central Bank rate, therefore, sets a trend throughout the system. There are various factors and political/economic dynamics which influence the federal bank rate.

- If the government is attempting to stimulate the economy because of a recession and lower the inflation rate, it may attempt to lower rates throughout the money system by lowering its bank rate. Conversely, if the economy is too buoyant and there is too much debt building up, the central bank could attempt to increase the overall lending interest rates through increasing the Central Bank rate.

- Government treasury bills or bonds are sold to investors who place their money where they believe they will be getting their best return on their money. The highest interest rate will attract the highest interest.

All of these factors influence mortgage short-term and long-term interest rates at any given time. This is why, when you are applying for a mortgage, you may wish to have a six-month open mortgage if you think interest rates are going to decrease. Then you would convert to a three- or five-year closed mortgage when you see that interest rates are heading up. This is just one of many considerations you have to take into account when determining your mortgage needs and selection. Other factors to consider are discussed in Chapter 7.

Excess or Shortage of Supply of Money. Real estate cycles were discussed earlier. There is a natural connection to the general economic cycle. When lenders have an excess supply of money to lend due to an inflow of customer deposits, for example at RRSP deadline time in the spring, then interest rates tend to be more attractive and competitive. This is because the lender needs to make money; that is, a "spread" on the difference between what it pays the depositor and what it charges for lending money. This spread could be 1% to 2% or more depending on various factors, including competition. Lenders realize that there is a high degree of consumer awareness to get the best rate. This is further reinforced by charts published regularly in daily and real estate newspapers comparing mortgage rates of various banks, trust companies, and credit unions. Depositors must earn enough money on their savings to be comparable to the returns that they would earn on other investments, relative to the same degree of risk and liquidity. The willingness of people to place money in a savings account is where the pool of mortgage money is created.

A situation where the inflow of deposit funds is high and the interest rates are low and the lender has funds to lend is referred to as a "loose money" market. This affects the real estate market, of course. In this situation, real estate activity can be expected to increase, as more people will be able to afford financing to purchase a home. As there is more activity in the market place, there is a dynamic of supply and demand, and real estate prices can be expected to rise.

On the other hand, when interest rates are low the public realizes that it can get a better return elsewhere, and the lenders are left with a shortage of money for mortgages or other loans. This is referred to as a "tight money" market. Lenders may cut back on lending mortgage funds in many cases and be extra-selective where the money is lent. Developers and contractors could have difficulty getting funds to build and therefore real estate activity slows down. As potential purchasers could have difficulty obtaining funds they may choose to hold off, so real estate prices could drop due to the reduced demand. If mortgage interest rates are too high, many people may not be able to afford to buy as they may not qualify for a sufficient mortgage.

Type of Lender. Rates vary among lenders, depending on their policies and restrictions. A more conservative lender may charge a higher rate than another. In general terms, conventional lenders — banks, trust companies, and credit unions — tend to be fairly competitive in the rates they charge for mortgages. A private mortgage lender generally wants a greater profit and therefore will charge more.

Quality of Borrower. Lenders assess the creditworthiness of the borrower and the ability to pay. A borrower with fewer assets, recently employed, or self-employed, or who has a spotty credit record, will pay a higher rate of interest than a borrower who has the opposite profile. For example, this is graphically reflected in the case of loans to a business. The lowest-risk/no-risk customer could receive the prime rate of interest (lowest) for a loan. Higher-risk businesses could be paying prime +1% to prime + 8%.

Quality of Property. After the lender has appraised the property, assessed the type of location and resale potential of the property, and has determined the amount of equity the borrower is putting in, the lender will set the mortgage rate. If the place you are buying is a house or condominium in an economically stable community, you would probably obtain a competitive rate.

Priority of Mortgage. Basically, the security of the mortgage is greater depending on its date of registration relative to other mortgages. A mortgage that is registered first is referred to as a first mortgage, a mortgage that is registered second in line is referred to as a second mortgage, and so on. In the event that the borrower defaults on a mortgage and the property is sold, the first mortgage gets paid out first from the proceeds, followed by the second, etc. Therefore, the lower the mortgage ranks in terms of priority the higher the risk to the lender that could potentially lose money if there is a shortfall on sale. There is a direct relationship between risk and interest rate. A first mortgage could be at 7%, a second at 9% and a third at 12%. How much equity the owner has is also a factor. If the owner has lots of equity, no matter how many mortgages on the property, the lower the risk to the last lender of losing money on a forced sale.

Terms of Mortgage. The interest rate is affected by such factors as:

- The amortization period is the length of time the mortgage is paid out in full.
- If the mortgage is insured by CMHC or GE Capital there is a lower risk and therefore a lower rate.
- The length of the term before the mortgage is due for payment or renegotiation — (e.g., six months or a five-year term or longer). Generally, the longer the term, the greater the risk of uncertain interest rates, and the higher the rate, as a protective buffer. This is not always the case, however.
- If the mortgage is open, it can be paid at any time before the end of the term without penalty. If closed, it cannot be repaid or can be repaid but with a penalty (e.g., three months' interest or interest rate differential for the balance of the term, whichever is greater). Open mortgages have higher interest rates than closed mortgages.
- Is the interest rate calculated and compounded annually, semi-annually or monthly? The more frequent the interest calculation and compounding, the higher the effective rate of interest that you will be paying will be.
- The frequency of your payment schedule (e.g., weekly, bi-monthly, monthly, etc.) will have an impact on how much you pay.

Negotiating Skills of Borrower. This factor is an important one, in terms of the mortgage interest rate that you will be paying. A lot of people don't realize that the "posted" rate, that is the rate that is "posted" in the bank or that you see in the paper, is not necessarily the lowest rate that the lender will give you. But if you don't ask, you won't get any reduction.

Most institutions will reduce your mortgage rate by 1/2 to 3/4 % from the prevailing posted rate if you are getting a three year or longer fixed rate mortgage term. How much you get reduced is a function of the lender's policy at the time, the competitive marketplace, what negotiating leverage you have, in terms of using other bank services and other factors. For example, GICs, RRSPs, mutual funds, term deposits, car loan, personal line of credit, and business account (if you have a small business), are considered to show a multiple service relationship, with obvious additional profit benefits to the lender. You won't know the best rate that you can obtain, unless you do your research and comparison shop by phone or in person. If you decide to use a mortgage broker, one of the key questions you want to ask is who is giving the best rate. Refer to Chapter 5 for a discussion of mortgage brokers.

One important point to keep in mind, is that the mortgage rate is just one of the key factors that you look for. You want to look at the overall package before you make your final choice. For example, what about pre-payments privileges, sign-up incentives (e.g. payment of your legal fees, appraisal fees), and other features.

DETERMINING THE AMOUNT OF MORTGAGE AVAILABLE

The amount of mortgage funds available differs with various lenders. There is considerable flexibility and it is important to compare or have your mortgage broker do so in order to get the maximum amount of mortgage funds possible if that is important to you. Lenders use the Gross Debt Service (GDS) Ratio and Total Debt Service (TDS) Ratio as standard formulas for determining mortgage qualification. Naturally, any lender wants to be cautious and make sure you are not over-extending yourself in your ability to debt-service the mortgage. The last thing a lender wants is for you to default on your mortgage payments. If you are interested in what happens when one defaults on a mortgage, refer to Chapter 9 "The Legal Aspects."

In calculating principal and interest, you may want to purchase my mortgage payment book, *Mortgage Payment Tables Made Easy,* available at most bookstores. Refer to Chart 2-1 at page 21 which shows monthly mortgage payments for principal plus interest.

Gross Debt Service (GDS) Ratio

The GDS Ratio is used to calculate the amount you can afford to spend for mortgage principal (P) and interest (I) payments. Some lenders also include property taxes (T) as part of this formula, and possibly heating costs (H). Under the GDS Ratio, payments generally should not exceed 30% of your income, with some flexibility. Refer to Sample 2-3 at page 19 to calculate your own mortgage eligibility.

Total Debt Service (TDS) Ratio

Many people have monthly financial obligations other than mortgage and taxes, such as credit card payments, car payments, and other loans, and lenders want to know these in order to determine your ability to pay. In general terms, no more than 40% of your gross family income can be used when calculating the amount you can afford to pay for principal, interest and taxes, plus your fixed monthly debts. Refer to Sample 2-4 at page 20.

It is important for you to consider all your monthly obligations (e.g., insurance and electricity costs), some of which may not be taken into account by the lender, so that you get a good feeling for your financial standing. Sample 2-1 at page 12 should show you what your monthly income is and what you will have available for the mortgage payments plus other expenses.

APPLYING FOR A MORTGAGE

In applying for a mortgage, there are various steps you should follow to make sure you obtain the funds you need with the terms and conditions you want. If you go through a mortgage broker (see Chapter 5), some of these steps may not be required. Start out by checking with your existing financial institution as you already have a history and a relationship. However, make sure you comparison shop, as you could get a much better deal because of the competition.

Preparation for the Application Interview

Here is a summary of the steps that you should follow prior to your application interview with a lender.

- Do research on all the types of lending institutions from which you could obtain a mortgage. Check competing interest rates for different types of mortgages by contacting a mortgage broker or by referring to the business section of your local newspaper for comparative mortgage rates.
- Understand some of the jargon. This book should help you to determine what you want from a mortgage, and therefore negotiate the package that is suited to your purposes.
- Make up a list of questions that you want to ask the lender, using Checklist 6-1 at page 101 as a guide.
- Determine your financial needs. Complete the cost of living budget (Sample 2-1 at page 12) as well as the mortgage checklist.
- Calculate roughly the maximum amount of mortgage that you might expect from a lender (refer to the previous section

that provides the necessary formulas). Remember, th
guides only.

- Obtain a letter from your employer confirming your salary,
  your position, and the length of time you have worked there.
  If you are self-employed, you will be required to bring copies
  of recent financial statements and/or income tax returns
  (usually the last three years).
- Prepare a statement of your assets and liabilities and net
  worth (refer to Sample 2-2 at page 14).
- Complete the details on the amount of the down payment that
  you will be providing and where the funds are coming from.
  This could include savings accounts, term deposits, Canada
  Savings Bonds, RRSPs, a family loan, an inheritance, a divorce
  settlement, or other sources.
- Obtain a copy of the agreement of purchase and sale.

CHECKLIST 6-1

Mortgage Checklist

A. Ask Yourself These Questions

- Is your income secure?
- Will your income increase or decrease in the future?
- Are you planning on increasing the size of your family (e.g.,
  children, relatives) and therefore your living expenses?
- Will you be able to put aside a financial buffer for unexpected
  expenses or emergencies?
- Are you planning to purchase the property with someone else?
- If the answer is yes to the above question, will you be able
  to depend on your partner's financial contribution without
  interruption?
- If you are relying on an income from renting out part of your
  purchase, do you know:
  — If city by-laws permit it?
  — If the condominium corporation by-laws permit it?
  — If the mortgage company policies permit it?
- Have you thoroughly compared mortgage rates and features
  so that you know what type of mortgage and mortgage com-
  pany you want?

- Have you determined the amount of mortgage that you would be eligible for?
- Have you considered the benefits of a pre-approved mortgage?
- Have you considered talking to a mortgage broker?
- Have you considered assuming an existing mortgage?
- Have you considered the benefits of a portable mortgage?
- Have you considered having the vendor give you a mortgage?
- Have you determined all the expenses you will incur relating to the purchase transaction? (See Checklist 6-2 at page 104.)
- Have you completed your present and projected financial needs analysis (income and expenses)? (See Sample 2-1 at page 12.)
- Have you completed the mortgage application form, including net worth statement (assets and liabilities)? (See Sample 2-2 at page 14.)

B. Ask the Lender These Questions

Interest Rates
- What is the current interest rate?
- How frequently is the interest calculated? (semi-annually, monthly, etc.)
- What is the effective interest rate on an annual basis?
- How long will the lender guarantee a quoted interest rate?
- Will the lender put the above guarantee in writing?
- Will you receive a lower rate of interest if the rates fall before you finalize your mortgage?
- Will the lender put the above reduction assurance in writing?
- Will the lender show you the total amount of interest you will have to pay over the lifetime of the mortgage? (e.g., give you a computer printout)

Amortization
- What options do you have for amortization periods? (10, 15, 20, 25, 30 years, etc.)
- Will the lender provide you with an amortization schedule for your loan showing your monthly payments apportioned into principal and interest?
- Have you calculated what your monthly payments will be, based on each amortization rate?

- Are you required to maintain the amortized monthly payment schedule if annual prepayments are made, or will they be adjusted accordingly?
- What different terms are available? (6 months, 1, 2, 3, 5 years, etc.)
- What is the best term for your personal circumstances?
- What are the different interest rates available relating to the different terms?

Payments

- What is the amount of your monthly payments (based on amortization period)?
- Are you permitted to increase the amount of your monthly payments if you want to, without penalty?
- Does the lender have a range of payment periods available, such as weekly, bi-weekly, monthly, etc.? Does the lender have a standard and capped variable rate mortgage?
- What is the best payment period in your personal circumstances?

Prepayment

- What are your prepayment privileges?
  — Completely open?
  — Open with a fixed penalty or notice requirement?
  — Limited open with no penalty or notice requirement?
  — Limited open with fixed penalty or notice requirement?
  — Completely closed?
  — Some combination of the above?
- What amount can be prepaid and what is the penalty or notice required, if applicable?
- How long does the privilege apply in each of the above categories, if applicable?
- When does the prepayment privilege commence? (6 months, 1 year, etc.)
- Is there a minimum amount that has to be prepaid?
- What form does your prepayment privilege take: an increase in payments or lump sum?
- Is your prepayment privilege accumulative (e.g., make last year's lump sum prepayment next year)?

Taxes

- How much are the property taxes?
- Does the lender require a property tax payment monthly (based on projected annual tax), or is it optional?
- Does the lender pay interest on the property tax account? If yes, what is the interest rate?

Mortgage Transaction Fees and Expenses

- Is an appraisal necessary? What is the fee?
- Is a survey necessary? What is the fee?
- Will you be able to choose your own lawyer to do the mortgage work?
- Does the lender charge a processing or administrative fee?
- Does the lender arrange for a lawyer to do the mortgage documentation work at a flat fee, regardless of the amount of the mortgage?
- Does the lender know what the out-of-pocket disbursements for the mortgage transaction will be?
- Does the mortgage have a renewal administration fee? How much is it?

Mortgage Assumption Privileges

- Can the mortgage be assumed if the property is sold?
- Is the mortgage assumable with or without the lender's approval?
- What are the assumption administrative fees, if any?
- Will the lender release the vendor of all personal obligations under the terms of the mortgage if it is assumed?

Portability

- Is the mortgage portable; i.e., can you transfer it to another property that you may buy?

CHECKLIST 6-2

Real Estate Purchase Expenses Checklist

In addition to the actual purchase price of your home, there are a number of other expenses to be paid on or prior to closing. Not all of these expenses will be applicable. Some provinces may have additional expenses.

Type of Expense	When Paid	Estimated Amount
Deposits	At time of offer	$ _____
Mortgage application fee	At application	$ _____
Property appraisal	At application	$ _____
Property inspection	At inspection	$ _____
Balance of purchase price	On closing	$ _____
Legal fees re: property transfer	On closing	$ _____
Legal fees re: mortgage preparation	On closing	$ _____
Legal disbursements re: property transfer	On closing	$ _____
Legal disbursements re: mortgage preparation	On closing	$ _____
Mortgage broker commission	On closing	$ _____
Property survey	On closing	$ _____
Property tax holdback (by mortgage company)	On closing	$ _____
Land transfer or deed tax (provincial)	On closing	$ _____
Property purchase tax (provincial)	On closing	$ _____
Property tax (local/ municipal) adjustment	On closing	$ _____
Goods & Services Tax (GST) (federal)	On closing	$ _____
New Home Warranty Program fee	On closing	$ _____
Mortgage interest adjustment (by mortgage company)	On closing	$ _____
Sales tax on chattels purchased from vendor (provincial)	On closing	$ _____
Adjustments for fuel, taxes, etc.	On closing	$ _____

Type of Expense	When Paid	Estimated Amount
Mortgage lender insurance premium (CMHC or GE)	On closing	$ _____
Condominium maintenance fee adjustment	On closing	$ _____
Home insurance	On closing	$ _____
Life insurance premium	Built into mort-gage payments	$ _____
Moving expenses	At time of move	$ _____
Utility connection charges (hydro, telephone, etc.)	At time of move	$ _____
Redecorating and refurbishing costs	After purchase	$ _____
Immediate repair and maintenance costs	After purchase	$ _____
House and garden improvements	After purchase	$ _____

Other expenses (list): _____

_____

_____

The Application Process

The steps in the application process are as follows:

- Set up and attend a meeting, along with your spouse and any co-applicant or guarantor, with the lending institution.
- A formal mortgage application has to be completed. The application is typically divided into three main sections: description of the property, financial details relating to the purchase of the property, and personal financial information.
- Processing of the application by the lender normally takes one to five business days. During that time the lender will:
  — check your credit references and your credit rating;
  — verify your financial information;
  — have the property appraised (at your cost);
  — assess your application within the lender's approval guide-lines; and

— issue a formal commitment of approval in writing.

- Different lenders have different guidelines when assessing mortgage applications, but generally there are three main criteria: character, capacity, and collateral.

Character. The lender will assess your credit history and other factors to predict how you will meet your obligations in the future. For example, do you pay your bills on time? What is your credit rating in terms of paying off previous loans? Do you have a dependable employment history, or have you had a different job every three or four months?

Capacity. The lender is concerned about your ability to meet your financial obligation and will be concerned about such questions as: Does your GDS Ratio come within the guidelines? What are your other debts and obligations? Is your income sufficient to handle the mortgage payments? Is your income stable and does it appear as though it will continue to be so?

Collateral. Lenders are very much concerned with knowing that the security or collateral that has been provided for a loan (the home) is sufficient to cover the loan in the event that it is not repaid. They want to be satisfied that the property could be readily sold if necessary. That is why they prefer to select the appraiser for assessing the value of a property. When making an appraisal the following factors are considered: location, price, zoning, condition of the housing unit, quality of neighbourhood, size, appearance, municipal services available, and comparative sales in the same area.

Pre-Approved Mortgage

Pre-approved mortgages are fairly popular with most conventional lending institutions such as banks, trust companies, and credit unions. The purpose is to confirm in writing, in advance, the maximum amount of money on which you can rely for mortgage purposes. This will help you to be realistic when you are out house hunting and negotiating a purchase. You are offered a specific amount of mortgage for a period of time, for example $100,000, with an interest rate guaranteed for 90 days. If the rate drops before the lender advances funds, you are given the lower rate. There is always a condition, of course, that the lender must approve the actual property before you can finalize the agreement, so that the lender can make sure that the security is suitable.

Assuming An Existing Mortgage

One of the options you may have, is to assume the vendor's existing mortgage. You would have to obtain the consent of the vendor and the vendor's lender of course. The lender does the same type of credit assessment of you as they would if you were obtaining a new mortgage.

The reason you may wish to explore the above option only makes sense if the mortgage is more attractive in the interest being charged, than what you would otherwise pay for a new mortgage. Also, if there is enough time left in the mortgage term to make the exercise worthwhile. For example, if at the time you are seeking a mortgage the prevailing rate was 10% for a five year term closed mortgage, and you could assume an existing mortgage at 7% with three years left in the term, that would be a considerable financial saving in interest payments. In this scenario, the vendor is motivated to have you assume the mortgage because they would otherwise have to pay a penalty for the interest differential for the remaining three years. This could be a considerable penalty, depending on the amount of the mortgage. Refer to the earlier discussion on pre-payment privileges and penalties, as that is another issue for you to consider. That is, how attractive the mortgage is in terms of your pre-payment privileges (e.g. 10-20% a year) and other features.

Loan Approval

Once the lender has granted approval for the mortgage, it will suggest its own lawyer to protect its interests by checking on the title of the property to make sure that it is clear, and to perform any necessary duties, including the filing of the mortgage. However, the lender may allow the borrower's lawyer to perform the mortgage work. In either case, the borrower customarily pays all the legal fees and disbursements. If you are required, or prefer, to use the lender's lawyer, obtain independent legal advice about the provisions of the mortgage. Other legal aspects are covered in Chapter 9, "The Legal Aspects."

Mortgage Life Insurance

When you apply for a mortgage with a lender, you frequently have the option to buy life insurance designed to pay out the mortgage in full on your death. Naturally, there is a premium for this feature, and the premium is built into your regular mortgage payments. You should comparison shop with various lenders to see how competitive the insurance rates are for the coverage that you would be wanting. Naturally, when you sell the home, the mortgage life insurance is no longer in place. You would have to apply for it again when you get a mortgage for a new home.

It is also helpful considering the alternative of buying personal term life insurance to meet your existing and projected future needs. Do a comparison of the premium rates, features and benefits. You might find that you would be further ahead using your own personal term insurance coverage to clear out the mortgage debt on your death. You could find that the insurance premium rates are similar to the rate for the mortgage insurance. The other point is that you could be insurable now for personal life insurance coverage but may not be at some point in the future, for whatever reason, if you held off getting personal term insurance until some later date. So there are a number of financial planning issues to consider. Also, consider disability insurance to cover your mortgage payments should you become unable to work due to an accident, surgery, etc.

DEDUCTING HOME OFFICE EXPENSES

If you currently have, or are considering a part-time or full-time home-based business, there are significant tax advantages. You can legitimately write off a lot of home-related expenses that you would be incurring anyway. Indirectly therefore, you could be helping to reduce your mortgage debt by saving money on your home business taxes.

Many home business owners pay too much tax. Most of them don't know all the types of tax deductions available or how to take full advantage of them. Others overpay because they are conservative by nature. And some either receive poor tax advice, or no advice at all. Whatever the reason, if you're paying too much tax, it's time to stop. Keep in mind two key points.

- You have a right to maximize your tax deductions. It is important to adopt the mindset that a high percentage of your expenses legitimately relate directly or indirectly to earning business income.
- You should find a professional accountant with an equally aggressive attitude towards maximizing deductions. Accountants typically fall on the conservative side. You should locate one who adopts an assertive approach to planning, who enjoys the professional and intellectual challenges of knowing the fine line, and can bring you comfortably close to it. No professional accountant (e.g. CA or CGA) would choose to risk their reputation or livelihood by advising you to fall over the line.

Anyone can call themselves an accountant, and many do. So select an accountant with a professional designation, such as chartered accountant (CA) or certified general accountant (CGA). Even if you already have an accountant, obtain at least three other opinions from accountants who specialize in tax matters, to ensure the advice you're getting is appropriate. You need a benchmark for comparison. If you don't have an accountant, have an interview with at least three of them before you decide which one, if any, you want to rely on for advice. You can obtain names from friends in business or from the Yellow Pages under "Accountants." Most initial visits are free. Confirm this before the appointment. Before your meeting, put all your questions in writing in case you forget them, and prioritize them in case you run out of time.

Then, apply tax planning strategies to every decision you make. These strategies should be customized to your situation and updated regularly. With your new assertiveness, keep receipts of every expense you incur. Your accountant can advise you later what portion is usable.

Here are the deductions most frequently missed or ineffectively used by home business owners. These are guidelines only. You want to get customized personal advice and make sure the information is current.

Home

Deduct the portion of your home that is dedicated exclusively for business purposes. this could include work, office and storage areas. If you have customers coming to your home, claim a separate reception area and washroom for business use, or a portion of it if it's shared between personal and business uses.

To calculate the percentage of home office use there is a formula. Divide the total area (excluding basement, for example) by the overall square footage used for business-related purposes. Don't forget to include a portion of the "common area" used for business purposes, e.g., hallways and stairs. Use the committed office area percentage as a base. The normal home office space usages ranges from 10%-25% of the total home area.

Once you have figured out your business-use portion, apply it to your total house-related expenses to calculate your total home office business expenses. Allowable home expenses include: mortgage interest and property taxes (or rent), plus insurance, maintenance costs and utilities (e.g. gas, electric, water, sewer, telephone, cable). Make sure you obtain extended homeowner insurance protection to cover home-office use. This extra premium is 100% tax deductible.

Another formula option when calculating home office usage is to take the number of rooms you use for your home office, and divide that by the total number of rooms in the house to obtain a percent. You want to use whatever formula is to your tax advantage.

Car

If you have one car and use it for business 50% of the time, claim half your car-related expenses (e.g., gas, oil, maintenance, insurance, interest on car financing costs) as business expenses. You should maintain a mileage log book to support your usage claim. If you have two cars and use one exclusively for business, you can claim 100% of that car's expenses. Be sure to claim depreciation of 30% on your car and deduct the appropriate portion each year from income. Make sure you obtain insurance coverage for your car to cover your business usage. The additional premium is 100% deductible.

Furniture and equipment

Your office furniture, computer hardware and software, printer, fax, copier and other equipment have to be depreciated over time, using the capital cost allowance formula, which lets you deduct a portion (20% to 100%) each year. The concept of depreciation is that the cost of the asset has to be spread over the projected useful life of the asset. If you have an incorporated business, you can sell your personal business furniture, computer and car to your business at fair market value. In doing so, you pay no personal income tax on the proceeds, as you originally bought the assets with after-tax income.

Salaries

Salaries paid to children, spouse, relatives or others to perform work for your firm are all deductible expenses. Payments should be reasonable and the arrangements structured properly to avoid problems in case of an audit. You may want to structure your spouse's business involvement, in tax terms, as an independent contractor, that is self-employed.

Meals

You can deduct 50% of your total meal costs (e.g. including alcohol, taxes and gratuity) relating to promotion or other eligible purposes, for example, taking a prospective or existing customer out to lunch or dinner, or someone who is knowledgeable in the industry whose expertise and opinion you want to benefit from. If you attend a trade show and pay for lunch for yourself, you can take 50% of that cost.

Education

If you attend any seminar, conference, convention or trade show relating to your current or future business interest or operation, keep all receipts. They are 100% deductible except 50% for meals. Don't forget to include any parking costs. Also, all subscriptions to magazines and newspapers are tax deductible if you are incurring those expenses to keep your knowledge current, for example, keeping aware of trends, ideas, the competition, pending legislation, the economy, etc. Don't forget any Internet-related costs, such as Internet Service Provider (ISP) fees. You are incurring these expenses for research and other business-related purposes.

Travel

This is one deduction many people don't fully understand. With proper tax advice and planning, you should be able to claim up to 100% of all costs, except meals, which would be at 50%. The percentage and eligibility of deduction depends on whether your trip was deemed to be business-related exclusively (e.g. 100%) or partially (e.g. 50%). In the latter case, the other 50% could have been a personal vacation.

Remember to obtain professional tax advice on an ongoing basis. Obtain the current "Business and Professional Income Tax Guide" from Revenue Canada. Ask your accountant about all the tax saving strategies available to you. And stay assertive about maximizing your deductions. As the saying goes, it's not what you make, it's how much you keep that's important.

If you are interested in more information about succeeding in a home-based business or small business, refer to my books, *Home Inc.: The Canadian Home-Based Business Guide* and *The Complete Canadian Small Business Guide*, both published by McGraw-Hill Ryerson.

* * *

Now you understand the complexities of the various kinds of mortgages available to you and you have a good idea how much you can afford, but that isn't everything. Next you'll review the additional costs that must be considered when buying your home.

Chapter 7

ADDITIONAL COSTS

There are numerous direct and indirect expenses related to obtaining a mortgage and buying a home that you must budget for. Not all of these costs will apply in your case, but it is helpful to be aware of them. (Refer to Checklist 6-2, "Real Estate Purchase Expenses Checklist" at page 104.)

This chapter discusses additional costs related to the mortgage, and additional expenses not related directly to the mortgage itself.

COSTS RELATED TO THE MORTGAGE

Costs will vary considerably from one lender to another. The type of financing that you are obtaining will also be a factor. The following sections discuss some of the most common expenses related to the mortgage that you should consider and budget for. Costs will vary depending on the geographic location and province. Naturally you should have a contingency reserve fund for unexpected emergencies.

Mortgage Application Fee

Some lenders charge a processing fee or set-up fee for their administrative expenses in the processing of your mortgage application. Due to the highly competitive nature of the mortgage industry, normally, when purchasing a single-family dwelling, the mortgage application fee is waived.

Appraisal Fee

The lender will obtain its own appraiser to determine the value of the property for mortgage purposes. The borrower pays the cost of the appraisal which ranges from $150 to $350. Generally lenders will not give you a copy of the appraisal, although you should request it in advance.

You may be able to avoid the appraisal fee if a professional appraiser has evaluated the property within 60 to 90 days and the lender is prepared to accept it. Alternatively, if you are only obtaining the standard 70% financing, many lenders will waive an appraisal requirement because the risk is less. This waiver would depend on the state of the market, the age, size, and location of the home you are buying, etc. Ask the lender. Due to the competitive marketplace, some lenders will absorb the appraisal fee to get your business.

Standby Fee

Some lenders attempt to charge the borrower a fee for setting aside and reserving the money required until it is advanced. The rationale behind this is that the mortgage company will be losing revenue on this money in the interim. In principal residence mortgages this fee is fairly rare; it is more common for mortgages for new construction or real estate investment purposes.

Survey Fee

You may be required to obtain a property survey prior to mortgage funds being paid out. The survey would be done by a qualified professional surveyor, and the purpose is to make sure that the lender knows exactly the dimensions of the property. The lender may also want to be satisfied that the building meets the requirements of municipal by-laws. The cost of the survey would be deducted from the mortgage funds that have been advanced to you, or you would pay for it directly. Your lawyer normally arranges for this survey. You may be able to save yourself money by using an existing survey and having the previous owner sign an affidavit stating that there have been no changes since the survey was done. Many lenders will accept this. Ask the realtor if the owner has a survey. It is primarily older houses that lenders are concerned about, due to additions, etc. If you are buying a new or relatively new house, you can ask the lender if they will waive the survey requirement. Survey fees generally range from $150 to $300. Some lenders will absorb this cost.

A survey is not required for a condominium but the lender may require a copy of the condominium plan showing the location of the unit you are buying.

Mortgage Broker Fee

For purchase of a home you intend to live in, you will probably not have to pay a fee for obtaining the mortgage as such. This was discussed in Chapter 5 "Professionals and Other Experts." Most mortgage brokers would require an advance from you for appraisal and out-of-pocket costs that are incurred on your behalf. This is not the same as an application or administration fee, but could be included within such fees if they are charged.

Mortgage Insurance Fees (CMHC or GE)

If you are obtaining a high-ratio mortgage or the lender requires you to obtain mortgage insurance for other reasons, then you will be paying a mortgage insurance fee. The fee is approximately 0.5% to 3.0% of the amount of the mortgage that is being insured (generally the full first mortgage) and is either added onto the mortgage total or paid by you in a lump sum at the time of closing the mortgage transaction. Mortgage insurance was discussed in Chapter 6 under the heading of "High Ratio/Insured Mortgages."

Mortgage Life Insurance Premiums

Mortgage life insurance is not the same as mortgage insurance. Many of the lending institutions provide an option for you to purchase insurance that will pay off the mortgage in the event of your death, the premium for which is generally included in your monthly payments. You should compare the cost with term insurance from private insurance carriers to see if the rates are competitive. As an option you may prefer to protect yourself by taking out your own term insurance that would provide sufficient funds to pay off the mortgage in the event of your death. There could be situations though where you might not be insurable for basic term life insurance, but would be eligible for mortgage life insurance without a medical examination requirement.

In certain circumstances, for example, if the lender felt your health to be a risk factor, they may require that you take out mortgage life insurance as a condition of mortgage approval. Also, consider disability insurance.

Fire and Liability Insurance Premium

Primary lenders require that any borrower on a mortgage carry sufficient fire insurance to cover the amount of the mortgage, and that they be paid off first. The second and third mortgage lenders would want the same type of coverage and have it shown that they are paid off second, third, and so on. It is necessary for the borrower to purchase sufficient replacement insurance. The borrower is responsible for making insurance arrangements and paying the costs of the insurance policy. This has to be provided to the lender's lawyer before any mortgage funds are advanced. Refer to Chapter 5 on "Professionals and Other Experts" for a discussion of insurance brokers and insurance.

Contribution to Property Tax Account

Some lenders require that you pay 1/12 of the projected annual taxes each month. This would be built into your monthly mortgage payments and the lender would set up a separate tax account and remit the funds directly to the municipality at the appropriate time each year. Don't forget to ask about the interest that is going to be paid on your tax account. The interest paid is normally lower than that paid on deposit accounts.

In most cases, lenders will give you the option to be responsible for paying your own taxes directly after a year. Try to negotiate this option. Alternatively, attempt to have the property tax contribution requirement waived entirely. Perhaps in your situation you consider it to be a worthwhile "forced savings" plan. The interest you get on the tax fund deposit is generally very low. If you are paying a portion of the projected property tax every month, you will have to build that expense into the costs related to your mortgage.

Property Tax Adjustment Holdback

This concept is related to the previous topic. If the lender requires that you pay a portion of the property taxes every month, and if you purchase the property on April 1st with property taxes due in July, obviously there will be a shortfall in the tax account. Either you would have to come up with these funds additionally or the lender would subtract that amount of money from the mortgage proceeds being made available to you.

Interest Adjustment

When you pay rent you are paying in advance. When you pay mortgage you are paying in arrears. In other words, the mortgage payment you make on March 1st covers the funds and interest for the month of February.

Because the lender's internal system is geared on a monthly payment basis, the lender will want to be paid in advance for the use of the funds prior to March 1. This interest adjustment is then advanced from the mortgage funds provided to you so that the interest is prepaid up to March 1st. When your normal mortgage payment would be made on April 1st, it would cover the one-month interest charge for the month of March plus a small repayment of the principal. Not all lenders require this arrangement, but you should know in advance so that you are aware of the net proceeds that you will receive on the mortgage.

Interest

Interest is, of course, a cost of having the funds paid to you under a mortgage. What you will have to pay for interest, and the steps you should go through to obtain the most attractive interest rate, were discussed in Chapter 6.

Provincial Mortgage Filing Tax

Most provinces charge a tax for filing a mortgage in the land registry. In addition, there are filing fees for transferring title of the property, which are $50 to $100 per filing.

Legal Fees and Disbursements

You are responsible for legal fees as well as out-of-pocket disbursements that your lawyer incurs in preparing and filing your mortgage documentation. Disbursements would cover such things as preparing property searches, photocopy expenses, courier costs, and other costs associated with the preparing and registration of the mortgage. The disbursement costs would normally include the provincial mortgage filing tax or fee referred to above. It is the normal practice for lawyers to deduct the legal fees and disbursements directly from the money to be advanced under the mortgage. In addition, you would obviously have to pay your lawyer to do the transfer of the property.

Sometimes, lenders require you to use a particular law firm, or one of a limited number of firms, but often you can use the lawyer of your choice. In all cases you are responsible for the legal fees and disbursements. Using the same lawyer to do both the mortgage and transfer will mean savings on fees and disbursements by eliminating duplication of expenses. There is also efficiency of scale.

COSTS NOT RELATED DIRECTLY TO THE MORTGAGE

The following are additional expenses not related directly to the mortgage itself.

New Home Warranty Program Fee

This fee is either built into the price of your home or added separately. The fee is normally related to the cost of your home, generally with a maximum which can vary from province to province. If it is added separately, you will need to budget for this expense.

Provincial Property Purchase Tax Fee

Some provinces charge a tax for transferring title in property. The tax formula varies, depending on the province.

Federal and Provincial Government Taxes

You will have to pay the federal Goods and Services Tax (GST) of 7% on any service relating to your residential real estate purchase. In addition, you could pay GST on the cost of the property in some cases. In some provinces you have to pay provincial sales tax (PST) on real estate related services. Here is a summary of the key points relating to GST:

Services. The type of services covered by GST include lawyer's fees and disbursements (out-of-pocket expenses) for doing the mortgage and transfer work, survey fees, appraisal fees, and moving costs.

New Residential Property. GST applies to the sale of "new" residential property. The test being that the property has never been occupied as a place of residence or lodging after its construction.

Substantially Renovated Residential Property. GST also applies to a "substantially renovated property." A substantial renovation is one in which all or most of the building, except the foundation, external walls, interior supporting walls, floor, roof, and staircases are removed or replaced. Where a residential property was substantially renovated, GST will apply to the full value of the renovated property, including the value of the land.

GST Exceptions. The GST does not apply to sales of "used" residential housing. As a general rule, "new" residential premises become "used" once the premises are sold and lived in or used by the first purchasers. In other words, in most circumstances it is the first purchaser who pays the GST; subsequent purchasers do not.

GST Rebate on New or Substantially Renovated Property. If you buy a property valued at no more than $350,000 and pay GST on it, you are entitled to a rebate of 36% of the total GST paid. The net effect is that rather than paying 7% GST, you are paying 4.5%. You are only eligible for this if you are buying the home to live in it as your principal residence. You can sign the "GST new housing rebate form" before completing the transfer of property. This will let you pay only the net amount GST due on closing and you won't have to wait for the rebate. Discuss this issue with your lawyer prior to closing. Refer to Chapter 10.

Property Inspection

The benefits of having a professional inspection have been discussed earlier. The fees normally range from $200 to $400 and over.

Moving Expenses

Don't forget to budget for moving costs. Make sure you get from three to five estimates, as well as the information packages. Consider the middle estimate. Selecting a lowball price is not necessarily the best decision. Professional movers can be expensive. Attempt to negotiate a lower price if you are moving at the slow time of the month. Find out how long the mover has been in business and obtain references. Check the amount of insurance for loss or damage you are covered for. Consider obtaining additional insurance. Check for complaints with the Better Business Bureau. You may wish to rent a truck and move the goods yourself, if that option is feasible. Refer to Chapter 13, "The Move."

Renovating, Repair, and Redecorating Costs

Make sure you include these costs in your purchase budget. Depending on the condition of the home, your needs and budget, the costs could be low or high, necessary or discretionary. You also want to save for a contingency reserve fund for unexpected emergencies or expenses. For example, if you have an older home, you will probably have to repair or replace various items. If you had a professional home inspector provide you with a report and possible estimates for repair prior to purchase, you probably have a fairly clear idea of the "might do," "should do" and "must do" costs. You may have successfully negotiated a purchase price reduction to cover all or part of these costs. If you are covered by a New Home Warranty Plan, any major structural repairs should be covered. Check it out.

If you are buying your first house, you could have additional expenses such as new appliances, furniture, yard maintenance equipment, tools and supplies. You may be able to buy some of these from the present owner.

Due to the age of the house or your needs or style preferences, you may wish to redecorate all or a part of the house. This could include drapes, curtains, wallpaper, paint, flooring, carpeting, light fixtures, etc. You may wish to add on or renovate rooms for in-laws, renters, a growing family, or a home office. If you are buying a new home, there could be landscaping costs to factor in. Refer to Chapter 14 for a discussion of these subjects.

* * *

Now that you have a clear picture of the various costs associated with buying your first home, let us now examine how to go about putting a price tag on the home you want to buy.

Chapter 8
DETERMINING THE VALUE OF THE HOME

Before you can begin to put a price on the home you are considering buying, you should first understand how the real estate market works.

This chapter will cover real estate cycles and other factors that affect real estate prices, as well as various formulas for calculating how much a home is worth.

UNDERSTANDING THE REAL ESTATE MARKET

In order to have a better appreciation of how the real estate market operates, you need to understand the cycles and factors that influence prices and interest rates. No buying decisions should be made without market assessment.

The Real Estate Cycle

Real estate is a cyclical industry. As in any such industry, the cycle historically creates shortage and excess. This relates to the issue of supply and demand in the marketplace. Too much supply creates a reduction in value. Too little supply creates an increase in value. It is essential to know where you are in the cycle relative to the exact location you are considering. It is also important to appreciate that different provinces, regions, and communities are in different parts of the economic cycle. Timing in the cycle is important when making buying or selling decisions.

One of the reasons for the cycle is that many developers are entrepreneurial by nature and operate primarily by short-term planning. If financing and credit are available, developers tend to build without regard for the overall supply and demand. If a consequent glut occurs and the demand is not there, prices come down as houses and condominiums go unsold. The phases of the real estate cycle will be discussed later in the chapter.

External factors that can affect the real estate cycle include:

General Business Economic Cycles. The economy historically goes through periods of increased economic growth followed by recessionary periods. The economic impact is greater, of course, in certain parts of the country than in others in any given cycle. In a recessionary period, people lose their jobs and have to put their houses on the market. Real estate prices become depressed as potential purchasers decide to wait until the economy is more secure.

It is difficult to know for certain when the economy will turn around, but various indicators should give you some insight. If the economy has been in a recession for a sustained period of time, there could be definite opportunities to buy. Once the economy comes out of a recession, prices tend to climb. Conversely, if the economy has been on a buoyant growth trend for an extended period of time, be very cautious in purchasing because a change in the cycle, and therefore a drop in real estate prices, could be imminent.

Local Business Cycle. Each local economy has its own cycle and factors that impact on real estate prices. These factors may not be greatly influenced by the general (provincial or national) business cycles just discussed.

Community Cycle. Certain geographic locations within a community can have their own economic cycles as well as supply and demand, all of which affect real estate prices. In addition, a community has its own life cycle from growth to decline to stagnation to rehabilitation. Look for areas of future growth.

As you can see, being aware of economic, business, and community cycles is critical to prudent decision-making. Before buying or selling real estate in a certain area, determine what external factors are prevalent and how they impact on the cycle of the real estate market. Different types of real estate — for example, condominiums, new houses or resale houses — can be in different parts of a cycle.

There are four distinct indicators or phases to a real estate cycle. They go from a depressed market to an increasing market to a declining market to a depressed market. Each of these indicators exhibits certain characteristics that are identifiable and therefore helpful cues to assess the state of the real estate cycle. (Refer to Chart 8-1 on page 123.)

CHART 8-1
Criteria for Determining Real Estate Cycles

INDICATORS

Criteria	A	B	C	D	A
Values	Depressed	Increasing	Increasing	Declining	Depressed
Rents	Low	Increasing	Increasing	Declining	Low
Vacancy Level	High	Beginning to Decrease	Low	Increasing	High
Occupancy Level	Low	Increasing	High	Decreasing	Low
New Construction	Very Little	Increasing	Booming	Slowing	Very Little
Profit Margins	Low	Improving	Widest	Decline	Low
Investor Confidence	Low	Negative	Positive to Neutral	Slightly Negative	Low
Media Coverage	Negative and Pessimistic	Positive and Encouraging	Positive and Optimistic	Negative and Pessimistic	Negative and Pessimistic
Action	Buy	Second Best Time to Buy	Sell	Be Cautious	Buy

To assess where the real estate cycle may be at any point in time, look for the indicators that correspond with the criteria categories listed in the left hand column.

You are undoubtedly familiar with the common terms used to describe the three types of real estate markets. As a brief review, they are:

Seller's Market. In a seller's market the number of buyers who want homes exceeds the number of homes available. In this type of market homes will sell quickly, prices will increase, and a large number of buyers is available for a minimal inventory of homes. These characteristics have implications for the buyer who has to make decisions quickly, must pay more, and frequently has his conditional offers rejected.

Buyer's Market. In a buyer's market the supply of homes on the market exceeds the demand or number of buyers. Homes will be on the market longer, fewer buyers will be available compared to the higher inventory of homes, and house prices will be reduced. The implications for buyers in this type of market are more favourable negotiating leverage, more time to search for a home, and better prices.

Balanced Market. In a balanced market, the number of homes on the market is equal to the demand or number of buyers. Houses sell within a reasonable period, the demand equals supply, sellers accept reasonable offers, and prices are generally stable. The implications for the buyer of this type of market are that the atmosphere is more relaxed and there is a reasonable number of homes from which to choose.

Factors that Affect Real Estate Prices

There are many factors that influence the price of real estate. Whether you are a buyer or seller, you need to understand what factors are present that are impacting on the market, so you can make the right decisions at the right time and in the right location. Many of these factors are interconnected.

Position in Real Estate Cycle. As described in the previous section, the position of the particular real estate market in the cycle will have a bearing on prices.

Interest Rates. There is a direct connection between interest rates and prices. The higher the rates, the lower the prices. The lower the rates, the higher the prices. The lower the rates, the more people who can afford to buy their first home. This puts pressure or greater demand on the market. A further discussion of interest rates will follow shortly.

Taxes. High municipal property taxes can be a disincentive to a purchaser, and could cause real estate prices to drop. Provincial taxes, such as a property purchase tax will restrict some buyers. Federal tax legislation on real estate, such as changes in capital gains tax, could have a negative influence on investors. All these factors would affect the overall amount of real estate activity, including prices.

Rent Controls. Naturally, provincial rent controls and related restrictions could have a limiting effect on investor real estate activity, thereby resulting in fewer buyers in the market for certain types of homes.

Vacancy Levels. If there are high vacancy levels, this could reduce investor confidence due to the potential risk, and real estate sales could go down. On the other hand, if there are low vacancy levels, this could stimulate investor activity as well as first-time home-buyers. Renters who can't find a place to rent may borrow from relatives or find other creative ways to enable them to purchase a home.

Economy. Confidence in the economy is important to stimulate home-buyer and investor activity. If the economy is buoyant and the mood is positive, more market activity will occur, generally resulting in price increases. At the same time, however, strong economic growth can also be associated with an increase in interest rates. Conversely, if the economy is stagnant, the opposite dynamic occurs resulting in a decrease in activity and lower prices. If real estate purchasers are concerned about the same problem, a predictable loss of confidence occurs in the market.

Population Shifts. A geographic location with attractive business, employment, tourism, and retirement opportunities, will attract people from other areas. The increased demand will increase prices. Conversely, if there is net migration out of the area the opposite effect will occur — real estate prices will be forced down.

Location. This is an important factor. Highly desirable locations will generally go up in price more quickly and consistently.

Availability of Land. If there is a natural shortage of land, municipal zoning restrictions, limits on development or provincial land-use laws that restrict the utilization of existing land for housing purposes, these will generally cause prices to increase. Again, it relates back to the principal of supply and demand.

Public Image. The perception by the public of a certain geographic location or type of residential property or builder will affect demand and therefore price. Some areas or types of properties are "hot" and some are not at any given time.

Political Factors. The policy of a provincial or municipal government in terms of supporting real estate development will naturally have a positive or negative effect on supply and demand and therefore prices.

Seasonal Factors. Certain times of year are traditionally slow months for residential real estate sales, hence prices decline. There are ideal seasons for purchase and sale.

Having reviewed the various factors that affect the real estate cycle and house prices let us now examine the methods of establishing how much a particular home is worth.

HOW MUCH SHOULD YOU PAY?

It is absolutely necessary to determine the worth of the property you may be buying. In other words, how much should you pay for it? In theory, a property is worth whatever a buyer is prepared to pay. There are various appraisal techniques that you can use, and there are professional, qualified appraisers whose services you can hire. In addition, there are "rules of thumb" that are often used to calculate the worth of a property. These "rules of thumb" are only good for approximations. You will need an accurate and professional appraisal. Appraisers charge fees, of course, so are generally not called on until a serious offer is made and accepted, subject to an appraisal satisfactory to the purchaser and/or the lender.

Appraising a property's value is more an art than a science. Two seemingly identical pieces of property seldom are. When a professional appraiser writes up a report, the estimate of value is given as an opinion, not a scientific fact. This is helpful to you as a basis for negotiation with the owner. Anyone can have an opinion as to value. The appraisal, though, is only as reliable as the competence, integrity, experience, and objectivity of the appraiser, and the accuracy of information obtained. Real estate appraisal is only as reliable as the assumptions that are made. There are distinct benefits of having an appraisal, especially a professional appraisal. The main reasons you might want an appraisal would be to determine the following:

- To establish a reasonable price to offer when purchasing.
- The value of a property for financing purposes (your lender will require this).
- The value of a property at death for estate purposes.
- The value of a property when converting the use from principal residence to investment (rental) use, or vice versa. This would be for Revenue Canada capital gains determination purposes, unless you are exempt from this provision. Check with your accountant for more details.

- The amount of insurance to carry.
- Undertaking a feasibility study of a purchase.
- Preparation for a property assessment appeal.
- Preparation for litigation purposes.
- Preparation for expropriation negotiations.
- Preparation for taxation records or appeal purposes.

There are several professional designations for property appraisers in Canada. They subscribe to uniform academic, professional, and ethical standards, and are regulated by their professional associations. The most common national designations are AACI (Accredited Appraiser Canadian Institute) and CRA (Canadian Residential Appraiser). There are other national and provincial appraisal designations as well as specialty appraisal areas (e.g., industrial and commercial).

Here are some of the basic methods or "rules of thumb" used by professional appraisers, real estate lenders, or homebuyers. When buying a home to live in, you would normally only be interested in the market comparison approach and cost approach. The average of these two estimates is what most lenders use for value appraisal purposes. The lender then gives mortgage funds based on the purchase price or appraised value, whichever is lower. The purchaser pays for the appraisal cost (usually between $150 and $300) for the average house or condominium. The lender arranges for the appraisal.

If you intend to invest in real estate, there are many additional formulas to apply to determine value of revenue property. That is outside the scope of this book. If you are interested in investment real estate and evaluation criteria, refer to my book *Making Money in Real Estate: The Canadian Residential Investment Guide*.

Market Comparison Approach

This approach is probably the most easily understood concept for the first-time home buyer and is the most commonly used by real estate agents for single-family dwellings. In effect, it is comparison shopping. It involves a comparison of properties similar to the one you are considering. Because no two properties are exactly the same due to age, location, layout, size, features, upgrades, etc., you will want to compare homes that are as close as possible, and you will want to have current sale prices.

You may have to make adjustments to the comparable properties to make them become more realistic comparisons when you
review prices; for example, making price adjustments in the comparison properties for such matters as the circumstances of the
sale (e.g., forced sale due to financial problems, order for sale, foreclosure, etc. — refer to Chapter 10 for a description of these), special features of the property (flower garden, shrubs, arboretum,
etc.) and location of property (view, privacy, etc.).

The market comparison approach lends itself to situations where
the properties are more numerous and there are more frequent
sales, and therefore they are easier to compare. Condominiums,
single-family houses, and raw land are the most common types of
properties to use the market comparison method. At least it gives
you a feeling for the appropriate value. Refer to Checklist 3-1 at
page 36 as a guide for comparing properties. Generally, when an
appraiser is doing a market comparison appraisal, he compares
recent sales of similar properties, similar properties currently
"listed" for sale on the market, and properties that did not sell
(listings expired). The limitation of the market comparison
approach is that similar properties may not be available for comparison in a particular situation. Also, it is difficult to know the
motivations of the vendors of the comparable properties, so in
some cases the sale price might not reflect the fair market price.

For example, if you are comparing a condominium for sale
against two other similar units in the same complex that have been
sold very recently, that will give you a fairly close comparison. If
the price on the one you are considering is higher, you want to
know why. Perhaps it has a better view, is on a higher floor, or the
previous owner made a lot of improvements. The point is that the
market comparison approach does have its limitations and provides general guidelines only.

Cost Approach

This approach involves calculating the cost to buy the land and
construct an equivalent type of building on the property you are
considering with appropriate adjustments, and then comparing
the end prices. If you calculated that the replacement cost is below
market value, you might want to seriously consider the benefits of
buying a lot and building. That is a separate issue, of course, with
its own advantages and disadvantages. There are various steps
involved in arriving at a figure using the cost approach. These are
the types of steps a professional appraiser goes through.

Step 1. Estimate the land value, using the market comparison approach discussed earlier. The sale price of similar vacant residential lots in the area should be determined, with adjustments made for such factors as use (zoning), size, location, and features (e.g., view).

Step 2. Estimate the cost to construct a new building that is comparable in square footage, features, and quality to the one you are considering. For example, a modest quality construction could be $50 a square foot to replace, whereas a luxury quality construction could be $125 or more a square foot to replace. These costs vary depending on your geographic location.

Step 3. If the house you are considering is not new, you would have to calculate a depreciation factor (e.g., reduced value of the building because of wear and tear over time). Calculating the depreciation adjustment factor depends on the building's condition, age, and estimated useful life. Estimated useful life is the point beyond which the building is not economical to repair or maintain. In effect, it would have no market value. If that is the case, you might be buying primarily for lot value and intend to tear down the building or substantially renovate it. A professional appraiser would normally be required to calculate this depreciation factor.

Step 4. To determine estimated property value, add the depreciated cost of the building (Steps 2-3) to the cost of the land (Step 1).

* * *

Refer to the following Chart 8-2 for an example of how to estimate market value.

For single-family houses and condominiums, the appraiser normally arrives at an estimate of value as of a certain date by adding the market and cost approach values, and averaging them.

The limitation of the cost approach is that depreciation might be difficult to estimate correctly. In addition, construction costs vary, depending on location, supply and demand, and inflation. Again, the cost approach value is an estimate only.

* * *

This section has covered some of the most common types of techniques for establishing the value of a property. There are many other formulas that may be used in addition to the ones noted. It is important to understand the basic concepts to know how and when to apply them, and to know their limitations. The key bene-

CHART 8-2
Example of Estimate of Market Value

Note: Using market and cost approaches, this is the normal formula for properties such as houses and condominiums.

1. *Market Comparison Approach*

   Comparison with four similar properties whose prices were $150,000, $155,000, $160,000 and $157,500. Average price is therefore $155,375.

   Market Approach Estimate   (A) $155,375.00

2. *Cost Approach*

   Land (30 foot × 150 foot lot) = 16,500 square feet
   @ $5 per square foot $82,500.00

   Value of improvements on land such as shrubs,
   trees, fence, garden, toolshed $7,500.00

   Construction of building is 1,000 square feet at
   $75 per square foot construction cost (new) $75,000.00

   Less 5% depreciation per year because building being purchased is two years old:

   $75,000 – 5% = $71,250.00 (Year 1), and

   $71,250 – 5% = $67,687.50 (Year 2).

   Therefore, depreciated value of building $67,687.50

   Cost Approach Estimate   (B) $157,687.50

FINAL ESTIMATE OF MARKET VALUE (A + B / 2) $156,531.25

(Market estimate of $155,375.00 plus cost estimate of $157,687.50 divided by two).

fit of these methods is that they can often be quickly calculated to determine if the owner is asking too much, or too little. Remember, the rules of thumb are guidelines only. The calculations could also provide you with negotiating leverage to have the purchase price reduced. You will, of course, want to consider other factors before making your final decision.

Also keep in mind that the values are estimates of what that average person would pay. You may not be prepared to pay the estimated price for various reasons, including the following:

- Price is more than you can afford.
- Price is higher than your comfort level in terms of risk.
- Market is starting to decline.
- Economic turndown.
- Waiting for more attractive property.

Conversely, you might be prepared to pay more than the average person. Here are some of the factors that might cause you to consider paying more:

Why Pay More?

Confidential Information. You might be aware of a possible zoning change, subdivision potential, or proposed development nearby.

Financing. You might be able to obtain favourable financial terms (e.g., a low-interest vendor-take-back mortgage or high-ratio financing).

Potential for Increased Income. The property could have a basement suite which could be rented out.

Attractive Closing Date. You could get a long closing date, enabling you to get funds that you are expecting from various sources, get access to increased mortgage funds by closing, or sell the agreement of purchase and sale to someone else (almost like having an option).

* * *

It is not enough to understand about the real estate market, mortgages, and methods of determining the value of your home; you must also understand the legal aspects of buying a home. We turn to that next.

Chapter 9

THE LEGAL ASPECTS

It is important to have an understanding of the legal issues and terminology in order to discuss the appropriate matters clearly with your lawyer, make the correct decisions, and protect your interests. Every aspect of a real estate purchase involves legal implications, so you want to make sure you avoid legal problems.

However, do not be intimidated by this chapter. It provides a background for information purposes only. Your lawyer deals with these matters on your behalf. The following discussion gives you an idea of the process involved and the potential legal issues you should be aware of as an enlightened consumer or just for your interest's sake.

This chapter provides an overview of different kinds of property ownership, the legal documents involved in a purchase of real estate, options and implications of getting out of a signed contract, the services provided by a lawyer, and what happens if you default on a mortgage.

TYPES OF OWNERSHIP OF PROPERTY

Types of Interest in Land

There are several types of legal interests in land, the most common being freehold and leasehold.

Freehold. This type of ownership in land entitles the owner to use the land for an indefinite period of time and to deal with the land in any way desired, subject to legislation (e.g., municipal by-laws, hydro utility easements or rights-of-way, provincial mineral rights), contractual obligations (e.g., subdivision restrictive covenants), and any charges that encumber the title of the property and that are filed in the provincial land registry office (e.g., mortgages, liens, judgements, etc.). Another term for freehold is "fee simple."

Leasehold. In this example the holder of the interest in land has the right to use the land for a fixed period of time (e.g., 50 or 99 years). The owner of the property (landlord or lessor) signs an agreement with the owner of the leasehold interest (tenant or lessee) setting out various terms and conditions of the relationship. The leasehold interest can be bought and sold, but the leaseholder can only sell the right to use the land for the time that is remaining in the lease — subject, of course, to any conditions contained in the original lease. The mortgage implications of a leasehold property are covered in Chapter 6, "Mortgages."

Both freehold interest and leasehold interest can be left in your will as an asset of your estate or specifically bequeathed.

Types of Joint Ownership in Property

You may wish to have shared ownership in the property with one or more other persons. There are two main types of legal joint ownership: joint tenancy and tenancy in common. If you are considering investment property, there are many other options of buying with others. To get a more detailed explanation of the cautions and pitfalls, refer to my book *Making Money in Real Estate*.

Joint Tenancy. This is a situation in which an owner has an undivided but equal share with all of the other owners. No one person has a part of the property that is specifically his, because all of the property belongs to all of the owners. At the time of purchase, the names of all the people who are joint tenants will be listed on the title of the property equally and each of the joint tenants has the right in law to possession of the whole property.

One of the main features of a joint tenancy is the right of survivorship. This means that if one of the joint tenants dies, the others automatically and immediately receive the deceased person's share, equally divided. In other words, the deceased person's share in the joint tenancy is not passed on as an asset of his estate to beneficiaries, whether or not a will exists. It is fairly common for a couple to hold the legal interest in the property by means of joint tenancy. You should consider tenancy in common if you want to have your interest automatically go to other parties.

Tenancy in Common. In this form of ownership, the tenants can hold equal or unequal shares in the property. Each party owns an undivided share in the property and therefore is entitled to possession of the whole property. For example, there could be five people who are tenants in common, but four of them could own 1/10 of the property each, and the fifth person could own 6/10 of the property.

The holder of a tenancy in common can sell or mortgage his interest in the property. When a buyer cannot be found and the tenant in common wants to get his money out of the property, he can go to court and, under a legal procedure called partition, request that the court order the property to be sold and the net proceeds of sale be distributed proportionately.

Unlike joint tenancy, tenancy in common does not carry an automatic right of survivorship. In other words, if one of the tenants in common dies, the interest does not go automatically to the other tenants, but goes to the estate of the deceased, to be distributed under the terms of the will. If the deceased person does not leave a will, there is provincial legislation dealing with that type of situation, and the person's assets, which would include the tenancy interest, would be distributed to relatives according to the legislation.

There are various reasons why some people prefer tenancy in common to joint tenancy.

- If you are purchasing property with people who are not relatives, you may not want them to automatically have your interest in the property in the event of your death.
- If you have been previously married, have children from a previous relationship, and have since remarried, you may want to specify in your will that a certain portion of the worth of the estate goes to those children individually or collectively. The only way this can be dealt with is a tenancy in common, because the interest would be deemed to be an asset of one's estate.
- If you are putting unequal amounts of money in the property, a tenancy-in-common structure would reflect those different contributions in terms of the percentage interest in the property.

Written agreements should be signed by tenants in common setting out the procedures if one of them wants out of the situation. This is a prudent procedure that can be accomplished by giving the others the first right of refusal on a proportional basis to buy out the interest; or there could be a clause requiring the consent of the other tenants in common in approving a potential purchaser; or there could be a provision requiring a certain period of notice to the other tenants before the property is sold. Another case when tenancy in common might be preferable would be when one of the owners of the property wishes to have the personal independence to raise money for other outside interests (e.g., a business). The tenancy-in-common portion might be able to be mortgaged without the consent of the other parties.

UNDERSTANDING THE PURCHASE AND SALE AGREEMENT

The most important document you will sign will be the offer to purchase, which if accepted becomes the agreement of purchase and sale. It sets out the terms and conditions between the parties and, as in any contract, it is legally binding if no conditions exist in the contract that have to be met before it comes binding. Of course, there can be verbal contracts, but all contracts dealing with land must be in writing to be enforceable. That includes the purchase and sale agreement or a lease, which, of course, is also a contract.

Most purchase and sale agreements come in standard formats, with standard clauses, and are drafted by the builder, the local real estate board, or commercial stationers. There are generally spaces throughout the agreement for additional, customized clauses to be added. A contract prepared by a builder has distinctly different clauses from those of a standard form for resales, and there are considerable differences in the standard contract clauses used by builders and those used by real estate boards.

There is a high risk that the standard clauses, or additional ones that you may choose to insert, will not be comprehensive enough for your needs; you may not even understand them or their implications and sign the agreement regardless. That is why it is so important to have a lawyer review your offer to purchase before you sign it. Regrettably, only a small number of people do this because they either don't realize they should, think it is an unnecessary, costly legal expense, or are naive and too trusting. But it is false economy to try to save on legal fees, as the costs are relatively low and the risk involved in signing a bad contract is high. Alternatively, rather than seeing a lawyer before submitting an offer to purchase, some people may wish to insert a condition that the offer is "subject to approval as to form and contents by the purchaser's solicitor, such approval to be communicated to vendor within X days of acceptance, or to be deemed to be withheld."

There are many common clauses and features contained in the purchase and sale agreement, and they will vary from contract to contract according to various circumstances whether one is purchasing a new or a resale property, the type of property, etc. A brief overview follows with some of the common features of the agreement for purchase and sale.

Amount of Deposit

A deposit serves various purposes. It is a partial payment on the purchase price, a good-faith indication of seriousness, and an assurance of performance if all the conditions in the offer to purchase have been fulfilled. The deposit is generally 5% to 10% of the purchase price. If there are conditions in the offer, and these conditions cannot be met, then the purchaser is entitled to receive the full amount of the deposit back. This is one reason why it is important to have conditions or "subject to" clauses in the offer to protect one's interests fully. Most agreements for purchase and sale have a provision that gives the vendor the option of keeping the deposit as "liquidated damages," in the event that the purchaser fails to complete the terms of the agreement and pay the balance of money on the closing date.

When making a deposit, it is very important to be careful about who receives the funds. If you are purchasing on a private sale and no realtor is involved, never pay the funds directly to the vendor; pay them to your own lawyer in trust. If a realtor is involved, the funds can be paid to the realtor's trust account or your own lawyer's trust account, as the situation dictates. If you are purchasing a new property from the builder, do not pay a deposit directly to the builder. The money should go to your lawyer's trust account, or some other system that protects your funds. The risk is high in paying your money directly to a builder, because if he goes bankrupt, you could lose all your money. Although several provincial governments have legislation dealing with deposits on new property purchases as well as other risk areas, legislation provides only partial protection.

Another matter you have to consider is interest. You must ensure that an appropriate amount of interest is paid on your deposit. In many cases, deposit money can be tied up for many months, and that could represent considerable interest. Put your condition in writing.

Conditions and Warranties

It is important to understand the distinction between *conditions* and *warranties*, as it is very critical to the wording that you will be using in the agreement.

A *condition* is a requirement that is fundamental to the very existence of the offer (e.g. conditional on getting the necessary financing or a house inspection that is satisfactory to the purchaser). A breach of condition allows the buyer to get out of the contract and obtain the full deposit back. An inability to meet the condition set by a vendor permits the vendor to get out of the contract (e.g. a condition that the vendor can give you 72 hours' notice to remove any conditions that you have made or the deal would collapse. This happens if the vendor has another legitimate offer to purchase presented without any conditions).

A *warranty* is a minor promise that does not go to the heart of the contract. If there is a breach of warranty, the purchaser cannot cancel but must complete the contract and sue for damages. Therefore, if a particular requirement on your part is pivotal to your decision to purchase the property or not, it is important to *frame your requirement as a condition rather than as a warranty*.

Subject Clauses

Both vendors and purchasers frequently insert conditions into the agreement. These are also referred to as subject clauses and should:

- Be precise and clearly detailed.
- Have specific time allocated for conditions that have to be removed (e.g., within two days, 30 days, etc.). It is preferable to put the precise date on which a condition has to be resolved, rather than merely refer to the number of days involved.
- Have a clause that specifically says that the conditions are for the sole benefit of the vendor or purchaser, as the case may be, and that they can be waived at any time by the party requiring the condition. This is important, because you may wish to remove a condition even though it has not been fulfilled, in order to complete the contract.

Here is a sample of some common subject clauses. Many others are possible.

For the Benefit of the Purchaser:

- Title being conveyed free and clear of any and all financial encumbrances or charges registered against the property on or before the closing date at the expense of the vendor, either from the proceeds of the sale or by solicitor's undertaking.
- Inspection being satisfactory to purchaser by relative, spouse, partner, etc. (specify name).
- Inspection being satisfactory to purchaser by home inspector/ contractor selected by purchaser.
- Confirmation of mortgage financing. Be precise about the amount of mortgage, term, interest rate, monthly payments for principal and interest, and the amortization period.
- Deposit funds to be placed in an interest-bearing trust account with the interest to accrue to the purchaser.
- Approval of assumption of existing mortgage.
- Granting of vendor-take-back mortgage or builder's mortgage. Set out precise terms.
- Removal of existing tenancies (vacant possession) by completion date.
- Existing tenancies conforming to prevailing municipal by-laws.
- Interim occupancy payments being credited to purchase price.
- Review and satisfactory approval by purchaser's lawyer of the contents of the agreement of purchase and sale.
- Warranties, representations, promises, guarantees, and agreements shall survive the completion date.
- No urea formaldehyde foam insulation (UFFI) or asbestos having ever been in the building.
- Vendor supplying necessary legal documentation at the expense of the vendor within X days of acceptance of the offer.
- Vendor's warranty that no work orders or deficiency notices (inadequate or incomplete work that was performed) are outstanding against the property, or if there are, that they will be complied with at the vendor's expense before closing.

Additional Clauses if Purchasing a Condominium:

- Receipt and satisfactory review by purchaser (and/or purchaser's lawyer) of project documents, such as disclosure, declaration, articles, rules and regulations, financial statements, project budget, minutes of condominium corporation for past year, management contract, etc.

- Confirmation by condominium corporation that the condominium unit being purchased will be able to be rented, if so required.

For the Benefit of the Vendor:

- Removal of all subject clauses by purchaser within 72 hours upon notice in writing by vendor of a backup bona fide (legitimate) offer. This would be to protect the vendor from having you tie up the property with conditions, when another non-condition offer is made. You would have 72 hours to remove your conditions or your offer would collapse and you would receive your deposit back. The vendor could then accept the unconditional offer.
- Confirmation of purchase of vendor mortgage through vendor's mortgage broker.
- Satisfactory confirmation of creditworthiness of purchaser by vendor or vendor's mortgage broker, if a vendor mortgage.
- Issuance of building permit, if needed.
- Builder receiving confirmation of construction financing.
- Registration of a subdivision plan.
- Deposit funds nonrefundable and to be released directly to the vendor once all conditions of the purchaser have been met.
- Review and satisfactory approval by vendor's lawyer of the contents of the agreement of purchase and sale.

Risk and Insurance

It is important that the parties agree to an exact date when risk is going to pass (responsibility transfer) from the vendor to the purchaser. In some cases the agreement will state that the risk will pass at the time that there is a firm, binding, unconditional purchase and sale agreement. In other cases the contract states that the risk will pass on the completion date or the possession date. In any event, make sure that you have adequate insurance coverage taking effect as of and including the date that you assume the risk. The vendor should wait until after the risk date before termination of insurance.

Fixtures and Chattels

This is an area of potential dispute between the purchaser and vendor, unless it is sufficiently clarified. A fixture is technically something permanently affixed to the property; therefore, when the property is conveyed the fixtures are conveyed with it (e.g. a built-in dishwasher). A chattel is an object that is moveable; in other words, it is not permanently affixed. Common examples of chattels are clothes washer and dryer, refrigerator, stove, microwave, and drapes.

A problem can arise when there is a question of whether an item is a fixture or a chattel. For example, an expensive chandelier hanging from the dining-room ceiling, gold-plated bathroom fixtures, drapery racks, or television satellite dish on the roof might be questionable items. One of the key tests is whether the item was intended to be attached on a permanent basis to the property and therefore should be transferred with the property, or whether it was the intention of the vendor to remove these items and replace them with cheaper versions before closing the transaction.

In general legal terms, if it is a fixture and it is not mentioned in the agreement, it is deemed to be included in the purchase price. On the other hand, if it is not a fixture and no reference is made to it in the agreement, then it would not be included in the purchase price. To eliminate conflict, most agreements for purchase and sale have standard clauses built into them stating that all existing fixtures are included in the purchase price except those listed specifically in the agreement. In addition, a clause should list the chattels specifically included in the purchase price, and they should be clearly described.

Adjustment Date

This is the date that is used for calculating and adjusting such factors as taxes, maintenance fees, fuel, rentals, and other such matters. On that date, all expenses and benefits go to the purchaser. For example, if the maintenance fee has been paid for the month of March by the vendor and the purchaser takes over with an adjustment date as of the 15th of March, there will be an adjustment on the closing documents showing that the purchaser owes half of the amount of the prepaid maintenance fee to the vendor for the month of March. A discussion of adjustments for property tax is found in Chapter 12.

Completion Date

This is the date when all documentation is completed and filed in the appropriate registry and all money paid out. The normal custom is for all the closing funds to be paid to the purchaser's solicitor a few days prior to closing. As soon as all the documents have been filed in the land registry office and confirmation has been obtained that everything is in order, the purchaser's solicitor releases the funds to the vendor's solicitor. More discussion of the steps taken by the lawyers for the vendor and purchaser relating to the closing date is presented later in this chapter. *Note*: The adjustment date and the completion date are frequently the same.

Possession Date

This is the date on which you are legally entitled to move into the premises. It is usually the same date as the adjustment and completion date. Sometimes the possession date is a day later to allow the vendor time to move out; in practical terms, though, many purchasers prefer the adjustment, completion and possession dates to be the same, and make prior arrangements in terms of the logistics, if it is possible. One of the reasons is that the risks of the purchaser take effect as of the completion date, and there is always a risk that the vendor could cause damage or create other problems within the premises if he remains there beyond the completion date. As soon as your lawyer has advised you that all the documents have been filed and money has changed hands, your realtor or lawyer arranges for you to receive the keys to the premises.

Merger

This is a legal principle in most provinces to the effect that if the agreement for purchase and sale is to be "merged" into a deed or other document, the real contract between the parties is in the document filed with the land registry. To protect you, it should be stated in the agreement for purchase and sale that the "warranties, representations, promises, guarantees, and agreements shall survive the completion date." There are exceptions to the document of merger in cases of mistake or fraud, technical areas that require your lawyer's opinion, but it is important to understand the concept.

Commissions

At the end of most purchase and sale agreements there is a section setting out the amount of the commission charged, which the vendor confirms when accepting an offer.

LEGAL OPTIONS AND IMPLICATIONS OF GETTING OUT OF A SIGNED AGREEMENT

There are instances where either the vendor or the purchaser may wish to back out of the agreement. You have to be careful because legal problems can result in litigation, which is expensive, time consuming, stressful, and uncertain in outcome. If there are conditions or "subject to" clauses in your agreement, and the conditions are not met, the contract is normally null and void; in other words, is no longer legally binding. You want to get legal advice before you act. Some examples are discussed below.

Rescission

In several areas of Canada and the United States there is a "cooling-off" or rescission period, whereby the purchaser of a new property has a period of time (usually from three days to 30 days) to back out of the contract by giving notice to the vendor in writing before the deadline. The vendor is obliged to pay back, without penalty, all the money that the purchaser has placed on deposit. In cases where legislation does not give an automatic right to rescission, the documents that are a part of the property package may have a rescission period built in. If you do not have a statutory (by law) right to rescission, and it is not part of the documents relating to the purchase of a new property, you may want to make it a condition of your offer. "Subject clauses" can be a form of "cooling-off," depending on the clauses.

Specific Performance

If the vendor or purchaser refuses to go through with a purchase-and-sale agreement when there are no unfulfilled conditions attached to the agreement, the other party is entitled to go to court and request the court to order that the breaching party specifically perform the terms of the agreement (e.g., complete the transaction). The party who succeeds in obtaining the court order would be entitled to ask for the costs of the application from the court. Generally, court costs awarded represent about 25 to 40% of the actual legal costs incurred; therefore, those who "win" at court ultimately "lose" financially in terms of total cost recovery of legal costs expended.

Damages

If one party refuses to complete the agreement, instead of suing for specific performance of the terms of the agreement, the other party can sue for damages. Damages are the financial losses that have been incurred because the other party failed to complete the bargain. There is a basic legal maxim that says "to get financial damages (compensation), you have to prove you have suffered financial damages." This is a complex area of law and skilled legal advice is critical.

Conditional Contract

If the vendor or purchaser has preliminary conditions built into the purchase and sale agreement ("subject to" clauses), and those conditions cannot be met, no valid binding contract exists, and neither party is liable to the other.

Void Contracts

A contract is void and unenforceable if the required elements that make up a valid contract are not present (e.g., must be an adult, not have impaired judgement, not be under threat or intimidation, something of value must be exchanged between the parties, and the parties must intend to be bound). Another factor that would make the contract void is if it is prohibited by statute (e.g., municipal, provincial, or federal law).

Voidable Contracts

If one of the parties has been induced into entering the contract on the basis of misrepresentation, whether innocent, negligent, or fraudulent, that party may be entitled to void the contract. If the misrepresentation was innocent, generally only the contract can be cancelled and any money returned, and no damages can be recovered in court. If there is negligent or fraudulent misrepresentation, however, not only can the contract be cancelled, but damages can also be recovered in court.

These are just some illustrations of the types of factors that could impact on the validity or enforceability of the contract. You can see how competent legal advice in advance from a skilled real estate lawyer is necessary to minimize potential problems.

SERVICES PROVIDED BY THE PURCHASER'S LAWYER

There are many services provided by your lawyer at various stages before the agreement is signed, after the agreement is signed, just before closing the transaction on the closing day, and after closing the transaction. What follows is a partial summary of some of the matters discussed and services performed in a typical real estate transaction. Each situation will vary according to the complexity and nature of the transaction. The purchaser's lawyer does the bulk of the work in the process of completing the property purchase.

Before the Agreement is Signed

- Discuss the contents of the offer to purchase with your lawyer. If there is a counteroffer by the vendor (e.g. the vendor rejects your offer and presents you with a replacement offer), make sure that you continue your communication with your lawyer before accepting the counteroffer, unless it is simply a matter of the purchase price.
- Discuss with your lawyer the ways in which you intend to finance your purchase.
- Enquire as to all the various legal fees and out-of-pocket disbursement costs that you will have to pay.
- Ask your lawyer about all the other costs related to purchasing the property that you should be aware of. The most common expenses are shown in Checklist 6-2 at page 104.
- Discuss matters such as your choice of closing date, inspection of the property before closing, and any requirements that you want the vendor to fulfil.

After the Agreement is Signed

Once you have received a copy of the signed agreement, your lawyer will be going through a process of making sure that all your rights are protected and that you are getting what you contracted for. Here are some of the types of areas that your lawyer will commonly check for you.

- ***Title of property.*** An agreement for purchase and sale normally states that the vendor is going to provide title free and clear of all encumbrances. Therefore your lawyer has to make sure that there are no claims or other filings against the property. When searching the title, you will be able to discover the name of the registered owner, the legal description, the list of charges (matters affecting the property) registered against the property, and other documents that are filed against the property. The types of charges that may be shown against the property would include the fol-

lowing (different provincial jurisdictions may have varying terminology but the concepts are the same):

- mortgage
- right to purchase (agreement for sale)
- restrictive covenant (restriction on use of the property)
- builder's lien (claim for money owing)
- easement (right of someone else — e.g., next-door neighbour
  — to use your property)
- right of way (right of a government — e.g., municipal or
  provincial — or utility company — e.g., hydro or telephone —
  to use part of your property)
- option to purchase
- certificate under provincial family relations act restricting any
  dealing with the property
- judgment
- *caveat* (formal notice that someone has an interest in the property and the nature of that interest)
- *lis pendens* (an action pending relating to the mortgage, e.g.,
  foreclosure proceedings)
- lease, sub-lease, or option to lease
- mineral rights by the government
- condominium project documents
- condominium by-laws.

- **Survey certificate.** Obtaining a current one if the vendor has
one, or arranging for a survey if the mortgage company requires it.

- **Property taxes.**

- **Outstanding utility accounts.**

- **Zoning by-laws.**

- **Status of mortgages being assumed or discharged.**

- **Ensuring financing will be sufficient and in place on closing.**

- **Compliance with restrictions, warranties, conditions, and
agreements.**

- **Fixtures and chattels that are included in the purchase price.**

- **Documents prepared by solicitor acting for vendor** (if applicable).

- **All documents required relating to property purchase** (e.g., depending whether a new or re-sale house or condominium: building regulations, project documents, by-laws, rules and regulations, financial statements, disclosure statement, estoppel certificate, and other documents as required).

- **Maintenance fee.** If a condominium, determining the monthly maintenance fee.

- **Security deposit.** If there are any existing tenants in dwelling, determining the amount of rent, security deposit plus interest.

- **Insurance confirmation obtained.** That is, that you have arranged for an insurance company to cover your home from the date of purchase. The mortgage company will require this.

- **Mortgage reviewed.** This would be necessary if another lawyer prepares the mortgage for the lender. You would want your own lawyer to review the mortgage. Conversely, you may be able to get the lender to approve your lawyer handling the mortgage as well as the property transfer. There could be cost savings to you if one lawyer handles both matters.

- **Determining GST payable by purchaser** (if applicable).

Just Before Closing the Transaction

Just prior to closing there are various steps that your lawyer will go through, including the following:

- Preparing documents relating to any sales tax for the chattels that you may be purchasing.

- Preparing any mortgage documents necessary and making arrangements for funding to the lawyer's trust account from the mortgage proceeds on filing.

- Showing you a purchaser's statement of adjustments, which gives the balance outstanding that you must come up with before closing the transaction. Includes deposit, any necessary financial adjustments, mortgage net proceeds, legal fees and disbursements (photocopies, couriers, etc.), filing fees, provincial property purchase tax (if applicable), CMHC high ratio insurance fee (if applicable), etc. You normally have to provide the advance of funds to your lawyer two to five days or more beforehand. Preparing the vendor's statement of adjustments which is sent to the vendor's lawyer.

- Receiving for forwarding any postdated cheques or "void" cancelled cheque for automatic withdrawals, that may be required for the mortgage lender.
- Preparing all documents for filing in the land registry office on the closing date; if a different lawyer is involved in preparing the mortgage, that has to be coordinated for concurrent registration.

On Closing Day

On the date of closing the transaction, your lawyer will perform various services, including the following:

- Checking on the search of title of the property to make sure that there are no last-minute claims or charges against the title.
- Releasing funds held in trust after receipt of mortgage proceeds from the lender if applicable, and sending an amount to the vendor's lawyer based on the amount they are entitled to as outlined in the vendor's statement of adjustments.
- Receiving a copy of the certificate of possession from the New Home Warranty Program, as applicable.
- Paying any money required on the date of closing as outlined in the purchaser's statement of adjustments (e.g., sales tax on chattels being purchased, land transfer tax as applicable, and balance of commission owing to the real estate company paid from the proceeds of the purchase funds due to the vendor and as outlined in the vendor's statement of adjustments).
- Holding back any "withholding tax" if you purchased the property from a nonresident of Canada. If you fail to have the appropriate funds held back from the purchase funds, Revenue Canada could attempt to collect the appropriate taxes from you. Your lawyer can tell you more.

After Closing the Transaction

Once the purchase has been completed, your lawyer will confirm this with you and you can make arrangements with the realtor or lawyer to obtain the keys to your home. Your lawyer will also:

- Send you a reporting letter with all the filed documents and all the other related documents attached for your records, including an account for fees and disbursements that have been taken from the funds that you provided your lawyer in trust prior to closing.

- Arrange to obtain and register the appropriate discharges of mortgages that were paid off from the funds you paid for the purchase, unless the vendor's lawyer is attending to this obligation.
- Ensure that all the vendor's promises have been satisfied.

There are numerous costs involved in purchasing new property, as shown in Checklist 6-2 at page 104. Your lawyer will outline the legal fees and costs so that you can budget for them. Most lawyers charge a fee based on a percentage of the purchase price. In the case of condominiums, there is generally a higher charge for the extra documentation and responsibility involved on the lawyer's part, due to the nature of the transaction. Although fees can vary from place to place because of market competition and other factors, between 3/4% and 1% of the purchase price is normal (this relates only to legal fees and not to disbursements, which can vary considerably according to the nature of your transaction). Remember to compare fees before you decide upon which lawyer to use.

SERVICES PROVIDED BY THE VENDOR'S LAWYER

The lawyer acting for the vendor will perform a wide range of services, the extent of which depends on each transaction. As a purchaser, it is important and helpful that you understand the process. Some of the services that will be performed at various stages are discussed below.

Before the Agreement Is Signed

Before the agreement is signed, the vendor should have selected a lawyer and have discussed the contract with him. Once the vendor is presented with a written offer, there are basically three options open to him:

- Accept the offer in the form in which it is presented by signing the offer. In this event there is a binding contract between you and the vendor, once all conditions have been removed.
- Alter the offer by making changes and having the offer resubmitted to the purchaser. By making changes to the purchaser's offer, the vendor is in effect rejecting the offer and countering with a new offer. The purchaser can either accept these changes or make further changes and return the agreement to you, which constitutes another new offer.

- Ignore the offer completely, if it seems unrealistic or otherwise unsatisfactory.

After the Agreement Is Signed

Once the agreement has been struck in writing, the vendor's lawyer might request various documents from the vendor to assist in completing the transaction. Otherwise the lawyer will get copies directly himself if required. Generally, the vendor's lawyer just waits to receive all the documents from the purchaser's lawyer.

Just Before Closing the Transaction

The vendor's lawyer might prepare a deed or transfer document that must be signed before title can be passed to the purchaser, and will also review the vendor's statement of adjustments. In most provinces or regions the custom is for the purchaser's lawyer to prepare the conveyancing (property transfer) documents for the vendor to sign and prepare the vendor's and the purchaser's statement of adjustments. These would then be forwarded for review to the vendor's lawyer before the vendor signs.

If a mortgage exists on the home, it is the responsibility of the vendor to discharge the mortgage in order that clear title to the property can be transferred. After obtaining a copy of the mortgage statement showing the balance outstanding as of the closing date, the vendor's lawyer would then "undertake" (legally promise) to the purchaser's lawyer that the mortgage would be paid off first from the proceeds of the purchase, received from the purchaser's lawyer. Alternatively, the purchaser's lawyer could discharge the mortgage.

On Closing Day

On the date of closing, the vendor's lawyer or agent will meet the purchaser's lawyer or agent at the land registry office in order that the transfer documents can be filed, changing title.

After Closing the Transaction

After the transaction has been completed, and the vendor's lawyer has received the appropriate money based on the vendor's statement of adjustments, he will clear off any existing mortgages with those funds and have the mortgages discharged from the title of the property, and advise the purchaser's lawyer accordingly.

You would than receive the balance of funds after the legal fees and disbursements have been deducted.

Finally, your lawyer will send you a reporting letter setting out the services that were performed and enclose any appropriate documents for your files.

DEFAULTING ON YOUR MORTGAGE

As long as you meet the payments and the terms as agreed with the mortgage company, the lender has no right to interfere with you in any way. Only if you are in arrears, can the lender take legal action against you. On the other hand, if you have difficulty with your payments or breach any terms of the mortgage, there are very severe remedies that the lender has available to protect its security, including foreclosure or power of sale. Defaulting on a mortgage has other potentially serious consequences. If you are consistently late, this could affect your credit rating, and also your ability to renew your mortgage or obtain other mortgages in the future.

The term "foreclosure" means the lender takes action in court to have your name removed from title and the lender's name put on, or alternatively have the right to sell the property to get the mortgage money back. The foreclosure procedure has to go through the courts. The term "power of sale" means that the lender has the right, contained in the mortgage documents, to put your home up for sale, generally within 30 days' notice, without having court approval. Depending on what province you are in, the process could be foreclosure or order of sale.

Common Areas of Default

The mortgage agreement sets out in considerable detail the requirements of the borrower. The most common areas of default could be:

- Failure to make your mortgage payments
- Failure to pay your taxes
- Failure to have insurance, or sufficient insurance
- Failure to obey municipal, provincial, or federal law as it relates to the premises that you have mortgaged
- Failure to maintain the premises in a habitable condition
- Failure to keep the premises in proper repair

- Deliberately damaging the property that secures the mortgage
- Leaving the place vacant for an extended period of time

Options if You are Behind in Payments

If you are having difficulty maintaining payments under the mortgage, there are many options to consider. You can, for example:

- Make arrangements with the lender to waive payments for a period of time (e.g. three or six months) or arrange for partial payments to be made. This is normally done in a situation where the borrower is sick, injured, or laid off, or has a reduced monthly income to debt-service the mortgage due to a marital separation, a spouse who has been laid off, or other such factors
- Reschedule the debt and make new payment arrangements
- Refinance the mortgage with another lender on terms that are more flexible and appropriate in the circumstances
- Provide additional security to the lender in order to negotiate concessions
- Put the property up for sale
- Transfer the property to the lender. This is not always feasible or desirable. Most lenders will not agree to this
- Exercise your right of redemption. You are generally entitled to this by law, especially if the home is your primary residence. This means you "redeem" yourself, by paying the arrears outstanding under the mortgage, which prevents the lender from commencing or from continuing foreclosure proceedings. You generally have a right of redemption up to six months in order to pay the lender, or the lender would be entitled to take over the property, or sell it, among other remedies. An exception to this is if there is an acceleration clause, which some mortgages have, whereby the lender can claim the full amount of the mortgage immediately due and payable. In that event you would have to pay the full amount of the mortgage in order to stop foreclosure proceedings. You can ask the court to have this acceleration clause waived however, and just pay the arrears. Depending on the circumstances, you could be successful. Some provinces do not permit acceleration clauses.
- Ask the court for more time. If you can see that you are not able to pay off the lender within the right of redemption

period, you are entitled to request of the Court an extension of time. Whether the court grants an extension depends on the circumstances. For example, it is in your favour if you had previously lost your job and you are now employed, you are expecting proceeds from an inheritance, or you are having family members raise funds for you. All of these are factors that could show that the delay request is based on a realistic assessment of the ability to make the necessary payment. Having a substantial equity in the property would also assist you.

The main options that lenders have would be to: sell the property at the end of the order for sale period; sue the borrower personally for the debt outstanding; or foreclose against the property. In a foreclosure situation, the lender requests that the court extinguish your property rights and transfer all legal interest that you have, including the right of possession and legal title, to the lender. In practical terms, this option is seldom utilized for a variety of reasons.

As you can see, there are many factors to consider if you are having financial difficulties on your mortgage. The circumstances of your default will make a difference in terms of what steps you wish to take. Contacting the lender and attempting to negotiate a resolution is clearly the first step that you should take to resolve the problem. If that does not turn out to be a satisfactory procedure, it would be prudent to obtain advice from a lawyer specializing in power of sale or foreclosure matters so that you are fully aware of your available rights and options.

* * *

The legal aspects of buying your first home can seem complicated, but remember, your lawyer is there to advise you. You, personally, do not need to know all the complications of the law, but it is important that you understand the process. It is also important that you understand the implications of taxes as a home buyer, especially if you will be renting out part of your home or running a business from it. We will discuss taxes next.

Chapter 10

THE TAX ASPECTS

A s you can appreciate, tax implications with respect to your
purchase are particularly important. The information and tips
presented below will either save you money or at least help you to
understand the key options you can utilize to save money. As
income tax provisions can change at any time, before making any
real estate purchase, make sure you contact a tax accountant to
obtain current income tax advice. Everyone's tax situation is
unique to his personal circumstances.

The following discussion highlights the main categories of local,
provincial, and federal government taxes that may apply when a
home to be used as a principal residence is purchased.

If you have a second property or other revenue property, there
are different tax considerations that apply. Check with your professional accountant for further information.*

LOCAL/MUNICIPAL/REGIONAL TAXES

Municipalities assess taxes for various purposes. Some include
all taxes within one assessment, while others separate the taxes.
The main taxes are as follows:

Property Taxes

These are generally due on an annual basis with assessment of
value determined within six months prior to the property taxation
year. Some municipalities (e.g. Toronto) have not reassessed value

---

*See also Gray, *Making Money in Real Estate: The Canadian Residential Investment
Guide* (Toronto: McGraw-Hill Ryerson Ltd.) and *The Canadian Snowbird Guide*
(Toronto: McGraw-Hill Ryerson Ltd.)

on an annual basis and therefore have fallen behind. The problem in this situation is that property taxes could take a large jump in the future when assessments are brought up to market value. This is an important issue and significant consideration to take into account. For residential property, a "mill rate," is generally determined annually and multiplied by the assessed value of the property, including the building on the property, to determine the actual tax due. In many provinces there is a homeowner's grant that is subtracted from the gross taxes assessed for your property to determine the net payable tax you owe. Seniors (over 65) receive a larger grant than other homeowners.

If you believe your property taxes are unfair because they are based on an artificially high property assessment you can appeal the assessment notice. For example, when a real estate market has gone down, it is not uncommon for property assessment appeals to increase because of the time lag before the assessment reflects the reduction in value.

Property taxes are generally assessed for municipally supplied services such as schools, education, roads, hospitals, etc.

Utility Taxes

These taxes tend to be for services such as water, sewer, garbage pick-up, etc.

Further Information

To obtain further information about the taxes noted above, and other taxes, contact your lawyer, realtor, local city hall, or regional assessment authority.

PROVINCIAL TAXES

Many provincial governments levy a property purchase tax when you buy a property. This is the main form of provincial tax dealing with property. However, there could also be provincial tax on various real estate transaction expenses and ongoing homeowner expenses (e.g., services, products, utility costs).

Property Purchase Tax

Basically this tax is charged based on the purchase price of the property. It is assessed and paid at the time of purchase. The formula for determining the amount payable varies from province to province. If it is your first home, or you have a high-ratio mortgage, some provinces have tax relief in terms of a partial or full rebate. Check it out.

Further Information

To obtain further information about provincial taxes, contact the local branch of your provincial government Land Titles office, your realtor, or lawyer.

FEDERAL TAXES

There are two main federal taxes — the Goods and Services Tax (GST) and Income Tax.

Goods and Services Tax (GST)

The GST, which became effective January 1, 1991, applies to every "supply" of real property (with some exceptions). This includes not only sales and leases of real property but also transfers, exchanges, barters, and gifts. Most services dealing with the real estate transaction are also covered by the GST. In other words, whenever you consume a "good" — i.e., buy a product or use a service — you will be required, in most cases, to pay the 7% tax.

The following overview discusses how certain types of real estate purchases are affected by, or exempted from, the GST, and how the GST rebate system operates.

How the GST System Works. The GST is paid by the purchaser to the vendor at the time of purchase. The vendor then remits the tax to Revenue Canada Customs and Excise Division. Sometimes the vendor includes the GST within the purchase price and other times it may be added on separately. There are also several categories of GST exemptions relating to real estate. Although the basic rate of the GST is currently 7%, that could be changed at any time, and most countries who have brought in a similar tax have increased it over time.

If you are the purchaser who must pay the GST, you may be able to receive a partial rebate.

Resale Home or Other Residential Dwelling. If you buy a used residential property as a principal residence, you **do not** have to pay GST. Revenue Canada defines "used residential property to include an owner-occupied house, condominium, duplex, apartment building, vacation property, summer cottage, or non-commercial hobby farm."

The "used property" definition requires that the vendor must not be a "builder" as defined in the legislation; that is someone who builds or substantially renovates the property as a business. Used property can also mean a recently built house that is substantially complete but has been sold at least once prior to your purchase of it.

If you purchase a resale home that includes a room used as an office, and you are self-employed, the entire house still qualifies for the GST exemption if you use it primarily as your residence. However, if you purchase a home that is used primarily for commercial business purposes, and it is zoned for that type of operation, at the time of purchase you would only be GST exempt from the portion that you would reside in.

When purchasing a resale home, you can request that the vendor provide you with a certificate stating that the property qualifies as "used" for GST purposes.

New Home. When you purchase a newly constructed home from a builder as a principal residence, the entire purchase price including land is taxable. The word "home" refers to a residential dwelling and includes a simple family house, condominium (apartment or townhouse format), or mobile home. If the home is going to be your principal residence, it may qualify for a partial GST rebate depending upon the sale price.

Purchasers of homes priced up to $350,000 will qualify for the maximum rebate of $8,750, or 36% of the GST paid on the purchase price, whichever is less. Since the $8,750 amount is 2.5% of $350,000, a purchaser is really paying the GST at a rate of 4.5% on a $350,000 home instead of 7%.

If you are purchasing a home priced at more than $350,000 but less than $450,000, the rebate is gradually reduced; in other words it declines to zero on a proportional basis. There is no rebate for homes selling for $450,000 or more.

Here are some examples of how the rebate is calculated. The term "purchase price" refers to the price paid to the builder for the home and lot before the GST is calculated, and does not include any associated realty or legal fees.

EXAMPLE 1
Formula used for a home selling for $350,000 or less

If you buy a new home for $150,000, you would calculate the rebate like this:

GST paid (7% of $150,000)	$10,500
Amount of GST rebate ($8,750 or 36% of $10,500 — the smaller amount must be claimed)	$ 3,780
Net GST paid (GST paid minus rebate)	$ 6,720

EXAMPLE 2
Formula used for a home selling for more than $350,000 but less than $450,000

If you buy a new home for $400,000 you would calculate the rebate like this:

GST paid (7% of $400,000)	$28,000
Step 1 of rebate calculation ($8,750 is the amount because 36% of $28,000 is $10,080 and you must use the smaller amount)	$ 8,750
Step 2 of rebate calculation ($8,750 [Step 1] × [$450,000 − $400,000 purchase price] / $100,000 =	$ 4,375
Amount of GST rebate	$ 4,375
Net GST paid (GST paid minus rebate)	$23,635

EXAMPLE 3
Sample new-home rebates

Purchase Price	GST Paid	GST Rebate	Net GST Paid
$100,000	$ 7,000	$2,520	$ 4,480
150,000	10,500	3,780	6,720
200,000	14,000	5,040	8,960
250,000	17,500	6,300	11,200
300,000	21,000	7,560	13,440
350,000	24,500	8,750	15,750
400,000	28,000	4,375	23,625
450,000	31,500	none	31,500

When the home is purchased, the builder can either pay the rebate directly to you or deduct it from the GST you owe on the purchase price. You have to complete a form called "GST New Housing Rebate," which you can obtain from real estate agents, the builder, or a Revenue Canada Excise Office.

Owner-Built Home. If you build your own home or hire someone to build or substantially renovate a home for you as a principal residence, you will qualify for a GST rebate if:

• You paid the GST on construction materials and contracting services;

• You or a relative are the first occupants of the home; or

• You sell the home and ownership is transferred to the purchaser before it is occupied as a place of residence.

The amount of the rebate will depend on the fair market value (FMV) of the home and whether or not the GST was paid on the acquisition of the land.

If you did not pay the GST on the acquisition of the land, the rebate for homes valued up to $350,000 is a maximum of $1,720 or 10% of the GST paid, whichever is less. For homes valued at more than $350,000 but less than $450,000, the rebate is gradually reduced. There is no rebate for homes valued at $450,000 or more.

Here are some formulas to show how to calculate the rebate on an owner-built home, when the GST has and has not been paid on the land. Remember, FMV stands for "Fair Market Value."

GST PAID ON LAND
Example 1

If the FMV of the home, including land, is $350,000 or less, the rebate calculation is $8,750 or 36% of the GST paid on the land, building, contracting services and building materials, whichever is less.

Refer to the previous "New Home," Example 1, for a similar calculation example.

Example 2

If the FMV of the home, including land, is more than $350,000 but less than $450,000, the rebate calculation is based on the following formula:

$$\frac{A \times (450,000 - B)}{\$100,000}$$

A = $8,750 or 36% of the GST paid on the land, building, contracting services, and building materials, whichever is less.

B = the fair market value of the home.

Refer to the previous "New Home," Example 2, for a similar calculation example.

GST NOT PAID ON LAND
Example 1

If the FMV of the home, including land, is $350,000 or less, the rebate calculation is $1,720 or 10% of the GST paid on the building, contracting services and building materials, whichever is less.

Example 2

If the FMV of the home, including land, is more than $350,000 but less than $450,000, the rebate calculation is based on the following formula:

$$\frac{A \times (\$450,000 - B)}{\$100,000}$$

A = $1,720 or 10% of the GST paid on the building, contracting services, and building materials, whichever is less.

B = the fair market value of the home.

Renovated Home. Under the GST, sales of substantially renovated homes are treated as new housing. "Substantial renovations" means that all, or substantially all, of the house except the foundation, external walls, interior support walls, floor, roof, and staircases are removed or replaced. At least 90% of the items on the Revenue Canada guidelines must be removed to constitute a substantial renovation. For GST purposes, this substantially renovated home, when sold, will be treated like a new home. If you purchase this substantially renovated home, you will pay the GST on the purchase price and be entitled to claim the GST New Housing Rebate, if the price is under $450,000. Refer to the GST on "New Home" section discussed earlier.

A substantially renovated home is considered a resale home if the renovator owns it and lives in it, even for a short time. That is an important point to keep in mind, especially if you are buying from another homeowner or renovating yourself, and in both instances the renovations are substantial. You should be able to get more money on resale if the purchaser does not have to pay GST.

Land. There is no GST on the sale of vacant land or recreational property such as a hobby farm owned by an individual or by a trust for the benefit of individuals. Certain sales and uses of farmland are also exempt.

If you did pay GST on the land because its previous use was such that it was covered by GST, the rebate would be the same as for a new home. See the GST on "New Home" section.

If you build on the land and sell it, refer to the GST discussion relating to "Owner-Built Home" above.

Real Estate Transaction Expenses. Most of the services associated with completing a real estate transaction have GST applied. Real estate commissions, paid by the vendor, are GST taxable, even if the total GST owed is reduced by a rebate or the sale is exempt from GST. Other real estate related services on which GST is charged include fees for surveys, inspections and appraisals, and legal and tax advice. GST is charged on these fees regardless of whether the house you purchase is exempt from the tax. All moving charges are taxed.

There are several exemptions from GST, however. Mortgage broker fees are not taxed if the fees are charged separately from any taxable real estate commissions. Also, mortgage and interest on mortgages are exempt from GST.

Condominium Maintenance Fees. If you own a condominium, the monthly fee charged by the condominium corporation is not subject to GST. However, the condominium corporation will be charged GST on all services employed to maintain the building and grounds. These additional GST costs will obviously be passed on to the condominium owners in the form of increased monthly fees.

Homeowner Expenses. Any service you employ around the house, such as gardening, plumbing, carpentry, etc., will carry a 7% charge. You will already have noted a GST charge on your cable, hydro, and telephone bills.

Income Tax

There are positive tax considerations you should be aware of when selling your home, renting out part of your home, or operating a home office. The following discussion only highlights the common areas to consider. It is not intended to be complete or go into detail. It is important that you obtain advice from a professional tax accountant so that you can maximize all the tax benefits and savings. Laws and regulations dealing with taxation matters are complex and constantly changing. Also, you want to have specific advice based on your personal circumstances. In addition, there are forms, guides, information criteria and interpretation bulletins available from Revenue Canada, Taxation. Look in the Blue Pages of your telephone directory under "Government of Canada."

Tax Benefits of a Principal Residence. Most people start their first real estate "investment" by purchasing their own home to live in. Your principal residence may be a house, apartment, condominium, duplex, trailer, mobile home, or a houseboat.

A property will quality as a principal residence if it meets various conditions:

- It is a housing unit, a leasehold interest in a housing unit, or a share of the capital stock of a cooperative housing corporation.
- You must own the property solely or jointly with another person.
- You, your spouse, your former spouse, or one of your children ordinarily inhabited it at some point during the year.
- You consider the property your principal residence.

One of the key benefits is that the capital gain (increase in value from your original purchase price) that you realize on the sale of the home that was your principal residence is not subject to tax. For example, if you bought the property originally for $50,000 and sell it for $250,000 in a "hot" market, you would not pay tax on this increase in value of $200,000.

Getting A Tax Break on Your Moving Costs. You could be entitled to a tax deduction for your moving costs. However, there are various requirements for eligibility. Refer to Chapter 13 for a discussion of this aspect.

Deducting Home Office Expenses. There could be considerable tax savings to you if you are operating a part-time or full-time home-based business. The reason is that you are entitled to claim a lot of expenses that relate to your home that you are incurring anyway, from the income you make in your business. Naturally, this will help your overall finances, and could enable you to pay down your mortgage more quickly. Refer to Chapter 6, under "Deducting

Home Office Expenses" for a discussion of eligibility requirements, what to write off and how, and other issues to consider.

Renting Out Part of Your Home. Some people prefer to have a "mortgage helper," by renting out part of their house for example, to a student. There are various municipal by-law issues that you need to check out, in terms of rentals, as private homes are generally zoned for single family only, not multiple family, which would be the case if you rent out part of your house to an unrelated person. However, as you are probably aware, many people do have "mortgage helpers." You can anonymously check out what the policy of your munipicality is on the issue.

If you are renting out part of your house, you need to complete and file a special form and include it with your annual personal income tax form. You can get this form and a booklet entiled, "Rental Income Guide" from Revenue Canada. Basically, the tax aspects work out the same way as discussed above for the home office use, except you don't need to fill out this form for a home office. On the "Rental Income" form, you simply fill out the income from the rental and the portion of the home-related expenses that you are writing off relative to the portion of the square footage that you are renting. Generally, one offsets the other, so that you have no taxable income from your rental.

Further Information

As mentioned earlier, to obtain further information on the GST, contact Revenue Canada, Customs and Excise, or your accountant. To obtain information on income tax matters, such as moving costs, home office expenses or renting out part of your home, contact Revenue Canada, Taxation, or your professional accountant. All government listings are located in the Blue Pages of your telephone directory under "Government of Canada."

* * *

Some of these tax considerations may not apply to you but it is best that you understand all the possibilities before moving on to actual house hunting.

Chapter 11

FINDING THE RIGHT HOME

Now comes the really important part. That is how to find the right home for your needs and wants, taking all your budget realities into account.

This chapter will cover where to find a home for sale, including such sources as a real estate agent, the Internet, open houses, and pre-sales. Also discussed will be the common types of home descriptions. In addition, tips when choosing a home are covered — from condition of building, style and layout to noise, light, and security. Avoiding the hidden costs are also discussed.

WHERE TO FIND A HOME FOR SALE

There are some preliminary considerations you need to work through before you begin house hunting.

- Be clearly focused on what type of real estate you want and where it is to be located in order to save time and stress.
- Target specific geographic areas. Restricting your choices to specific communities or areas within a community will make your selection much easier and give you an opportunity to get to know specific areas thoroughly. Obtain street maps of the areas as well as zoning maps from city hall.
- Know the price range that you want based on your available financing and real estate needs.
- Determine the type of ideal purchase package that you want (e.g., price and terms) as well as your "bottom line" fallback position. You want to know the maximum you are willing to pay and the most restrictive terms that you can live with. Make sure that you don't compromise your own position.

- Do comparisons and short list choices. That way you can ensure you get the best deal in comparative terms.
- Be realistic in your expectations in terms of the current market situation. Many people fantasize about buying real estate for 20% less than the fair market value and keep searching for this elusive purchase. The reality is that this situation could be very difficult to find.
- Don't necessarily wait for mortgage rates to go down before looking. Higher mortgage rates generally mean less demand in the market and therefore lower prices and more negotiating leverage for the purchaser. Conversely, lower mortgage rates generally mean more demand in the market, higher prices and less negotiating leverage. These are guidelines only. The key factor is to buy at the right price, taking all the factors outlined in this chapter and others into consideration. If mortgage rates come down, you can renegotiate a lower rate with or without a penalty, depending on the mortgage you originally negotiated (see Chapter 6).
- Remember, the location of a property is very important, especially for a principal residence, but it has to be balanced against things such as appreciation and resale potential.

There are various methods of finding out about real estate for sale. Here are some of the most common approaches.

Real Estate Agent

A good real estate agent is an invaluable asset. He can save you time, expense, and frustration, and provide advice and expertise. Remember that the vendor pays the real estate commission whether the agent is a listing or selling broker. Refer to Chapter 9 "The Legal Aspects" for a discussion of real estate listing agreements, and to Chapter 5 "Professionals and Other Experts" for a discussion about realtors. There are many advantages to using realtors. You can use their services to source out property listed on multiple or exclusive listings, or for property being "sold by owner." You can also use them to contact owners of property which is not currently for sale. Another advantage of using a realtor is that they can negotiate with the vendor or vendor's agent in a business-like manner, without emotions clouding the picture.

If you use a realtor to assist your search, be loyal to that realtor if you purchase the property. On the other hand, if the realtor is turning out to be disinterested or you don't feel comfortable with them, then find another. Make sure you give your agent a list of your requirements so he or she can be precise while searching for you. For example, when looking to buy a house, provide the following information:

- your price range
- preferred location
- style of house
- age of house
- number of bedrooms
- square footage
- basement/non-basement
- self-contained suite/no self-contained suite
- lot size
- exposure of lot
- fireplace
- en suite
- zoning
- special features.

Multiple Listing Service (MLS)

MLS is an excellent tool for obtaining information. You can only access this through a realtor. The information consists primarily of an MLS book that generally comes out weekly, and a daily "hot sheet" of new listings. Realtors can access MLS information from a computer, and the type of information available was discussed in Chapter 5 "Professionals and Other Experts." If you are looking at an MLS book, look for specific factors that will give you cues as to vendor motivation or the appropriateness of the property. This could assist you in negotiating a lower price. For example, look for how long the property has been listed, if it has been relisted, whether the property is vacant, if any price reductions have occurred (how much and when), and whether there has been a previous collapsed sale. Also look in the remarks/comments section in the MLS listing book. For example, it could say why the property is for sale, such as foreclosure action, order for sale, relocation, vendor has bought another house, etc. All this information is important.

Using the Internet

If you have not used the Internet yet for your home search, you are in for a pleasant and rewarding experience. It is a goldmine of helpful information at your finger tips, that will save you a lot of time and energy and give you many creative ideas in terms of short-listing your search. One of the many benefits of the Internet is the ability to calculate your mortgage eligibility, including payment schedules right on the screen and then print out the information. You can get instant gratification in terms of knowledge. Not only are there colour pictures, in many cases showing the home from different perspectives, but some web sites also have audio and video features, if your computer has that compatible capacity to access those features.

The Internet is now being used extensively for marketing houses, condominiums and other types of real estate. In the past, you had to thumb through several MLS (Multiple Listing Service) weekly books of listings, which you may still prefer to do. You will find the Canadian Real Estate Association (CREA), real estate companies, individual real estate firms, individual realtors, real estate developers, individual Real Estate Board Multiple Listing Services (MLS), and real estate investment companies on the Internet. CREA has the MLS listings of many of the real estate boards across Canada. CREA has more than 150,000 properties on its database and updates it daily. You will also find banks, trust companies, credit unions, mortgage companies and mortgage brokers with web sites on the Internet.

Here are some tips for narrowing your search.

If you are familiar with the Internet, the following will be familiar to you. If it is a new experience, here is the process. You need your computer, modem, software and Internet connection and you are ready to go. One of the first things to do is to select the list of directions. The web browers, Netscape Navigator and Internet Explorer, as well as others, offer directions on how to use the Internet. Once you know the basics, navigating around the Internet is quite easy. If you need help, you have a number of options. You can access the "Help" section of the web browser, or the particular website itself that you are looking at. You can also access the FAQ (frequently asked questions) section of the browser or website. The process will be learning curve for you, but a positive and exciting one.

There are two main ways of accessing the real estate Internet sites.

Going Directly to the Specific Website. This is the easiest route. If you know the web (world wide web or WWW) site address, you simply type it in and push enter. For example, when you type the CREA (Canadian Real Estate Association) MLS (Multiple Listing Service) address, http://www.mls.ca, you will land (no pun intended) on the MLS homepage. It contains a series of easy-to-understand icons or buttons to help you navigate through the system.

The next step on the CREA website is to position your cursor over "Properties for Sale" and you will see a new page giving you a choice of residential, recreational, industrial or commercial properties. If you are looking for a house or condo, choose residential. The next page is a map of Canada. Choose the province, either on the map or by name in a box on the side. Whenever you choose a province, you will be given a choice of different regions. You keep selecting ever smaller areas until you arrive in the city, town or district where you want to concentrate your search.

The next selection allows you to choose the criteria for your search. You can choose from a house, condo, triplex, or raw land, for example. You can also choose whether you want an oceanview or lakefront, and the number of bedrooms and bathrooms. Finally, you select the price range of your home. Select the search button and the MLS site consults its database. After a few seconds, the computer will show you a selection of homes that meet the criteria that you have set. Click "View" to see them, normally in colour.

Occasionally, you will receive a notice that no matches meet your criteria. In that case you will have to make a few adjustments to your selection. You can do this in three ways: change the location and view the maps again, change the type of property you are looking for, or change the details such as the number of bedrooms, bathrooms, lot size, and price.

After you have made any changes, press "OK," and MLS site updates the number of properties that match your search. You can change the options again, and keep looking, or you can press "View" when you are ready to look at the properties you have selected.

To read the details about the property, click on its picture and a larger image appears along with specific information about it. If you are interested in a particular property, it is easy to contact the realtor involved. Often there is an e-mail link directly to the realtor's computer. If not, you should find the realtor's address and phone number listed.

Searching the Internet for Real Estate Web Sites. In this example, you don't have a specific real estate web site address to go to, or you simply want to do research in find out what websites are available to you that cover the geographic area that interests you.

There are various search engines that can assist you in your search. There are many large search engine companies and smaller ones as well. Some have more Canadian content than others. Once you are on the Internet, you will see the various options available to you.

You simply type in the "key words" and the search engine than attempts to find web sites that contain content with those key words. The more key words you put in the more fine-tuned the result. For example, you could type in "real estate" + "Canada" + "province" + "city" + "house" or "condo." That will help refine your search. You might only get 40 listings of web sites for example, rather than 10,000 if you just had "real estate". Remember to put the "+" sign between words, so the search engine will look for web sites that contain **all** those words. If you didn't put the plus sign, than the search engine will look for all sites that contain **any** of those words. The result could be overwhelming in terms of the volume of sites.

Another tip is to put a "-" sign if you want to delete a city. For example, if you had a number of key words, plus Vancouver, you might wish to put "-Washington", so that the search engine would not look for web sites containing the key words "Vancouver" and "Washington" state, as there is a community called "Vancouver" in Washington state. In this example, you would want to restrict your search to sites dealing with Vancouver, British Columbia.

After you have looked at all the offerings available, don't forget to "bookmark" those web sites that you want to come back to quickly and directly. Otherwise, you will have to go through the whole search process again like you did the first time.

Take time with your searching and enjoy the process. You will find it a productive research exercise.

Newspaper Ads

Look in the classified section of your local newspaper under "Houses for Sale," "Homes for Sale," "Condominiums for Sale," or "Apartments for Sale." The weekend section tends to have the most listings. Ignore the harmless sales puffery. Many ads are designed to entice you with the impression that the owner is anxious, implying that you may be able to get a better price. This may or may not be the case. Pay particular attention to ads that may imply an owner is under time pressure, such as "estate sale," "owner transferred" or "foreclosure sale." Also refer to the weekly real estate newspapers that are available free in most major Canadian cities.

Develop a system that works for you when looking at ads. Circle with a coloured pen those ads that interest you, clip them out, and staple them to an 8.5" × 11" sheet of three-hole punched paper. Collect these in a binder. Date the ads and write the information in summary form when you speak with the realtor or owner. Your checklist of questions will keep you on track so that you have information for comparative purposes. Keep the ads for interesting properties for six months, if you are still looking, so that you can track the property to see if it has gone down in price, whether it is still on the market, etc. The types of ads described could be listed or "for sale by owner." Clearly, the suggestions relate more to a "for sale by owner" research approach. If it is listed, you would be going through a realtor.

Real Estate Channel on Cable TV

If you are on cable, there is a good chance that there is a real estate channel that covers local real estate for sale. The size of your community has a lot to do with whether there is a channel or not. Generally, the format is a colour photo of one or more views of a home, plus a "voice-over" giving a description of the highlights of the home, plus pertinent details such as price, location, size, and other facts. As well, the realtors name, company and contact number is also shown.

Putting Ads in Newspapers

You may wish to locate property owners who have not yet put up their property for sale, but who are considering selling. One way is to insert an ad in the "Real Estate Wanted" or "Property Wanted" section of the newspaper in the area in which you are interested. Be as precise as possible about your needs in the ad or you could have a lot of people wasting your time phoning you for clarification. You will have to be clear as to the questions you are going to ask the callers. Develop a standard checklist that will save you time and frustration. Get right to the point to obtain the information you need.

Drive Through the Neighbourhood

As mentioned in Chapter 3, it is important to develop a familiarity with the area you are interested in. Drive through the area on a regular basis and look for "for sale" signs, both property listed with a realtor and "for sale by owner." Take down addresses, names, and telephone numbers.

Open Houses

This is another effective way to view homes to see what features interest you. Open houses tend to be on the weekends . You can see what homes are open and when by looking for ads in your local daily or community newspaper, local real estate newspaper, current MLS (Multiple Listing Service) book for area of interest and by contacting a realtor. Another way is to drive throughout the geographic area of the community that interests you, looking for "open house" signs. If you have a realtor actively searching on your behalf, let them know what you intend to do, so that they can tell you the protocol. That is, to let the realtor hosting the open house know that you have another realtor assisting you. That way, there won't be any discomfort on the issue of the commission split between the realtors. As discussed earlier, the vendor pays for the commisson, not the buyer.

Direct Offer to Owner

In the process of becoming familiar with a particular neighbourhood, you could look for indications that the owner of a property not currently for sale might be interested in selling. Look for cues that the property is vacant, lawns are not cut, paint is peeling, windows are broken, fence is in disrepair, etc.

Once you have determined which properties might seriously interest you, you can find out who the owner is by doing a search in the local Land Titles office. The documents are on public record. You could do the search yourself or through a lawyer or realtor. You would also be able to discover other information in your search, such as when the existing owner bought it and for how much, the nature and amount of mortgage financing, and if there are any legal problems relating to the property such as liens, judgments, foreclosures, or power of sale. The latter two mortgage default legal procedures were discussed earlier. If you want to pursue it further, you could contact the owner yourself, or preferably have your lawyer or realtor do it.

Buying by Pre-Sale

You will probably encounter the option of buying a house or condo before it is completed. The popularity and availability of this format depends on market conditions, the amount of available homes on the market, and other factors.

There are pros and cons of this option. One of the potential advantages is that you are buying at today's prices. If construction costs go up during construction (e.g., over a 9 to 12+ month period), then the builder suffers that loss in appreciated sale price. Another potential benefit is that some builders offer incentive packages to potential buyers. Also, lenders working with the builders often offer mortgages at a reduced rate at the time of pre-sale and hold that price until the project is completed and closing occurs. If the interest rate goes down further, you get that benefit. If the interest rate goes up, you don't pay any more than the rate at which you had originally signed. Attempt to get at least 1/2% off the "posted" lender's mortgage rate. Lenders also have inducements such as waiving the appraisal costs, and possibly some other closing costs. In addition, the lender could cover any legal fees for closing the deal, or contribute to them, often up to $1,000, depending on local market and competitive conditions.

Another potential advantage is that you have a greater selection of homes before completion. You can normally customize features to suit your tastes and needs, with finishing touches such as colour schemes, grade of carpet, paint, or type of tile.

There should not be any hidden costs in your purchase. You don't want surprises, so make sure that everything is spelled out in writing in the contract, concerning, for example, GST, provincial property transfer tax (if applicable), maintenance fees (if condo), and appliances.

Depending on the market economy, some lenders will require that a builder have at least 75% pre-sales from committed purchasers, before the lender will fund the builder's project. That is one reason why you will see "pre-sales."

There is always a flip side, however. Some disadvantages could include: the project is delayed in completion, thereby causing you inconvenience because you were counting on the closing date and have given notice at your apartment. Sometimes the quality of construction in the final project is not the same as you saw in the "show home" or in the brochures or other promotional literature. Possibly the real estate market could drop before the closing date, and you end up paying more for the property than it is worth at the time of closing. You might be able to get out of the deal, depending on the wording of the contract, but even if you can, you would normally lose your deposit.

Here are answers to some frequently asked questions:

- **How safe is my deposit?** In most provinces of Canada, it is required that the deposit money be paid into a lawyer's or realtor's trust account. There are provincial statutes dealing with the protection of those trust funds. However, if the developer wants you to place your deposit with their company, do not do it. If the company goes under you would lose all your money. Always make sure that your deposit is held in one of the two types of trust accounts discussed above. You want to be sure that the contract states that you will be getting the maximum bank interest on your trust money and that that interest will be credited to you on closing. In the event that the builder fails to complete the project, all your deposit money, plus interest, must be returned to you immediately.

- **What if I am unhappy with the quality of the final construction?** Most contracts have a provision where you give permission to the builder for substitution of materials. It should state, however, that the substitutions must be of equal or greater quality, and in the event that items that you specify are altered, it must be with your written consent. Minor imperfections can occur and you should have several opportunities before you more in to inspect the dwelling and note any deficiencies that need to be corrected. Outline these deficiencies in writing and include the date that the builder promises to complete them to your satisfaction.

- **Can I change anything I want before completion?** Not usually, but it depends on what it is. For example, generally you can make any change you want if you pay for it as an extra. That is because the builder's original special prices were based on bulk purchases. So if you want a special colour, type, or quality carpet, or want hardwood rather than carpet, or a gas-burning fireplace rather than a wood-burning one, you will probably have to pay extra.

- **How do I know exactly what I am going to get for my money?** It depends on what is in the contract that you negotiate. You want to make sure that everything is fully spelled out in writing, for example, the including of window coverings or appliances.

- **What warranties and guarantees can I expect?** Again, it depends on what is in the purchase and sale agreement. If the builder is a member of the New Home Warranty Program

(NHWP), check exactly what that coverage involves, and what the exceptions or exclusions are. Are they in writing and do you understand them? What are the warranties or guarantees over and above the NHWP, and what are those extra protections? Are they in writing and clearly understandable?

You want to make sure that you check the builder's track record thoroughly. How long have they been in business? What other projects have they done? Will they give you references from buyers in their other projects? Is the builder covered by the New Home Warranty Program in your province? If they have had problems in the past, how have they dealt with them? It is critical that you satisfy yourself that the builder is reputable. You don't need the aggravation or risk that may otherwise be predictable.

Finally, make sure you read and understand the wording of all the documentation. Have a real estate lawyer review any documents and explain the key clauses to you before you sign anything. You may put any subject clauses or conditions into your offer you wish. It is another matter whether the developer will agree to them. For example, you may wish to have a penalty clause covering the payment to store your possessions, and a "fine" of up to $100/day for each day that the project completion date is delayed. You may also wish to have a clause that, at your option, you can get out of the deal if the project is not completed on schedule. In that event, you would get all your deposit money back, with interest.

Buying by Auction

Buying your home by auction may seem like a novel idea, and it is. Only a tiny fraction of home sales in Canada are sold this way. You probably would think that you are going to pay a good deal below market value. You might but you could also end up paying more than market value, especially if the emotion and competition runs high at the auction sale, and also depending on the format of the auction. Here, it is the buyer, not the seller, who pays the commission, which is the reverse of the conventional home sale format. Commissions can vary between 1% – 10%, depending on various factors. The seller generally pays the cost of the advertising and marketing, which could run about 1.5% to 2% of the selling price.

Auctions sales are generally advertised about six weeks prior to the auction. There are open houses prior to the auction. Auctions are effective in a situation where the seller wants to sell the house quickly, for example, in a declining or overbuilt market.

There are various types of auction formats:

Absolute Auction. In this situation, the property is sold to the highest bidder, without any restrictions, limitations, or required minimum price.

Published Minimum Bid Auction. In this case, the seller sets an advertised minimum price and the property will be sold for the highest amount above that price.

Confirmation Auction. This option allows the seller to reject any offer for any reason. Naturally, this is not too exciting a format for a potential buyer.

Sealed Bid Auction. All bids have to be sealed. Therefore no one knows who else is bidding and how much.

There is a simple format to the process. You view the property and register to attend. If you are serious about submitting an offer, you are normally required to bring a certified cheque, bank draft, or money order for $1,000–$5,000+ depending on the auction policy. These funds are made out to you. If your offer is accepted, you sign the funds over to the auction company or seller and make up the difference, if any, with a personal cheque. You also sign all the documents at the site, including the closing date, etc. However, you can put conditions, such as subject to financing or review of documentation by your lawyer, and to be to your satisfaction. Many auction companies arrange for a lending institution to attend to give prompt mortgage approvals. After the auction, the closing process is very much like that for a conventional home purchase.

Word of Mouth

You could let your friends, neighbours, relatives, or business associates know that you are looking to buy property in case they hear of someone who is thinking of selling, or if they see a property for sale in their neighbourhood that might interest you. But beware of the pitfalls of this approach. It can get "personal" and hurt feelings may arise when you look but decide not to buy cousin Louie's house. The anonymity of a real estate agent or newspaper ads is lost.

* * *

After you have done your search using several of the methods outlined above, you will eliminate possibilities until you have a short list of preferred homes. It may take several trips to see the house with fresh eyes, etc. Rank the houses on your short list according to features you want or need (e.g. big yard, privacy, quiet neighbourhood) and once you have a "winner", look at it again. Buying your first house is an exciting and emotional time but you must not make the mistake of letting your heart rule your head. Don't just fall in love with one place and ignore the others. Remember, this isn't a car you can trade in for a new model in a couple years. You could be in this home for a lifetime.

Once you have made your decision, there are other things to consider.

UNDERSTANDING HOME DESCRIPTIONS

When shopping around for a home or when selling your own home, it is helpful to understand the jargon of the trade. There are common ways of describing a home, whether it is a house or condominium.

Most realtors, real estate companies and real estate ads use the same basic terminology when describing the seven key types of homes. This consistency provides some uniformity when searching for the right house for your needs, although the features or dimensions can differ, of course.

Here are the four main categories of houses.

Detached Bungalow

A detached, three-bedroom single storey home with 1&1/2 bathrooms and a one-car garage. It has a full basement but no recreation room, fireplace or appliances. Using outside dimensions (excluding garage), the total area of the house is 111 sq. meters (1,200 sq. ft.) and it is situated on a fully-serviced, 511 sq. metre (5,500 sq. ft.) lot. Depending on the area, the construction style may be bricks, wood, siding or stucco.

Executive Detached Two-Storey

A detached two-storey, four-bedroom home with 2 1/2 bathrooms, a main floor family room, one fireplace, and an attached two-car garage. There is a full basement but no recreation room or appliances. Using the exterior dimensions (excluding garage), the total area of the house is 186 sq. metres (2,000 sq. ft.) and it is situated on a fully-serviced, 604 sq. metre (6,500 sq. ft.) lot. Depending on the area, the construction style may be brick, wood aluminum siding, stucco or a combination like brick and siding.

Standard Two-Storey

A three-bedroom, two-storey home with a detached garage. It has a full basement but no recreation room. Using outside dimensions, the total area of the house is 139 sq. metres (1,500 sq. ft.) and it is situated on a fully-serviced, city sized lot of approximately 325 sq. metres (3,500 sq. ft.). The house may be detached or semi-detached and construction style may be brick, wood, siding or stucco.

Senior Executive

A two-storey, four- or five-bedroom home with three bathrooms, main floor family room plus atrium or library. Two fireplaces, a full unfinished basement and an attached two car garage. The house is 279+ sq. metres (3,000+ sq. ft.) and is situated on a fully-serviced 627 sq. metre (6,750 sq. ft) lot. Construction may be brick, stucco, siding or in combination.

The three most common types of condominium options are:

Standard Townhouse

Either leasehold or freehold, the townhouse (rowhouse) has three bedrooms, a living room and dining room (possibly combined) and a kitchen. Also included are 1&1/2 bathrooms, standard broadloom, a one-car garage, a full unfinished basement and two appliances. Total inside area is 92 sq. metres (1,000 sq. ft.). Depending on the area, the construction may be brick, wood or stucco.

Standard Condominium Apartment

A two-bedroom apartment with a living room, a dining room (possibly combined) and a kitchen, in a high-rise building with an inside floor area of 84 sq. metres (900 sq. ft.) Amenities include standard broadloom, 1&1/2 bathrooms, 2 appliances, a small balcony and 1 underground parking space. Common area includes a pool and some minor recreational facilities.

Luxury Condominium Apartment

A two-bedroom apartment with a living room, a dining room (possibly combined) and a kitchen, with family room or den, in a high-rise building with an inside floor area of 130 sq. metres (1,400 sq. ft.) Amenities include upgraded broadloom. 2 full bathrooms, ensuite laundry and storage area, 5 appliances, a large balcony and 1 underground parking space. Common area includes a pool, sauna and other major recreational facilities.

TIPS WHEN CHOOSING A SPECIFIC HOME

Condition of Building and Property

As mentioned, you want to be satisfied that you have an objective and accurate assessment of the condition. Having a home inspector look at it is one recommendation. (Refer to Chapter 5 for tips on selecting an inspector.) In addition, have the vendor answer specific questions, preferably in writing so you have proof of the answer. There is a trend in several provinces for real estate boards to request that the vendor complete and sign a "property condition disclosure statement" which should form part of the agreement of purchase and sale. You also want to make sure you include appropriate conditions in your agreement of purchase of sale in terms of obtaining or confirming information. Some of these key conditions or "subject clauses" are discussed in Chapter 9 "The Legal Aspects." Some of the common questions that should be asked follow. Address these to your lawyer, real estate agent, vendor, and home inspector. Not all of these questions may be applicable to you.

Questions of a General Nature

- Does the property contain unauthorized accommodation?
- Are you aware of any encroachments, unregistered easements, or unregistered rights of way?
- Are you aware of any local improvement levies/charges?
- Have you received any notice or claim affecting the property from any person or public body?
- Are the premises connected to public water system?
- Are the premises connected to public sewer system?
- Are the premises connected to a private or a community water system?
- Are you aware of any problems re: quality or quantity of well water?
- If well water, how many gallons of water per minute are available?

- Are you aware of any problems with the septic system?
- When was the septic tank last serviced?

Questions About the Structure of the Dwelling
- Are you aware of any infestation by insects or rodents?
- Are you aware of any damage due to wind, fire, or water?
- Are you aware of any moisture and/or water problems in the basement or crawl space?
- Are you aware of any problems with the electrical system?
- Are you aware of any problems with the plumbing system?
- Are you aware of any problems with the swimming pool and/or hot tub?
- Are you aware of any roof leakage or unrepaired damage?
- How old is the roof?
- Are you aware of any structural problems with the premises or other buildings on the property?
- Are you aware of any problems in terms of the building settling?
- Are you aware of any additions or alterations made without a required permit?
- Has the wood stove, fireplace or insert been approved by local authorities?
- To the best of your knowledge, have the premises ever contained urea formaldehyde insulation (UFFI)?
- To the best of your knowledge, have the premises ever contained asbestos insulation?
- To the best of your knowledge, is the ceiling insulated and to what R-factor?
- To the best of your knowledge, are the exterior walls insulated and to what R-factor?
- If a newly constructed home, has a final building inspection been approved or a final occupancy permit been obtained?

Questions Regarding a Condominium Property
- Are there any restrictions on pets, children, or rentals?
- Are there any pending rules or condominium by-law amendments which may alter the uses of the property?
- Are there any special assessments voted on or proposed?

Type of Construction

Is the construction made of wood, brick, concrete, stone, or other material?
Is this important for fire safety concerns you might have?

Structure

Check for any cracks in the basement, ceilings, or walls. Is the foundation solid? Are there any signs of insect infestation or dry rot in the wooden part of the structure? Is there any sign of settling, in terms of the house being uneven? If the doors or windows stick, or the floors are not level, that should cause concern. Do the floors squeak? Is the chimney in good condition?

Quality of Construction Materials

Examine your building and the surrounding development thoroughly to make an assessment of the overall quality of the development. If you are buying a condominium, keep in mind that you are responsible for paying a portion of the maintenance costs for the common elements. You may wish to hire a home inspector or a contractor you trust, to give you an opinion on the quality and condition of the construction before committing yourself. An older building is clearly going to cost more money to repair and maintain, possibly considerable amounts within a short time.

Common Elements and Facilities

If you are buying a condominium unit, review all the common elements that make up the condominium development. Consider them in relation to your needs as well as the maintenance or operational costs that might be required.

Owner Occupiers vs. Tenants

If you are buying a condominium, ask how many tenants as opposed to owners there are in the complex, and the maximum number of tenants allowed. The higher the percentage of owner/occupiers, the better the chance that there will be more pride of ownership and therefore more responsible treatment of common elements and amenities and less maintenance costs. When purchasing a house, the same principal applies to the neighbourhood. Generally you should be concerned if there are 25% or more tenants, and especially if it is increasing.

Condominium Management

If you are buying a condominium unit or apartment building, enquire as to whether the building is being operated by a professional management company, a resident manager, or self-managed. Ideally, you should check out the condominium unit or property that you are interested in at three different times, during the day, in the evening, and on the weekend, before you decide to purchase. That should give you a better profile of noise factors such as children or parties, and the effectiveness of management's control.

Size

How many rooms do you need now and how many will you need in the future? What is the type and size of each room? How much overall living space is there? Is this all usable space? Is there a room for a home business, rental or in-law suite if you so wish, or will you need to renovate?

Style

What type of style do you prefer? A single-storey rancher or bungalow, a one-and-a-half-storey (second floor is one-half the size of the main floor and built into the slope of the roof), a two-storey home, or a split-level home where each floor level is half a storey apart? Would you like a full or partial basement below ground which is finished or unfinished? Would you prefer a detached (stand-alone dwelling) or semi-detached house (two single-family dwellings joined by a common wall; e.g., duplex) or a rowhouse (several dwellings joined by common walls? Would an apartment condominium (one level) or townhouse condominium (two or more levels) be preferable? Do you prefer a new dwelling, an older one, or possible a conversion (from a previous rental apartment building, warehouse or historical building)? Do you prefer an older home with its own character or a new modern one?

Design and Layout

When looking at a building and overall layout, consider your present and future needs and lifestyle. For example, if you are buying a condominium, although you are entitled to use the interior of your unit as you wish, there are restrictions relating to the exterior of your unit. For example, you may find that the balcony is very windy and you would like to have a solarium built to enclose it. There is a very good chance that you would not be able to do so without the consent of the condominium council, because it would affect the exterior appearance of the development.

How is the home laid out? Is the living area an open design, without walls between living room, dining room and den? Or does each room have four walls? Is there at least one bathroom on each floor? What is the view from the kitchen? If you have children, you may want to be able to see the backyard. Where are the high traffic areas? Where is the laundry room located? Does the traffic flow from room to room, or is there a centre hallway joining the rooms together?

Light

Is the home dark inside because shrubs or trees block the light or the windows are too small and too few? Or does the home have lots of natural light because of the number and size of windows and possibly skylights?

Noise

Thoroughly check the noise levels. Consider such factors as location of highways, driveways, parking lots, playgrounds, and businesses. If you are buying a condominium, also consider the location of the garage doors, elevators, and garbage chutes as well as the heating and air-conditioning equipment.

Privacy

Privacy is an important consideration and has to be thoroughly explored. For example, you want to make sure that the sound insulation between the walls, floors, and ceilings of your property is sufficient to enable you to live comfortably without annoying your neighbours or having your neighbours annoy you. If you have a condominium or townhouse unit, such factors as the distance between your unit and other common areas, including walkways, parking lot, and fences, are important.

Storage Space

Is there sufficient closet and storage space? Is the location and size suitable? Are the kitchen, hall, and bedroom closets big enough for your needs? Is the basement or other storage area sufficient for sports and other equipment, tools, and outdoor furniture?

Yard and Landscaping

Are the yards fenced and are the fences in good repair? Are they of legal height and design, e.g. located correctly on your property line? Is the garden well maintained or over grown? Is the grass in good condition? Would it be easy to mow? How big are the back and front yards? What is the nature and condition of the landscaping? How much work would you estimate and how much would it cost to maintain the yard? Is that within your comfort zone?

Driveway and Garage

Is the driveway paved, concrete, or interlocking brick? How has it been maintained? Is there a garage or car port? Does security present a problem?

Drainage

This has been discussed earlier. Check around the house to see if it is adequate. Does the basement show evidence of any water seepage from outside?

Roof

What type of roof is it, shingles, shakes, tile, etc.? Are any pieces lifting or missing? Is there any moss on the roof? When was the roof last shingled? Are drainspouts and eavestroughs properly attached and in good condition?

Plumbing

Check to see if there are any visible signs of leaking. Are there water stains on the ceilings, walls or floors, or around sinks or faucets? Are there rust stains around the toilets, bathtubs, sinks or hot water tank? Flush the toilets and turn on the taps. Is the water pressure strong or weak? What types of pipes are being used — galvanized steel, copper, lead, or plastic?

Electrical

What type of wiring is in the house — aluminum or copper? Are there sufficient outlets in every room? Is the power supply adequate for your needs (e.g., computer equipment)? Has there been any wiring done that has not been inspected by the city?

Heating

How is the house heated and is the system efficient for your needs (e.g., natural gas, oil, forced air, hot water, radiators, electric baseboard, wood burning stove, or fireplace)? How old is the furnace? Has it been serviced regularly and is it still covered by warranty? Do you have any air conditioning or ceiling fans? Is there a heat exchanger system in the fireplace? Are there double- or triple-paned windows and/or other forms of insulation to minimize heat loss? What are the annual heating bills?

Insulation

What type of insulation is used? Is it adequate for your purposes? In addition to the attic, are the ceilings and walls also insulated? If so, it will also add a soundproofing factor. Has there ever been any asbestos or UFFI used? Are the windows single-, double- or triple-paned? Are the windows and doors weatherstripped to avoid heat loss?

Interior Condition

What kind of locks and other forms of security are there? What is the condition of the flooring or carpets? What is underneath the flooring surface — fir, pine, oak, plywood floorboards, or cement? What is the condition of this flooring material? What is the condition of the wallpaper or paint?

Exterior Condition

Is the paint peeling or blistering? Are the eavestroughs and downpipes in good condition? Does the porch need replacing? The stairs? What is the condition of the mouldings or windowsills? Do they need to be replaced? If a brick house, are there any signs that the mortar might be deteriorating? What do other buildings look like in the neighbourhood? Are they new, old or renovated? Or are they poorly maintained with signs of broken windows, uncut grass, litter, and peeling paint? Would the appearance of the property be attractive to someone else on resale?

AVOIDING HIDDEN COSTS WHEN BUYING A HOME

You have many things on your mind when buying a home, including carefully balancing your pre-purchase and closing day budget. One of the areas you don't want to ignore, however, is the physical inspection of the home and property by a qualified and objective professional home inspector. Buying a home, especially a resale home, without a physical inspection would be like buying a used car without taking it to a mechanic first. The cost of a home inspection will range from $250 and up depending on the size of the house and other variables. This is cheap money for peace of mind, to minimize potential surprises and to protect your largest life investment. Refer to Chapter 5 on how to select a home inspector.

You can have a home inspection done on a house or a condominium, apartment or townhouse. A thorough professional home inspection lasts approximately 2–3 hours or more. During the inspection, the inspector examines the house from the ground up, covering 100's of items in the home. This would include heating, air conditioning, plumbing, electrical, appliances, structural components of the roof, foundation, basement and exterior and interior.

The previous section covered some tips to follow when choosing a specific home. Here is an overview of some additional areas you may wish to check yourself. However, there is no substitute for the benefits of using a professional home inspector.

Roof — Average Life Spans

- Composite Shingles   15–22 years
- Wood Shingle   15–20 years
- Heavy Shake   25–30 years
- Tile   40 plus years

Naturally, exposure to the elements and upkeep affect life expectancy.

Electrical System Overview

- Check all of the outlets with an electrical tester.
- Look for exposed wiring.
- Check the service panel for "tripped" breakers or "blown" fuses.

Heating/Cooling

- Activate the thermostat to the "on" position.
- Walk around the house and check the vents for air flow.
- Do not test the air conditioning unit if the outside temperature is below 15°C.

Water Pressure

- Go into the bathroom, turn on sinks, shower, and flush the toilet.
- Check all plumbing fixtures in the kitchen.

Pipes/Plumbing

- Examine floor areas around the tub and shower.
- Check all pipes, especially at joints for visible corrosion, especially at the water heater.

Doors/Windows

- Open and close all windows and doors:
  — windows should open easily,
  — doors should close easily in the frame.

Drainage

- Look for evidence of ponding (standing water), discolouration, sunken elevations, trees that are growing at angles.
- Check the gutters and downspouts.

Structural/Room Additions

- Check the year the structure was built, zoning, etc. with the tax rolls or the local city/municipal building inspection department regarding permits.

Appliance Check

- Oven — turn oven to 350°F — check the oven temperature in 10 minutes.
- Range — ignite burners and smell for any gas odour, or, for electric ranges, check to see if they are hot.
- Dishwasher — let the cycle run through.
- Other appliances — check garbage disposal, hood/fans, trash compactors, etc.

* * *

So, you have used the tips and ideas outlined here and have a list of homes in which you are interested. The next step is to negotiate the best offer you can.

Chapter 12

NEGOTIATING

Understanding the art and science of negotiating is going to be important for you, if you want to make money when buying or selling real estate. As a first-time home-buyer, you will benefit from the practical tips, strategies, and insights in this chapter.

Most interaction with people — personnel, professionals, business associates, suppliers — involves some dynamics of the negotiation process. If you are attempting to sell, persuade, convince, or influence another person's thinking or feeling to accord with your own wants and needs, you are using negotiating skills. If, at the same time, you have defined and satisfied the other person's needs, you have attained an optimal or "win-win" type of negotiation. However, in practical terms in real estate negotiations, you will not always satisfy the other person's needs, as these may differ dramatically from yours.

There are psychological negotiating games and techniques abundantly used in the real estate market by different players. They will help you save more money and therefore make more money on any type of real estate purchase or sale.

This chapter will discuss the necessary steps to follow to prepare for real estate negotiation, understanding the reasons why the property might be for sale, and what to put in the offer. As mentioned before, using the services of a realtor to assist you is very important. A realtor has access to an extensive amount of computer database information to assist your research and therefore buying strategies.

PREPARING FOR REAL ESTATE NEGOTIATION

There are various preliminary steps you should go through to maximize your success before any offer is made:

- Determine the amount of mortgage that you are entitled to, the maximum price that you are prepared to pay, and the terms that you would prefer.
- Have alternative properties so that you have options.
- Have your realtor thoroughly check out the property. The services a realtor can offer in this regard were covered in Chapter 5. Find out such factors as how long it has been for sale, why it is for sale, how the vendor determined the asking price, recent market comparisons in the area, and any vendor deadline pressure.
- Be thoroughly prepared.
- Ideally, use a realtor as a negotiating buffer between you and the vendor.
- Obtain legal and tax advice on the implications of your purchase.
- Don't get too emotionally involved with the property. Be totally objective and realistic; otherwise it could taint your judgment.
- Train yourself to appear patient and unemotional to the vendor or his agent.
- To increase your bargaining leverage, look for negative features of the property in advance. All properties can be found to have something negative. For example, it could be a large lot with a high property tax. Some people want a large lot, but others see the negative aspects in terms of maintenance (cutting grass, etc.). Make a list of the positive and negative features.
- Establish a relationship with a home inspector in advance; you might need their inspection services on short notice.

REASONS WHY THE HOME IS FOR SALE

It is important to determine the real reason the owner is selling the property. This will assist you in knowing how to negotiate in terms of your offer price, terms, and general strategies. The motivation for selling could be positive or negative. If the vendor is selling in a buyer's market, be particularly thorough about finding out why he is selling when it is clearly disadvantageous to him in terms of the negotiating climate and eventual sale price.

Some of the frequent reasons for selling a home include:

- Separation or divorce.
- Death of owner or co-owner.
- Loss of job of one of the principal wage earners, especially when two wage earners are necessary to pay for the home expenses.
- Job relocation.
- Ill health of one of the home owners.
- Retirement of vendor and relocation to a smaller house, or desire to take some of the equity out of the house for retirement purposes.
- Owner lost money in a business or investment and needs to sell the house to pay off the debt.
- Owner has not made payments on the mortgage due to personal or financial problems, resulting in court proceedings by the lender. This could be in the form of an order for sale or foreclosure proceedings. The length of time before the house could be sold in the above circumstances varies depending on the provincial jurisdiction. In Canada, though, all distress sales of real estate, especially principal residences, are sold by the lender with or without court approval of the price, depending on the nature of the litigation and province. In practical terms, a current real estate appraisal is obtained by the lender, and legitimate and sincere attempts are made to sell the property at fair market value. Otherwise, the owner could complain to the court or sue the lender, claiming that the sale price was not fair market value.
- Municipal property tax sales in Canada are also a rarity. In normal circumstances, depending on the province, a municipality waits for approximately three years worth of arrears before a tax sale by sealed bid or auction can take place. The purchaser of the tax sale property cannot obtain title to the property until one year after the sale, to give the owner more chance to pay the arrears. For all these reasons, in practical terms, an owner of a principal residence is not going to let the property go, and lose all the equity built up, for the relatively small amount of property tax arrears. One way or the other, the owner will raise the money, or alternatively put the house on the market and sell it at fair market value.
- Owner wants to sell in a seller's market.
- Owner is concerned that the market is changing and could become a buyer's market.

- Owner is testing the market to see what the market will pay, without any serious attempt to sell.
- Empty nesters are downsizing the size of their house.
- A larger home is needed because of increasing family size, whether children or live-in parents or relatives.
- To trade up to a nicer home or better neighbourhood.
- To buy a house with a rental suite as a "mortgage helper."

NEGOTIATING TIPS AND TECHNIQUES

After you have gone through the preparation steps, the next negotiating stage is the presentation of your offer to the vendor. Following are some guidelines when presenting your offer.

Deposit

Try to put the smallest deposit down. You don't want to tie up any more money than you have to. Also, if you back out prior to closing, your deposit funds could be at risk of being kept by the vendor. Never pay the deposit money you put down directly to the vendor. Always have it paid to a realtor's or lawyer's trust account. Make sure you write in the offer that your deposit funds are to accrue interest to your credit pending the closing date.

Price

Attempt to offer the lowest possible price the market and circumstances allow. Always start with your ideal price and terms. You never know what the vendor will find acceptable, so don't anticipate disfavour. Be positive. If the vendor counter-offers, you may want to extract concessions due to the variation of your original offer.

Closing Date

Depending on your objectives, you may want to have a long closing date such as three or four months. Maybe you will be receiving funds by then. Maybe the market will have gone up in an escalating market, and you would be entitled to a higher mortgage on closing.

Financing Terms

You may want to ask the vendor for vendor-back financing for a first or second mortgage. Depending on your objectives, you may want to ask for a long-term open mortgage (say, five years), with an attractive interest rate, and assumable without qualifications. This latter provision would make it easier for resale. The vendor may be willing to provide such favourable terms if the market is slow and he is anxious to sell.

Conditions

Conditions are sometimes referred to as "subject" clauses. You should include as many conditional clauses as you feel are appropriate for your needs, such as, subject to "financing" or "building inspection satisfactory to the purchaser." Also include any warranty confirmations from vendor. Examples may include the vendor's assertion that "the furnace is functioning property and still covered under a manufacturer's warranty" or "the house was built under the New Home Warranty Program." Also, request that the vendor leave all warranty information, receipts and operating manuals. Refer to the section "Understanding the Purchase and Sale Agreement" in Chapter 9 for further "subject clause" examples.

* * *

You have now successfully negotiated your first home purchase using the things you learned in this chapter and elsewhere in the book. The next step is to take possession and move in.

Chapter 13

THE MOVE

Now that you are getting ready to move, there are many decisions you have to make. Do you decide to do it yourself, rent a truck or trailer and arrange for friends and family to help you pack or contract with a moving company to do it all for you? There are pros and cons of all these options, depending on whether it is a local move or one that is a long distance away, and whether you have the time, desire and budget to do it yourself. You may decide to just use the moving company for some of the heavier items and carry the rest yourself. If you are using a local moving company, you can pay by the hour or the job. Generally a job quote is safer, as you have a benchmark for comparison and you know how much to budget. You want to get comparative quotes in writing that are firm price commitments. You also want to ask questions such as how many men will be involved in the move (eg. driver and one or two others), how large the truck is (eg. will it carry everything in one trip or require two trips) etc. Lots of questions and lots of options.

As many people do use moving companies, it is helpful to know the process. This chapter will cover how to select a mover, understanding the legalities of using a moving company and common consumer questions relating to using a moving company. The chapter will also include who to notify of your move and how to might be able to get a tax deduction for your moving expenses. The Moving Day Countdown Checklist 13-1 should be helpful for you.

SELECTING A MOVER

Here is an overview of the key points to remember:

- Obtain names of possible moving companies from the Yellow Pages under "Moving and Storage" and references from family, friends and colleagues. Ask who they used and why they would recommend them.

- Use a company that has been in business for a long time. Obtain references which you should call. Also, check with the Better Business Bureau to see if there are any complaints.

- Many of the major international van line companies have consumer education brochures that have helpful tips and advice. Contact all the major companies and ask them to send you one of each of their brochures. You will also find that the major van line companies can provide you with value added services, such as information on key community resources with contact numbers, along with an overview of the key community features for the city you are moving to. In addition, some companies have made arrangements with other service companies for discounts on services a new home purchaser may require.

- Make sure you understand how much insurance the carrier has and what it covers. You may need to purchase extra insurance to protect your possessions.

- Compare and contrast your various moving company options. Obtain at least three written estimates in writing. Keep in mind that the lowest bid may not necessarily be the best when you consider insurance, training, experience, quality of vehicle, etc. Verify that the cost estimate includes all the items you want moved.

- Make sure that you get any verbal promises **in writing**. Make sure the contract specifies the dates and times of your move. Do not sign any contract with sections left blank. Carefully read and understand the contract before signing.

- Make an inventory of the goods to be moved. Supervise the loading and unloading of the truck or arrange for someone else who has a copy of your inventory to do so. It is important to have a responsible person stay at the truck during loading and unloading.

- If damage or loss occurs, have the driver make a special note on the inventory and/or delivery receipt and initial it. Then promptly notify the company in writing, keeping a copy for your own files.

- If your belongings will be left overnight in a truck be sure to use a company with proper climate controlled vehicles.

• Remember, if the moving company packs everything, **they** are responsible; if you pack things, **you** are responsible for those items packed.

UNDERSTANDING THE LEGALITIES OF HIRING A MOVER

There are terms and concepts that you should be aware of that have legal implications. Here is a discussion of some of the main terms that you might encounter.

Binding Estimates

Binding estimates must clearly describe the shipment and all services provided.

When you receive a binding estimate, you cannot be required to pay any more than the amount of the estimate. To be effective, a binding estimate must be in writing and a copy given to you before you move. A copy of the binding estimate must also be attached to the bill of lading.

If you agree to a binding estimate, you are responsible for paying the charges by cash, certified cheque, or money order at the time of delivery, unless the mover agrees before you move to extend credit or to accept payment by charge card. If you are unable to pay the amount required at the time the shipment is delivered, the mover may place your shipment in storage at your expense until the charges are paid.

Non-Binding Estimates of Approximate Cost

A non-binding estimate does not bind the mover. When you receive a non-binding estimate there is no guarantee that the final cost will be the same as the estimate.

Non-binding estimates must be in writing and clearly describe the shipment and all services provided. If you are given a non-binding estimate, do not sign or accept the order for service or bill of lading unless the amount estimated is entered on each form when prepared by the mover. In a non-binding estimate move, the mover should not require you to pay more than the amount of the original estimate plus 10 percent, at the time of delivery. You should then have at least 30 days after the date of delivery to pay any remaining charges.

Order For Service

Moving companies are required to prepare an order for service on every shipment transported for an individual shipper. You are entitled to a copy of the order for service when it is prepared.

The order for service is not a contract. Should your move be cancelled or delayed or if you decide not to use the services of the mover, you should promptly cancel the move.

Should there be any change in the dates on which you and the mover agreed that your shipment will be picked up and delivered, or any change in the non-binding estimate, the mover may prepare a written change to the order for service. The written change should be attached to the order for service.

The Bill Of Lading Contract

The bill of lading is the contract between you and the mover. The mover is required to prepare a bill of lading for every shipment it transports. The information on a bill of lading should be the same information shown on the order for service. The driver who loads your shipment must give you a copy of the bill of lading before loading your furniture. You must also sign the bill of lading and, in your own handwriting, put the amount of valuation you want your shipment to move under.

It is your responsibility to read the bill of lading before you sign it. If you do not agree with something on the bill of lading do not sign it until you are satisfied that the bill of lading shows what service you want.

The bill of lading requires the mover to provide the service you have requested, and you must pay the mover the charges for the service. The bill of lading is an important document. Do not lose or misplace your copy. Have it available until your shipment is delivered, all charges are paid and all claims, if any, are settled.

Inventory

At the time the mover's driver loads your shipment he or she, usually inventories your shipment listing any damage or unusual wear. The purpose of this is to make a record of the condition of each item.

After completing the inventory, the driver will usually sign each page and ask you to sign each page. It is important before signing that you make sure that the inventory lists every item in your shipment and that the entries regarding the condition of each item are correct. You have the right to note any disagreement. When your shipment is delivered, if an item is missing or damaged, your ability to recover from the mover for any loss or damage may depend on the notations made. The driver will give you a copy of the bill of each page of the inventory. Attach the complete inventory to your copy of the bill of lading. It is your receipt for the goods.

At the time your shipment is delivered, it is your responsibility to check the items delivered against the items listed on your inventory. The driver usually places a small numbered tag on each item as the inventory is prepared. The number should correspond to the numbered items on the inventory form and facilitate checking off the items as they are brought into your new home. Check each item for damage that did not exist when the shipment was loaded. If new damage is discovered, make a record of it in the space provided on the inventory form. Be sure to call the damage to the attention of the driver and request that a record of the damage be made on the driver's copy of the inventory.

After the complete shipment is unloaded, the driver will request that you sign the driver's copy of the inventory to show that you received the items listed. Do not sign the inventory until you have assured yourself that it is accurate and that proper notations have been entered on the form regarding any missing or damaged items. When you sign the inventory at the time of unloading, you are giving the driver a receipt for your goods.

Weight Shipments Subject To A Minimum Weight Or Volume Charges

Movers usually have a minimum weight or volume charge for transporting a shipment.

If your shipment appears to weigh less than the mover's minimum weight, the mover should advise you on the order for service of the minimum cost before agreeing to transport the shipment. Should the mover fail to advise you of the minimum charges and your shipment is less than the minimum weight, the final charges are normally based on the actual weight instead of the minimum weight.

Picking Up And Delivering Shipments On The Agreed Dates

Agree with your mover on set times for pickup and delivery. You and your mover must reach an agreement as to when your shipment is to be picked up and delivered. It is your responsibility to determine on what date, or between what dates, you need to have the shipment picked up and on what date or between what date, you require delivery. It is the mover's responsibility to tell you if the service can be provided on or between those dates or, if not, on what other dates the service can be provided.

In the process of reaching an agreement with a mover, it may be necessary for you to alter your moving and travel plans if no mover can provide service on the specific dates you desire.

Do not agree to have your shipment picked up or delivered "as soon as possible." The dates or periods of time you and the mover agree on should be definite.

Once an agreement is reached on the dates service is to be provided, the mover is required to enter those dates on the order for service. Do not sign or accept an order for service that does not have the agreed dates for service entered on the form. Do not sign or accept an order for service which has dates for the pickup entered on it which are different from those dates to which you have agreed. The dates you have agreed upon must also be entered on the bill of lading and become part of your contract with the mover.

Once your goods are loaded, the mover is contractually bound to provide the service described in the bill of lading. The only defense for providing the service on dates other than called for in the contract is the defense of "force majeure." This is a legal term which means that if circumstances which could not have been foreseen and which are beyond the control of the mover prevent the performance of the service as agreed to in the bill of lading, the mover is not responsible for damages resulting from the non-performance.

If the mover fails to pickup and deliver your shipment on the date entered on the bill of lading and you have expenses you otherwise would not have had, you may be able to recover those expenses from the mover. This is what is called an inconvenience or delay claim. Should a mover refuse to honour such a claim and you continue to believe that you are entitled to be paid damages, you may sue the mover. Every province in Canada has a small claims court. Depending on the province, it could be up to a $10,000 ceiling. You don't need to use a lawyer for small claims court.

Space Reservations, Expedited Service, Exclusive Use Of A Vehicle, And Guaranteed Pickup And Delivery

It is customary for movers to offer price and service options.

The total cost of your move may be increased if you want an additional or special service. Before you agree to have your shipment moved under a bill of lading providing special service, you should have a clear understanding with the mover what the additional cost will be. You should always consider that you may find other movers who can provide the service you require without requiring you to pay the additional charges. Here are various service options:

Space Reservation. If you agree to have your shipment transported under a space reservation agreement, you are required to pay a minimum number of cubic feet of space in the moving van regardless of how much space in the van is actually occupied by your shipment.

Expedited Service. This is designed to aid shippers who must have their shipment transported between specific dates which the mover could not ordinarily agree to do in its normal operations.

Exclusive Use of Vehicle. If for any reason you desire that your shipment be moved by itself on the mover's truck or trailer, most mover's will provide such service.

Guaranteed Service on or Between Agreed Dates. If you take this service option you enter into an agreement with the mover that provides for your shipment to be picked up, transported to destination and delivered on specific guaranteed dates. If the mover fails to provide the service as agreed, you should be entitled to be compensated regardless of the expense you actually might have incurred as a result of the mover's failure to perform. You want to know in advance in writing what the compensation formula will be.

Before requesting or agreeing to any of these price and service options, be sure to ask the mover's representative about the final costs you will be required to pay and consider all possible alternatives if you feel that the charges will be more than you are willing to pay.

Receipt For Delivery Of The Shipment

At the time of delivery the mover expects you to sign a receipt for your shipment. This is usually accomplished by having you sign each page of the mover's copy of the inventory.

Movers should not have you sign a receipt which relieves the mover from all liability for loss or damage to the shipment, regardless of an accident or its negligence or responsibility. Do not sign any receipt which does not provide that you are signing for your shipment in apparent good condition except as noted on the shipping documents. Also check into what insurance coverage protection you have, and what exclusions of coverage or deductibles there might be if you have a claim.

COMMON CONSUMER QUESTIONS

There are many recurring questions that people have about the moving process. Here are some of the frequently asked questions, along with the answers.

When Is The Best Time To Move?

If you are able to choose your moving dates, most moving companies will advise you to schedule your move at any time other than: school holidays, the middle or end of the month, weekends, and especially any combination of those times. This is because the demand placed on vans, containers, equipment and personnel are highest during those periods.

If you must schedule your move for a peak period, try and make your moving arrangements as far in advance as possible.

How Long Does It Take To Move?

This depends on many factors. The weather conditions, time of the year, weight of your shipment and your origin and destination may all influence the time it takes to move your possessions.

The delivery period will take place on the given day or within the time period entered on your bill of lading. If your household goods are not delivered on the promised date or within the guaranteed period, make sure you receive reimbursement for overnight and meal expenses for you and your family in accordance with a compensation schedule agreed on in writing in advance.

Do I Need An Estimate?

You want to have one. Obtain competitive quotes from at least three moving companies. At your request, a moving company representative will come to your home and do a survey of your household goods to be transported. There should be no charge for this estimate.

The estimate is based on:

- your origin and your destination
- other charges related to your move such as ferry crossing, extra pick-up, etc., if applicable
- any extra service you are planning to order such as packing, valuation, appliance service, etc.

Note that some of those charges may not be known until after arrival at destination and therefore cannot be included in the estimate. You want to have these unknown matters clarified in writing.

How Much Will My Move Cost?

The cost of your move will generally depend on:

- the actual scaled weight of your entire shipment
- the distance your goods will travel
- other charges, where applicable, such as storage-in-transit, valuation, extra pick-up or drop-off of goods, etc.
- other services ordered by you, such as packing/unpacking, housecleaning, appliance service, etc.

How and When Should I Pay For My Move?

Unless other arrangements have been made prior to the move, payment must be made in cash, by money order, or certified cheque before your shipment is unloaded at destination. Some companies permit credit card charges. Check in advance. If your shipment goes into storage-in-transit, payment is most easily arranged through you moving company at the outset.

Are My Goods Protected Against Loss and Damage?

It depends. The extent of your protection depends on the decision you make before your move. You have these two choices:

Released Rate Liability. You can release your shipment to a moving company at the carrier's liability rate of "x" cents per pound per article. There is no extra cost for this protection. However, it only provides minimum coverage since the repair, replacement or cash settlement value of the damaged or lost articles cannot exceed "x" cents per pound per article.

Replacement Value Protection. For an additional charge of "y" cents per $100.00 of valuation, you can place your own declaration of value on your entire shipment and protect its replacement value. This is subject to a minimum amount per pound. In this instance, repair, replacement, or the cash settlement value of a replacement or the cash settlement value of an article could be equal to, but no more than its replacement cost.

The costs "x" and "y" can vary so ask about the current rates.

Will You Move My Jewelry and Valuables?

While a moving company can move such valuables as important documents, stamp collections, or other items of extraordinary value, you should carry irreplaceable and expensive articles with you. Your local bank may also recommend the services of a commercial courier with the special facilities to provide the security such items warrant. However, if you wish the moving company to assume responsibility for items of extraordinary value, they will require a list of those items and their respective values prior to loading. Such information will clearly establish that the particular items are included in the shipment and extend the movers' liability for them. In that case, you should retain in your personal possession sufficient description and proof of value so as to substantiate a claim in the event of loss or damage.

What Documents Do I Have To Sign?

The following documents will be presented for your signature:

- Inventory listings. Basically, an itemized account of all the possessions that you are having a moving company transport for you, and their conditions.
- Bill of Lading. This is a receipt for your belongings and contract for their transportation.
- Certificate of packing and unpacking (if applicable). This confirms your agreement that the mover has completed the task.
- Notice of third party service requirements (if applicable). This would occur if some other company, e.g. house cleaners, were contracted on your behalf.

You should receive a copy of each document you sign.

Can My Goods Be Stored Temporarily?

Yes, if you cannot take immediate possession of your new home, a moving company can arrange for your goods to be stored in a warehouse at origin or destination.

The moving company will be liable for your goods in storage to the same extent as during transportation for a period of 60 days, more or less, following delivery into the warehouse. After that period, storage-in-transit becomes long-term storage and it is necessary for you to deal directly with the warehouse where your goods are stored.

If your goods travel by container, you may place them in short-term storage for a low daily rate. This may result in considerable savings for you.

What Do I Have To Pack?

Nothing, if you don't want to. If you would rather do your own packing, understand that the carrier does not assume responsibility for the contents of cartons the customer has packed because of the absence of control over the manner in which those cartons were packed. That is why most people prefer to have the packing done professionally.

How Do I Get Rid Of Possessions I Don't Want?

Part of preparing to move to your new home means getting rid of unnecessary possessions. Give yourself plenty of lead time to remove items to make the process more acceptable and less stressful. You may have to allocate three or four months of weekends before you have cleaned out the excess. Many people are packrats and have a mental block about letting go of possessions accumulated over time. They feel more comfortable about being surrounded by familiar items, no matter how unattractive, junky or impractical. Ask yourself about each item if you are having difficulty about whether to keep it or not. For example, ask yourself if you have used the item over the past year. If so, consider keeping it as long as it is still usable. If not, then ask yourself if it has any real value to you, or considerable sentimental value. If not, then get rid of it by selling it at a garage sale, giving it to friends or family, or donating it to charity. If you phone the Salvation Army, they generally have a pick-up service to take away items you don't want. Alternatively, they have a depot you can drop your items off at.

What About Dangerous or Hazardous Goods?

Explosive or flammable goods must not be packed with your household goods. You have to discard them before you move. You cannot have the following items travel in your shipment:

- Aerosol cans of all kinds
- Ammunition
- Acid batteries with the exception of those included in a vehicle transported with your shipment of household goods
- Chemistry sets
- Cleaning fluids
- Explosives
- Fire extinguishers
- Fireworks
- Fertilizers containing ammonium nitrate
- Flammable goods of all types
- Flares
- Gasoline
- Kerosene
- Lighter fluid
- Liquified petroleum gases of all types
- Matches
- Oily cloths
- Paints
- Pesticides containing an arsenic, strychnine or cyanide base
- Starter fuel
- Tanks of compressed gases such as barbecue tanks and diving tanks.

As a matter of public safety, federal and provincial legislation govern the transportation of dangerous goods. Some commodities may be included in your shipment under controlled conditions. Others are prohibited by law. Obtain a list from your moving company.

Most municipal landfill sites have the facilities to handle the disposal of dangerous goods. You don't want to conceal these categories of goods within your shipment. This could place the van, its contents and the driver in serious danger, as well as invalidate your liability protection and insurance, and place you at risk of being sued for damage or injury.

What About My Pets?

Pets cannot be shipped with your household goods. If it is not convenient for you to take your pet(s) in the family car, consult your moving company for alternate methods of shipping your pet(s) to your destination.

What About Moving Perishables?

Just like plants, other articles such as food which require temperature control can only be accepted for shipment at your own risk, as the carrier cannot assume the responsibility for their condition or flavour.

Wine cannot be transported without risking alteration. Homemade wine, in particular, could re-ferment on being moved. In any case, wine containers could leak or break, spilling the contents on other goods.

What About My Car?

If you wish, your car can be transported on board the furniture van along with your other possessions. As an alternative, you can have your car shipped by rail or car carrier.

What About Boats and Trailers?

Small boats and trailers and other similarly bulky articles can be transported. However, under certain circumstances, your transportation charges may have to be computed differently.

What About Re-Directing My Mail?

There are three handy services for the re-direction of your personal mail. Permanent Re-direction, Temporary Re-Direction, and Hold Mail. Visit your local Canada Post outlet at least two weeks before you move so that they have time to process your address change.

Permanent Re-Direction. Available in six month periods, to give you extra time to notify everyone of your new address. The service begins on the date you indicate on the "Change of Address Notification Form." You can also buy an additional six months service when you make your initial purchase. After this, extra six month periods can be purchased with a new request form and fee.

Temporary Re-Direction. This is handy for those who spend their winters down south or travel for long periods. This service is available at monthly rates but must be purchased for a minimum of three months.

Remember to take into account your travel time between addresses. For example, if you're taking six days to drive home from another address, is your mail still heading south while you're driving north? Remember to either file a mail re-direction notice at your temporary address or consider the "Hold Mail" option for that interim period.

Hold Mail. If you are going out of town for a short period, ask about the "Hold Mail Service." Sold by the week (with a two week minimum), this service assures that your mail is held for you for a specified period of time — during which, nobody can access your mail. When your hold mail period ends, the mail is delivered to your regular delivery address.

What Are the Disadvantages of Packing Myself?

* Responsibility for damage to goods in a carton which you pack is difficult to prove if there is no visible damage to the outside of the carton. You may wish to have the moving company professionally pack the fragile, expensive or irreplaceable articles or to supply special containers to protect your clothing, mattresses, pictures, etc. Your moving company will give you an estimate of the cost and explain your protection against damage and loss.

* Professional packers can pack an average household in one day, usually the day before the loading of the van or container. It will take you much longer to accomplish this chore because you must sandwich the job in between your regular daily schedule and other pre-move arrangements. All packing will have to be completed by the evening before moving day. The time and aggravation you will spare yourself and the peace of mind you'll have during your move might well be worth the extra charge you'll pay. However, if you decide to do your own packing, start planning four to six weeks before moving day.

* If your packing is improperly done or if the cartons are not properly sealed, the mover can refuse to load the cartons until

they are properly packed. If you choose to have the mover re-pack, a charge will apply.

What's the Best Way to Prepare Children for a Move?

While there are probably as many answers to this question as there are children, here are some general tips provided by experts:

- Talk to your children freely and often about the move and what it will mean. Talk about the positive and exciting features (e.g. new friends, new experiences, etc.).
- Keep to your normal routine as much as possible
- Keep familiar items (toys, books, blankets, teddy bears, etc.) out in the open and available, before, during and after the move
- Take photos and videos if possible, of the new home, neighbourhood and schools to show to your children before the move.
- If possible, take your children to your new home and community *before the move* to acquaint them with their new surroundings
- Above all, listen to what your children have to say, and keep communication open and honest.

Why Do Movers Sometimes Consolidate Shipments?

In order to keep moving costs down for the customer, they put more than one household on a van. The average van can carry from three to four households worth of furniture.

What's the Best Way to Prepare a Personal Computer for Safe Transport?

As with any delicate piece of electronic equipment, a few precautionary measures will ensure its safe arrival. For example, make back-up copies of all your data files. Remove any diskettes from the disk drives and replace them with "scratch diskettes" to park the hard drive. PCs, of course, move best in their original carton. Also, ask your local computer dealer where you bought the equipment for advice. You may even decide to take it in your own car instead.

What About Insurance Coverage for My Goods?

You want to make sure that all the aspects are covered in writing beforehand. The moving company will have insurance for the items they move. Your car insurance could cover certain items damaged, lost or stolen from your car. Check on this. Your homeowner insurance policy for the home you are moving to should be effective as soon as you have transferred title to your name. It could cover under a "floater policy" any personal possessions you are personally carrying during the move. That will cover you for any loss, theft or damage to them. Ask about the limit of that coverage, any limitations and deductibles. Refer to the next chapter for a detailed discussion of home insurance.

What Do I Do When My Goods Arrive At My New Home?

- Tape a large floor plan in a prominent place by the entrance of the new house to facilitate the proper placement of your household goods.
- Tour your new home — inside and outside — with the driver and his helpers to familiarize them with the placement of your belongings.
- If your mover packed any boxes for you, have him complete the unpacking of these boxes before he leaves.
- The boxes you packed yourself can be unpacked at your leisure.
- If you move in winter, allow television sets and appliances to warm up for an hour or so before plugging them in.

WHO TO NOTIFY OF YOUR MOVE

In addition to your friends and relatives, here is a summary of others to notify of your new address, phone number and date of move. You can get the change of address notice forms from any Canada Post outlet. You can probably think of additional people to add to this list.

Government and Public Offices:

Federal

- Post Office
- Veterans Office

- Income Tax
- Family Allowance
- Old Age Security
- Canada Pension Plan
- Unemployment Insurance
- Maternity Benefits

Provincial

- Health & Hospital Insurance
- Vehicle Registration
- Driver's License

Local

- Schools
- Library

Publications

- Newspapers
- Magazines
- Mail Order Houses
- Book & Record Clubs
- Others

Business Accounts

- Banks
- Finance Companies
- Credit Cards
- Diaper Service
- Charge Accounts
- Department Stores
- Insurance Agencies
- Real Estate Agency
- Service Stations
- Dairy
- Baker
- Laundry
- Dry Cleaner

- Drug Store
- Housecleaning Service

Professional Services

- Doctor
- Dentist
- Lawyer
- Financial Planner
- Investment Broker
- Insurance Broker
- Others

Utilities & Services

- Electric
- Gas
- Water
- Garbage (special pick up)
- Telephone
- Appliance Services
- Cable TV
- Fuel
- Water Treatment
- Others

GETTING A TAX DEDUCTION FOR YOUR MOVING EXPENSES

You may be able to deduct your moving expenses from income you earn from the time you move to the new geographic area. You can deduct your expenses if **all** of the following apply:

- You moved to start a job or a business, or to study full-time at an educational institution that offers post-secondary courses.
- Your new home is at least 40 kilometres (by the shortest normal public route) closer than your previous home to your new job, business or school.
- Your move was from one place in Canada to another place in Canada.

To make a claim, get the "Claim for Moving Expenses" form. You have to complete this form to determine how much you can deduct. You can get this form from Revenue Canada. Also contact them if you have any questions. Their phone number can be located in the blue pages of your telephone directory, under "Government of Canada."

If you cannot utilize all of your claim in this taxation year, you can carry forward the remaining expenses against income you earn next year. Do not include your receipts or form with your paper return. However, you have to keep them in case Revenue Canada asks to see them.

* * *

Now that you have gone through a moving experience and are the proud owner of your new home, you want to take care of it as much as possible. The next chapter discusses various ways of doing so.

CHECKLIST 13-1

Moving Day Countdown Checklist

Eight Weeks Before:

___ Decide which items are to be moved.

___ Select a mover to make arrangements for moving day.

___ Start to use up items that are not easy to move, such as frozen foods.

___ Contact the Visitors or Tourism Bureaus in your new community for information.

Six Weeks Before:

___ Inventory and evaluate your possessions.

___ Compile a list of everyone you need to notify about your move, such as friends, creditors, professionals, insurance, clubs or organizations, financial institutions, motor vehicle, or other licenses or registrations, subscriptions, etc.

___ Make arrangements, if required, to store any goods.

___ Contact schools, dentists, doctors, lawyers and accountants, and obtain copies of personal records. Ask for referrals where possible.

Four Weeks Before:

___ Notify Post Office of new address.

___ Fill out change-of-address cards.

___ Arrange special transport for your plants and pets.

___ Arrange to disconnect utilities at old home.

___ Arrange to connect utilities at new home.

___ Confirm loading and delivery dates with mover.

___ Arrange with telephone company for connection.

___ Purchase packing boxes from your local mover if you are packing some items yourself.

___ Make your personal and family travel plans.

___ Arrange to close accounts in your local bank and transfer accounts in your new location.

___ List all your questions as they come up. Ask them as soon as possible.

Two Weeks Before:

___ Collect clothing items to clean, repair.

___ Send out rugs and draperies for cleaning and have them delivered to your new address.

___ Collect items loaned, return things borrowed.

___ Have a garage sale or give away unwanted items to eliminate articles you don't want to move.

___ Draw up a floor plan of your new home, and indicate the location of all furniture. Give a copy to the moving company.

___ Arrange for babysitting, if necessary, for moving day.

___ Arrange any necessary insurance for transit or storage, as well as insurance for your new home.

One Week Before:

___ Set things aside to pack in car.

___ Take down curtains, rods, shelves, etc., if mover is not doing so.

___ Make up "Do not move" cartons for articles to be taken in the car.

One Day Before Moving:

___ Clean your range.

___ Empty freezer and refrigerator.

___ Finish packing personal items.

___ Set aside personal and other items you will be moving yourself.

___ Get a good night's sleep.

Moving Day:

___ Be at the old home or have someone else there to answer questions.

___ Make final check of appliances to be sure they are working.

___ Record all utility meter readings.

___ Review and sign and save all copies of bills of lading. Be sure delivery address and place you can be reached are accurate.

___ Tell driver exactly how to get to new address. Draw a map.

___ Have your vacuum ready to clean behind hard-to-move items.

___ Before leaving the house, check each room and closet, make sure windows are closed, doors are locked, lights are out, and water is shut off. If there is going to be a time period before the new owner comes in, consider shutting off the electricity.

___ Call and inform your insurance agent.

___ Notify landlord, realtor and/or lawyer that the home is vacant.

Delivery Day:

___ Arrange to make sure that you or a relative or friend is at the new home.

___ Review floor plan with moving company foreman.

___ Examine all goods as they are unloaded. Check off the inventory numbers as a protection against loss.

___ Arrange to have appliances installed, if applicable.

___ Arrange to have movers re-assemble any furnishings that were dismantled.

___ Re-check all items to make sure no damage exists before signing final moving documents.

Chapter 14

TAKING CARE OF YOUR HOME

Now that you are the proud owner of the biggest investment of your life, you want to make sure that your home is kept in good shape at an affordable cost. Not only do you want to fully enjoy your home in very way, but want to make sure that when the time comes to sell your home, that you will get the best price for it.

This chapter discusses various matters to consider that will enhance and protect your home. Sections include insuring your home, how to avoid common fire hazards, burglar-proofing your home, selecting alarm systems, maintaining your home and renovating your home.

INSURING YOUR HOME

You have heard of people whose homes have burned down without insurance or adequate insurance. You don't want that to happen to you. As many people are confused about insurance terms and options, it would be helpful to discuss some of the key concepts that you should know, so that you can be an informed consumer when comparing various insurance companies. Also refer to the Chapter 5 section on selecting an insurance broker, and the need to have adequate additional insurance if you have a home office.

Types of Property Coverage

Inflation Allowance. This coverage protects you against inflation by automatically increasing your amounts of insurance during the term of your policy, without increasing your premium. On renewal, the insurance company will automatically adjust your amounts of insurance to reflect the annual inflation rate. The premium you pay for your renewal will be based on those adjusted amounts of insurance.

Inflation allowance coverage will not fully protect you if you make an addition to your building or if you acquire additional personal property. This is why you should review your amounts of insurance every year to make sure that they are adequate.

Special Limits of Insurance. The contents of your dwelling are referred to as "Personal Property." Some types of personal property insurance such as jewellery, furs and money have "Special Limits of Insurance." This is the maximum the insurer will pay for those types of property. If these limits are not sufficient for your needs, you can purchase additional insurance.

Your policy automatically includes some additional coverages to provide you with more complete protection. Each of the individual coverages that are included are listed under the heading "Additional Coverages."

Insured Perils

A peril is something negative that can happen, such as a fire or theft. Some policies protect you against only those perils that are listed in your policy. Other policies protect you against "all risks" (risk is another word for peril). This means you are protected against most perils.

All insurance policies have exclusions. Even if you have selected "all risks" coverage, this does not mean that "everything" is covered. It is important that you read the exclusions carefully in order to understand the types of losses that are not covered by your policy. For example, floods, earthquakes, etc. may not be covered if you reside in a high risk location for these types of perils.

Loss or Damage Not Insured

This is the "fine print" — the section that tells you what is not covered. They are also known as "exclusions." Exclusions are necessary to make sure that the insurance company does not pay for the types of losses that are inevitable (e.g. wear and tear) uninsurable (e.g. war) or for which other specific policy forms are available to provide coverage (e.g. automobiles).

Basis of Claim Settlement

This section describes how the insurer will settle your loss. It's the real test of the value of your policy and the reason why you purchased insurance.

Replacement Cost. You should purchase replacement cost coverage for your property. This is particularly important for your personal property (e.g., the contents of your dwelling and personal effects). Otherwise the basis of settlement will be "actual cash value" which means that depreciation is applied to the damaged property when establishing the values. You therefore would get less money, possibly considerably less.

"New for old" coverage is available. All you have to do is ask for "replacement cost coverage" and then make sure that your amounts of insurance are sufficient to replace your property at today's prices.

Guaranteed Replacement Cost. This is one of the most important coverages available to a homeowner. You can qualify for this coverage by insuring your home to 100% of its full replacement value. If you do, then the insurance company will pay the full claim, even if it is more than the amount of insurance on the building. Make sure this is shown on your policy.

The Guaranteed Replacement Cost coverage applies only to your building — not your personal property.

There is usually an important exclusion. Many insurance companies won't pay more than the amount of insurance if the reason the claim exceeds that amount is the result of any law regulating the construction of buildings. Check this out.

By-Laws. Some municipalities have laws that govern how high you can build a house, what materials you have to use, or even where you can build it. These are known as by-laws. If the insurance company has to rebuild your house to different standards, this can increase the amount of your claim significantly.

Your policy doesn't cover this increased cost, because the insurance company has no way of knowing what laws may apply in your municipality. But you can find out. Then, make sure that your amounts of insurance are high enough to cover the increased cost, or increase them if necessary, and ask for a By-laws Coverage Endorsement. It'll cost a bit more now, but it can save you a lot later.

Deductible. There is a deductible and the amount is shown on the Coverage Summary Page of your policy. It means that you pay that amount for most claims, for example $250 or $500. The insurance company pays the rest.

As you can imagine, the cost to investigate and settle a claim can be considerable, often out of proportion when the size of the claim is relatively small. These expenses are reflected in the premiums you pay. By using deductibles to eliminate small claims, the insurance company can save on expenses and therefore offer insurance at lower premiums.

Conditions

This is a very important section of your policy. It sets out the mutual rights and obligations of the insurer and the insured. These govern how and when a policy may be cancelled, as well as your obligations after a loss has occurred.

Purchasing Adequate Amounts of Insurance

Purchasing adequate amounts of insurance that reflect the full replacement value of everything you own is without a doubt the single most important thing you can do to protect yourself. The penalty is, that insurance companies will not pay more than the amounts of insurance you have purchased. So it is up to you to make sure the coverage is adequate and realistic. Review it annually.

Establish how much it would cost to rebuild your home from scratch. This is the amount for which you should insure your house, in order to make sure that you are fully protected.

If you put an addition onto your house or carry out major renovations, you should recalculate the replacement value, as your current amount of insurance doesn't take this into consideration. Notify your insurance company representative. The Inflation Allowance feature of your policy does protect you against normal inflation, but is not sufficient to cover major changes.

You may also want to check with municipal authorities to see whether there are any by-laws that govern the construction of houses in your area, as you may need a higher amount of insurance so that the reconstruction of your home will be fully covered.

Contents Coverage

Your policy provides coverage for your contents. You should make sure that this amount is enough to replace all your possessions at today's prices.

If you have a claim, the insurance company will ask you to compile a complete list of everything that you have lost. Ideally, you should maintain an inventory of everything, furniture, appliances, clothes and other possessions. Estimating what it would cost you to replace them is a good way to check if your amount of insurance is enough.

At the very least you should keep the receipts for all major purchases in a safe place.

Another good idea is to take pictures of your contents, or make a video of everything by walking from room to room. In addition, most insurance companies will provide you with a checklist, so you can compile a list of your contents. This may seem like a chore right now, but it can really save time and aggravation if you do have a claim.

As you could lose your inventory or photographic evidence in a major loss, you should store your records away from your house. The best place is a safety deposit box. Whatever method you use, remember that you should update it periodically, ideally annually, to make sure that it remains accurate.

How Insurance Companies Calculate a Premium

The pricing of insurance is governed by a principle known as the "spread of risk". This means that the premiums paid by many people pay for the losses of the few.

When more dollars in claims are paid out than taken in as premiums, then the premium paid by everyone goes up.

The premium you pay therefore represents the amount of money needed by the insurance company to pay for all losses, plus their expenses in providing the service, plus a profit factor divided by the number of policyholders.

The potential for loss assessment is based upon a number of risk factors. Most of these risk factors are based upon where you live. Here are the three most important ones:

Fire. Although theft losses occur more often, fire still accounts for most of the dollars insurance companies pay out in claims. The potential severity of a fire is therefore based upon a municipality's ability to respond to, and put out, a fire.

If you live in an area with fire hydrants, your premium will be lower because the fire department will have access to a large water supply. Fires in hydrant-protected areas can be extinguished at an earlier stage than those in less well protected areas.

If you live in an area without hydrants or even a fire department close by, the premium will be even higher.

Theft. Statistics show that theft is narrowing the gap with fire for dollars paid out. Generally, there is a much higher number of break-ins in cities than in rural areas. Insurance companies track the loss experience caused by theft, by area, and this is reflected in the premium you pay.

Weather. If your geographic area has a history of severe weather storms, such as windstorms, snowstorms, hail, or flooding , insurance companies obviously look at these risks as well.

Ways to Reduce Your Premiums

Higher Deductible. Many people don't realize there are ways to reduce the premium payment significantly. What exactly do you want protection for? What you are really concerned with is the possibility of a catastrophe, or a total loss. If so, you can save money by increasing your deductible. By doing so, you save the insurance company the expense of investigating and settling small claims. That saving is passed back to you in the form of a reduced premium.

Discounts. You can reduce your premium if you qualify for any of the discounts insurance companies offer. Generally, discounts recognize a lower risk category. For example, buying a newer home, installing an approved burglar alarm system, non-smoking, seniors, etc. Always ask what discounts are available and see if you are eligible.

Claims Free Discount. This is a discount you don't have to ask for. Most insurance companies will reduce your premium automatically if you have been claim free for three or more years.

You should never reduce your amount of insurance so that you pay a lower premium. If you ever do have a claim, it could cost you a lot more than any amount you might save.

Personal Liability Protection

This is the part of the policy that protects you if you are sued. If someone injures themselves on your property, i.e., falls on your stairs, slips on your driveway, etc., and a court determines that you are responsible, your insurance company should defend you in court and pay all legal expenses and the amount up to the limit of the policy. The normal minimum limit is $1 million.

There are specific exclusions that apply to this section of this policy. They are listed under the heading "Loss or Damage Not Insured." Make sure you read this carefully.

How to Avoid Being Sued

Every year, many people are injured while visiting the premises of others. The last thing you want is to be sued. The process is stressful, time-consuming, negative, protracted and uncertain. Here are some suggestions to avoid problems.

Maintain Your Premises. Most injuries are caused by "slip and fall." They are usually the result of a lack of maintenance. In winter, you should clear ice and snow from all walkways on your premises and the stretch of sidewalk in front of your house. Exterior steps should be kept in good repair and a handrail provided.

Inside your house, carpets should be secured to stairs and floors and kept free of toys or objects that could trip a visitor.

Alcohol. If you serve alcohol to guests, you could be found responsible, to some extent, for their subsequent actions. Some courts have gone to extraordinary lengths to assign responsibility to a host. Good judgement is required. In particular, never allow an intoxicated guest to drive a car.

Other Hazards. You are potentially responsible for everything that happens on your premises. If you have a swimming pool, you are responsible for the safe use of the pool. If you have a dog, you are responsible for the actions of the dog. The list is almost endless.

The good news is that most injuries can be avoided by using nothing more complicated than common sense. All you have to do is be alert to the potential hazards on your own premises.

AVOIDING COMMON FIRE HAZARDS

Whether a fire is minor or major in nature, it is an incredibly traumatizing experience. Even if no one is injured, there can be the loss of treasured family photos, memorabilia and memories. However, with some advance planning, you can go a long way in avoiding a fire occuring by accident. Here are some tips.

Overfusing

Fuses are the safety valves in your electrical circuits. They prevent wires from overheating, which can cause a fire. If a fuse keeps blowing, then the circuit is overloaded. Never try to circumvent blown fuses by the use of pennies or foil. Call a qualified electrician.

Permanent Wiring

All additions or alterations to permanent wiring should be done by a qualified electrician and must be inspected and approved by your local city hall electrical inspector.

Careless Smoking

This is possibly the only cause of fire that is 100% preventable. If you have a no-smoking policy that should include any guests as well, so that your policy is 100% non-smoking. This will also have the added advantage of making your home more saleable when the time comes to re-sell. A lot of people are allergic to smoke and can detect the odour of smoke in a home, no matter how hard one tries to conceal or mask it.

Wood Stoves

All types of auxiliary heating appliances, such as wood stoves or portable heaters, require extra caution.

To avoid problems, you should note the following guidelines:

- Always look for a ULC or CSA label on the unit (Underwriters' Laboratories of Canada and Canadian Standards Association). This will tell you that the unit meets the minimum safety standards and has been approved for use in Canada.
- If you install the unit yourself, follow the installation instructions precisely. In particular, pay close attention to the clearances required between the unit and any combustible material. Even better, have it installed by a professional.
- Use the unit strictly in accordance with the instructions.
- You can call your local fire department or fire prevention bureau for information and advice on any fire safety related topic, including wood stoves.

Fireplaces and Chimneys

Always use a fireplace screen and dispose of the ashes in a closed metal container. Chimneys (for wood stoves as well as fireplaces) require cleaning by a chimney sweep service at least every two years to remove and prevent the build-up of creosote deposits. Creosote is flammable and can be ignited by the hot gases from

your fireplace. This can spread to any combustible material, such
as your roof.

Fire Extinguishers

Buy at least one portable fire extinguisher and keep it in an easily accessible place in the kitchen. If you have a workshop, keep an
extinguisher there, too. Ideally, you should have one extinguisher
for every level of your house. Try to select an extinguisher with
chemical contents to deal with A (paper and wood), B (flammable
liquids, e.g. oil) and C (electrical) types of fire coverage.

Smoke, Fire and Gas Alarms

These are absolute necessities. They are inexpensive and effective. Smoke alarms should be placed outside bedroom doors,
kitchen, workshop area and other key areas. When you are
researching which units to buy, you will see the recommended
home sites on the box. Some alarms are heat sensitive, rather than
detecting the by-products of a fire (i.e. smoke). If you are using natural gas in your home, make sure you get detectors for that risk as
well (e.g. carbon monoxide). Don't forget to replace the batteries
twice a year on a memorable date (e.g. when you change your
clocks for daylight saving time (forward or back)).

BURGLAR-PROOFING YOUR HOME

Given the time and the opportunity, a thief can break into almost
any home. It is possible to discourage residence entries by following simple and effective security measures.

Locks

Install one-inch single cylinder deadbolt locks on all exterior
doors. This type of lock has a keyhole on the outside and a "thumb-
turn" relocking control on the inside.

Locks which have the keyhole in the knob can be easily forced
or "jimmied" and should be replaced with deadbolts. If keys are
lost, locks should be changed promptly.

Doors

Exterior doors should be solid construction with the hinges
mounted inside. Door frames should be just as solid and equipped

with a proper strike plate, attached by 3 1/2 inch off-set screws. Install a door eye-viewer, as chain locks are poor security. Sliding glass doors (i.e. patio doors) can be lifted out of their tracks. Self-tapping screws can be installed in the upper tracks that prevent the door from being lifted out of its track. You should also install a secondary locking device consisting of a metal pin to be inserted where the inner and outer panels of the two doors intersect. A square-edged length piece of wood placed in the bottom tracks will resist lateral forcing.

Windows

Windows should be equipped with some type of locking device. While it may seem an obvious precaution, all windows, particularly basement windows, should be shut and locked when you are not at home. Most windows can be pinned for security purposes. Drill a 3/16" hole on a slight downward slant through the inside window frame and halfway into the outside frame. A nail or pin can then be placed in the hole to secure the window.

Basement Windows

Metal screens on basement windows can be an effective deterrent. In addition, basement windows can be re-enforced with a metal bar. Glazed windows that resist breakage are also effective and do not compromise your fire safety.

Garages

These are favourite entry targets for burglars. A garage door should be locked at all times, whether you are in the house or away.

Alarms

If you live in a high crime area, you may wish to consider installing a burglar alarm system. A good system can offer a high degree of protection and has the added benefit of reducing your insurance premium. Check with your insurance company. ULC and CSA approved systems are the most reliable. Depending upon the degree of protection you want, and the amount you are prepared to spend, some of these systems can even be monitored at a central facility. Alarms are covered in more detail later in this chapter.

Vacations

If you have ever experienced a home break-in or know someone who has, you probably know how frustrating, inconvenient and expensive it can be. You often feel a sense of personal violation that takes some time to lessen.

Here are some security tips to consider before you leave on a short or extended vacation:

• Keep a current inventory list of your belongings and other personal possessions. You can obtain free inventory booklets from many insurance companies.

• Keep receipts of your articles of value, such as cameras, jewellery, art, stereo equipment, furniture, etc.

• Take photographs or video of your rooms and belongings for additional support if you have to make a claim

• Mark your valuable assets for identification purposes, in case they are stolen. You can generally borrow a special marker from your local police department

• Keep a copy of your inventory list, receipts and photographs in your safety deposit box, in case your home burns down

• Check on the deductible amount you must pay if you make a claim. Generally it is $500. The higher the deductible, the lower the insurance premium.

• Get extra coverage for expensive items such as jewellery, as the limit may be $2,000 for any claim

• Don't leave a message on your answering machine that you are away

• Cancel newspaper delivery while you are away

• Arrange with Canada Post to forward your mail or hold it until your return

• Arrange for a neighbourhood friend or student to clear away advertising flyers

• If you are away in the winter, have a reliable neighbourhood friend or student clear the snow from your sidewalk or at least tramp it down

• Store small valuables in a safety deposit box. Store expensive items (e.g. TV or stereo) with a friend or relative if you are away for an extended time, or move them out of sight if they can be seen from a window

- Use clock timers to activate lights and radios when going out or away
- Keep garage doors locked and windows covered
- Secure air conditioners and other openings into your home
- Change your locks if keys are lost or stolen
- Make sure door hinge bolts face inside the house
- Install one-inch deadbolt locks on exterior doors. Door knob locks are unreliable and easily forced
- Insert a metal piece or fitted wood into sliding glass door tracks
- Reinforce basement windows with bars.

To obtain further information, contact the Canada Mortgage and Housing Corporation. Check the Blue Pages of your telephone directory for the closest office to you. Ask for their publication, "Protecting Your Home Against Burglary." In addition, you can obtain a free booklet entitled, "Guide to Safety and Security," by contacting the RCMP Crime Prevention branch, 1200 Vanier Parkway, Ottawa, Ontario K1H 0R2. Also check with your local police department for any consumer publications they have available on home security.

Taking a few precautions before you leave town could save you unnecessary anguish upon your return, and will give you peace of mind while you're away. Also, don't forget to check your insurance policy in terms of long absences. Many policies could be voided if the house is unoccupied over 30 days, unless arrangements are made to have someone check your home on a regular basis. The key concern from an insurance company's perspective is vandalism or arson. In the winter time, there is the added risk of pipes freezing and water damage. These concerns are more relevant of course to a house rather than a condo.

Additional Home Safety and Security Tips

- Keep emergency phone numbers handy.
- Do not leave notes that indicate that you are not home.
- Note licence numbers of suspicious vehicles in the neighbourhood and descriptions of suspicious persons. Telephone the police as soon as possible with the information.
- If you find a door or window has been forced or broken while you were absent, do not enter; the criminal may still be inside. Use a neighbour's phone to call police.

- Do not touch anything or clean up if a crime has been committed until the police have inspected for evidence.
- Join your local police "Operation Identification" program for marking your more valuable possessions.

SECURITY ALARM SYSTEMS

Electronic security alarm systems are recognized as an important contributor to the securing of life, property and possessions. A security system is an effective tool when used in conjunction with other sensible, overall crime prevention measures.

Independent studies clearly show that premises with alarm systems are less likely to be broken into. In one study it was discovered that premises without an alarm system experienced 38 times more break-in losses than those with a system.

Here is an overview of alarm features.

What an Alarm System Should Do For You

An alarm system is installed to deter and detect intruders. A basic security system will consist of both perimeter and space protection to secure your premises. The first stage secures vulnerable perimeter access points such as doors and windows; the second stage consists of space detection such as interior motion detectors which monitor movement inside the premise. The level of security you purchase is determined by the number of protective devices and the sophistication of the system you will have installed.

There are different types of sensors for any given application. Some of the most common are:

- Magnetic contacts — switches that detect the opening of a door or window.
- Motion detectors — various technologies designed to detect the movement of an intruder in a specific area.
- Glass break detectors — sensors designed to pick up the sound and/or vibrations associated with glass breakage.

There are two types of security alarm systems based on the manner of response:

Local System. This local system has a sounding device on the premises (either inside, outside or both), but does not transmit the alarm to a remote location. When the system is triggered, it sets off an audible warning device, usually a siren, to scare off the intruder and warn the occupants and/or neighbours. These systems are available through alarm companies, hardware stores, etc.

A local alarm system in conjunction with an effective Block Watch Program — may be an effective method to protect your property.

Monitored System. This system transmits the alarm signal to a remote location. A monitored system may either be silent (no warning sound on the premises) or set off local audible signals. The system is monitored by an alarm monitoring company, which notifies the police and the contact person. This would be the owner or someone chosen by the owner to give the police access to the premises in his or her absence. These systems are naturally more sophisticated and expensive.

Selecting an Alarm Company

When discussing your needs with a company, there are several questions you should consider asking to assess the capability of the company.

The following questions may be helpful to you as a guideline in your search for a security system. Continue to ask questions until you understand what you are purchasing and the level of security it will provide. Reputable companies should answer positively to all of these questions.

- Will the company provide a detailed written quotation, proposal and recommendations with accompanying rationale. What length of time will the quote be valid (30 days for example)? Ask for a sales representative from each company to visit your home to physically assess your needs. You would be wise to obtain a minimum of three written quotes before making a decision, and compare all features, benefits and limitations.
- How long has the company been in the security alarm business under its present name, and are they a registered or incorporated company?
- Has the company obtained all applicable provincial and municipal licenses?
- Does the company carry professional liability insurance and will they provide verification?
- Will the company provide names and phone numbers of people whom have used the service recently, as well as testimonial letters?

- Once an agreement has been reached, will the company provide you with a contract and if so, will it outline the applicable warranties, costs, and services included in the price? Are they clearly defined? Does the warranty include labour?
- Will the system be monitored 24 hours a day and who will be doing it? If servicing is required, what is the cost and how quickly can it be performed?
- How many employees are there in the installation and service department? Can it provide adequate after-sales service? What kind of training have the employees received?
- Is the proposed system user-friendly?
- Can the system be set up to allow for pets, if that is important to you?
- Will the company provide the necessary training on the system as part of the price?
- Does the company adhere to a false alarm reduction program?
- Does the company offer any protection for pre-paid monitoring in case the company goes under?
- Will you own the system or be leasing it?
- Is the company a member of the Canadian Alarm & Security Association (CANASA)?
- Is the company a member of the Better Business Bureau? (Note: Check to see if there are any complaints against the company.)
- Does the selected company and its equipment meet the standards of your home insurance carrier? Will you be able to get a discount on your home insurance premium?

CANASA is a non-profit Canadian association representing the electronic security industry. Members are to adhere to the ethics and business standards of the association. Contact CANASA at the following address and phone number to obtain a list of members in your area, as well as consumer information material: 610 Alden Road, Suite 201, Markham, Ontario, L3R 9Z1, telephone (905) 513-0622 or 1-800-538-9919. Or, see their web site at http://www.canasa.org.

Another important aspect in determining the capability of the alarm company is in their approach to you as a potential customer.

You should look for an alarm company that acts professionally by:

- Not criticizing a competitor; they will however, highlight their own strengths in providing a service
- Being properly dressed and discuss the potential sale of a system in a business-like and "non-pushy" manner
- Reviewing the premise as a whole and making recommendations regarding the overall protection of your assets. The review should include, but not be limited to:
  — reviewing the entrance ways
  — reviewing the lighting
  — reviewing the doors and windows
  — checking locks
- Providing you with written information needed to make an educated decision.

In deciding to purchase an alarm system, it is important for the consumer to understand their own responsibility. False alarms represent a problem that is of concern to both the industry and the users of alarm systems. A false alarm is an alarm that is generated by a system when no emergency exists. While the responsibility of the alarm company is to ensure that the system is designed and installed properly, the user has the responsibility of ensuring that the system is operated properly.

As an owner you will have to:

- Understand how to use the system and be sure that everyone who needs to use the system understands how to use it as well
- Inform the alarm company if changes are made to your premise (i.e. renovations) to be sure that the alarm system will continue to operate as designed
- Test the system on a regular basis as agreed to with your alarm company
- Have regular maintenance checks on your system.
- Make sure your pets don't trigger the alarm.

An electronic alarm system, when used properly, is a valuable tool in securing your family and assets.

Common Consumer Questions

What is a Monitoring Station? As discussed earlier, alarm systems can be installed to emit a local alarm using a bell or siren, and may be connected via a common carrier network (i.e. telephone lines) to a monitoring station which dispatches the appropriate response authority (police, fire, medical) when the system transmits a signal. In addition to the police dispatch, a monitored system may also emit a local internal and/or external siren when activated. A "local only" system does not in itself dispatch police.

In order to receive police response, you must either rely on a neighbour calling the police (in the case of a local system) or you must have the system monitored (24 hours) by a monitoring station. For this service, a nominal monthly fee is paid and can be arranged through your alarm installation company. In most, if not all municipalities, alarm systems may not be connected directly to the police as a result of municipal by-laws.

While there are a number of companies which install and monitor their own accounts, there are many more that install systems and contract with a third party monitoring facility. When you are deciding on which company to use, be sure to understand the service provided. The fact that the installing company subcontracts monitoring services is not a negative feature. It is simply a standard practice in this industry. Because of advances in telecommunications, it is also common practice to have your account monitored by an out-of-town station.

What's the Difference Between Wireless Systems and Hard Wired Systems? While there are many types of products available on the market, the actual system you purchase can be either hard wired or wireless. The difference is that for hard wired systems there is a wire connecting each device to the central control panel. A wireless system operates on batteries, has no wires and transmits its signal by radio frequency. The choice between a wireless or hard wired system is one you should make in consultation with your alarm company. Ask about the pros and cons.

What are False Dispatches? A false dispatch occurs when an alarm system is set off, the police are called and there is no intruder or emergency situation. User error is the number one cause of false dispatches. Studies show that 76% of all false dispatches are caused by users.

False dispatches result in a tremendous cost to society and threaten the safety of police officers and the community they protect. Quite apart from wasting time, when the police respond to alarms, they must be alert. The higher the false dispatch rate, the more apt they are to "let their guard down," resulting in a potentially life threatening situation. The other problem is that the police could be spending time on other priorities or real emergencies. Some municipalities levy a fine to homeowners who have a history of false dispatches or false external alarms annoying the neighbourhood.

How Do You Avoid False Dispatches? The following tips are simple steps that can dramatically affect the number of false dispatches you may experience during the life of your system.

At Home

Avoid objects that trigger your alarm:

- When leaving your premise, ensure that all doors and windows are locked
- If you have pets, be sure they are in an area not covered by motion sensors. Pets and motion sensors generally are not compatible and as a result, owners should consider other devices such as glass break sensors.
- Correct all drafts that may move plants and curtains, both of which may cause an alarm
- Insist that the keypad is easily accessible from the exit points, and that the arming delay is set for a reasonable period to reach it to turn it off.

With Your System

The following will help maintain your system and help make it more efficient and user-friendly:

- Replace the main battery every one to three years
- Insist that the system have a simple method for testing that will not result in a false dispatch, and then perform a test
- Insist that your system has a cancel signal that an authorized person can use to tell the monitoring company not to send police
- Insist on a service call as soon as possible after any unexplained alarms
- Request annual maintenance checks by the alarm company
- Before any household changes (remodelling, pets, etc.) contact the alarm company to be sure alterations do not affect the system

- Insist that the installing company adequately trains you on your system. Be sure you understand how to operate it before the technician leaves.
- Refer to your owner's manual or contact your alarm company.

With People

Enhance your alarm system's potential by:

- Ensuring that all key holders are trained in the proper use of the system
- Instructing domestic or repair persons on how to fully operate your system
- Never providing a key to someone who is not familiar with the system.

Other Safety Measures You Can Take

- Be sure you have proper locks and that all doors and windows can be secured
- Be sure you have well lit entrance ways and that all shrubbery is trimmed
- Be sure you have all ladders locked away so that they cannot be used by an intruder
- Be sure you review your property periodically to check for potential access points for burglars.

MAINTAINING YOUR HOME

As a matter of personal pride and investment protection, you want to maintain the quality and condition of your home. As a start, you need to know the condition that your home is in. This section covers some of the points you should know.

Home Inspection

You will probably have a professional home inspection done as a condition to buying your home. In other words, your offer includes the condition that the inspection must be satisfactory to you or the deal is off. Certainly a professional home inspection is to your advantage, in terms of having an objective person who is knowledgeable on what to look for, analyze the condition of your home, and in many cases give recommendations.

If you have an inspection done by a professional, you should have obtained a detailed report of the condition of all the key aspects of your home and property. That is your first starting point, in terms of the next step, which is prioritizing what areas need repair and maintenance.

Refer to the section in Chapter 5 on how to select a home inspector. There are also many books available in the library or bookstores on home inspection. In addition, you can obtain a booklet from Canada Mortgage and Housing Corporation (CMHC) called "Homeowner's and Homebuyer's Inspection Checklist for Maintenance and Repair." You can find your local CMHC office in the blue pages of your phone book, under Government of Canada.

Common Homeowner Maintenance Problems

Most people do not look on their home as a mechanical device, like a car, which should have regular maintenance check-ups. Yet a house does need to be maintained regularly in order to preserve the home value on re-sale. Simple, inexpensive maintenance can enhance the value of the house considerably.

Weather tends to be the main culprit when it comes to deterioration of the property. This involves the elements such as water, snow, ice or wind, in addition to sun.

A recent Canadian study has shown that the 10 conditions most neglected by homeowners are as follows:

Furnace Filters. Accumulated dust and debris on the furnace and filter require the motor and fan to work harder to pull air through the filter. The harder the furnace has to work, the shorter it's life expectancy. If you don't use a quality filter and replace it regularly, you might have to pay hundreds of dollars to replace the fan and motor, or several thousands of dollars to replace the entire furnace. In 80% of the homes, the furnace filters needed replacing.

Water Behind Walls. In three out of four houses, the caulking between the tub and surrounding wall (or shower pan and shower walls) is either deteriorated or missing altogether. If not corrected, this condition will allow water to migrate behind the walls, promoting dry rot and mildew. Eventually, the wall will fail. The removal of tile walls can be expensive.

Doors, Windows. Inoperable, improperly fitted or non-weatherstripped windows and doors are discovered in 60 percent of the houses that are 20 or more years old.

Windows and doors that don't open and close properly can be life threatening if they are needed as an escape route. If they are loose and improperly sealed, they allow warm or conditioned air to escape, creating climate control problems. This not only drives up your monthly heating and cooling bills, it forces your furnace and air conditioner to run overtime to attain the desired temperature, shortening their life span significantly.

Leaky Plumbing. Leaking water supply valves under sinks and faucets, found in one of every two houses, cause the floor (or wall if the faucet is also leaking) to deteriorate. If neglected, it could cost anywhere from $200 to $1,000 to repair the damage, depending on how long the leak has been ignored. Even when some owners are aware of this problem, the typical solution is duct tape and a bucket.

Overgrowth. Ivy growing up the side of your house is beautiful but terribly damaging. So are trees that hang over your roof. Yet, both conditions are found in two out of every five houses examined.

Retained water in vegetation contributes to accelerated deterioration and rot. The root of an ivy's system is so strong that it can move mortar and get behind siding and pop it out, and leaves deposited on a roof are a breeding ground for degeneration. Depending on the extent of growth, you may have to re-roof or re-side your house at a cost of several thousand dollars. At best, your roof's life expectancy will be reduced by 20 percent.

Poor Grading. About a third of all houses have grading problems. Even if the lot was graded properly when the house was built — it should slope away from the structure — the grade can shift over time.

The cause is usually heavy rain and erosion from overwatering shrubs placed too close to the house. But sometimes the ground simply settles. If the ground within 10 feet of the house slopes toward the house, water will pond adjacent to the building. This can be eliminated by a few wheelbarrows of dirt and some spade work. If water is allowed to remain over a period of time, it will migrate under the structure and weaken the foundation.

Clogged Gutters. A third of all houses also have gutters and downspouts clogged by roof debris of dead vegetation. This will allow water to back up on the roof, causing not only the roof to deteriorate more quickly but also erosion that leads to a negative grade at the foundation.

Broken Exhaust Fans. The exhaust fan in bathrooms without windows is either disconnected or inoperable in one out of every three houses inspected. This will allow condensation to accumulate, causing moisture damage. Eventually, the walls and flooring can rot out completely.

Worn-out Caulking. Fifteen percent of the houses examined have either worn out caulking or none at all. Deteriorated or missing caulking on exterior walls where dissimilar materials meet can allow water to intrude into wall cavities, where it will cause the framing to rot.

Caulking wears out. It shrinks, cracks, blisters and hardens, so it needs to be evaluated annually. If it's not checked and, when necessary, replaced, you may end up replacing sill plates, interior studs and framing at a cost of several thousand dollars.

Blocked Attic Vents. Many homeowners add new or additional insulation in the attic, and in many cases block the necessary attic ventilation passages. Blocked vents can create moisture build-up, mildew and rot in the attic.

TIPS FOR A HASSLE-FREE RENOVATION

Are you considering doing some renovation to your home? If so, you are one of the millions of Canadians who want to improve the value of their home this popular way.

Renovating a home can be an exciting and rewarding process, the outcome like a dream come true. Alternatively, the renovation process could be like a nightmare or at least a very bad migraine come true. Whether you are making modest changes in one or two rooms, or you are working on the whole home, it is critical to your emotional, financial and mental health that you plan your project carefully.

The following renovation chart is a national average profile. Different provinces could have different sequences. According to the Appraisal Institute of Canada, here are the top 10 home renovation projects in order of their potential enhancement of property value. The average potential payback is noted on the right hand column. Although getting your money back is one consideration, the other is the marketability of your home. The more attractive the renovation, the more likely you are going to get more demand, a quicker sale and more money.

Renovation	Average Potential Payback in %
1. kitchen	68%
2. bathroom	66%
3. interior painting and decor	66%
4. exterior painting and decor	62%
5. finished basement	50%
6. new furnace/heating system	50%
7. addition of main floor family room	49%
8. landscaping	45%
9. addition of a separate living unit to accommodate family members or generate rental revenue income	42%
10. addition of energy-efficient features	39%

Here are some step-by-step stages to go through to maximize the most out of the renovation experience.

Do Your Homework

Advance research is the key to getting what you really want. Study magazines and books to get an idea of the look you want. Watch renovation shows on TV. Borrow books and videos on home improvement from your local library. Visit home shows and display rooms to find out what products are available. Take seminars on renovation offered through your local school board, college or university continuing education department. Also, check with your local homebuilders or renovators association for any upcoming seminars on renovating. Talk to friends, family members and colleagues who have renovated recently. Consider your lifestyle and the needs of your family, both in the short and long term.

Determine How Much You Can Afford

Once you have a firm idea of the kind of renovation you would like to undertake, it is time to decide how you are going to pay for it. If you are thinking about using outside funds, discuss your borrowing needs and options with your lender. You will probably find that there are many financing possibilities to consider, from personal loans and lines of credit to home equity loans and homeowner's mortgages.

Look For a Professional Renovator

Call your local homebuilder or renovations association. Refer to the list of provincial home builders associations in the "Sources of Information" section in the Appendix. Ask family and friends for recommendations. Drive around your neighbourhood to see who is renovating, then talk to the homeowners about their project. Most people are pleased to share their renovation experiences.

Get Estimates

Obtain a minimum of three different bids. Make sure that you provide all the renovators with the same detailed information. It is important that they bid on the same job, or you will not be able to compare estimates. This information could be a description of the job including sketches, drawings, photographs and measurements.

For estimates involving major structural changes, such as additions or moving interior walls, renovators may also need a set of plans. An architect could be a great help here. The set of plans includes site and floor plans, elevations and detail drawings. The plan forms the basis for the estimating process and will also be used to obtain building permits. Be honest and open about your budget. The renovator will be able to make suggestions that will help you stay within your budget or provide alternative ideas to stretch you dollars.

Check References

Don't omit this step because you are too busy. Call your local homebuilders or renovations association (refer to the Appendix), the renovator's previous clients they give as references, and the building supply stores the renovator uses, to ensure that you are making the right choice. Ask the renovator which bank they use. Your bank can then check with their bank to see if they have a good banking business history. Check also with the Better Business Bureau to see if they have received any complaints.

Work Out a Contract

Don't automatically take the lowest bid, unless you are certain that the renovator has properly understood what you want. Sometimes low bids turn out to be the most expensive in the end.

If you accept the renovator's offer, it's time to write up the contract. Even the simplest of jobs should be outlined in writing because the contract is the basis of understanding between you and your renovator. Before signing a contract, read it carefully. Are you satisfied with the description of the work to be done? Does the payment schedule include holdbacks? Are the responsibilities of the renovator clearly spelled out? Remember that if something is not in the contract, then it's your responsibility. Have a lawyer examine the contract before you sign it. In addition, many provincial home builders' associations have sample renovation contracts you could use. Refer to "Sources of Further Information" in the Appendix.

Plan How You Will Live During the Renovation

Careful planning can greatly minimize the inconvenience of living in the midst of renovation. Talk to your renovator about the schedule of work to be done and how your daily routine might be affected. For instance, will the water be turned off for any length of time? Do you need to set up a temporary kitchen elsewhere in the home? Can major work be done in stages so you always have some liveable space? Discuss your expectations of the work crew and determine the work environment. The crew needs access to washroom facilities, telephones, water and electricity. Decide which areas of your home are off limits.

It is a good idea to let your neighbours know that you are going to be renovating. Show them your plans and explain how long the work will be going on.

Establish a Good Working Relationship With Your Renovator

Renovators and homeowners agree that a good working relationship is a vital ingredient in successful renovation projects. Mutual trust is essential. Keep lines of communication open at all times. Expect a brief report on the progress of your job at regular intervals, perhaps every evening. Be available to make decisions when they are needed so work is not held up, perhaps costing you more money. Don't hesitate to bring your concerns to the attention of the renovator.

Try To Stick With Your First Choices

Once work is underway, changes should be kept to a minimum. The details of your project, described in the contract, down to finishing touches, form the basis of both the price and the schedule of your job. Changes could affect both significantly. Most renovators want you to be satisfied with the final result, and will likely attempt to accommodate any alteration in plans, as long as you accept a possible delay in completion and/or a change in price.

Refer to Chapter 4 and the section "Buying a Lot and Building a House" and "Houses for Renovation" for additional tips and contract terms you should know when dealing with contractors or renovators.

* * *

As you have now finished all the chapters of this book, let's do a final wrap-up in the conclusion.

CONCLUSION

CONGRATULATIONS!

You have now completed all 14 chapters. Hopefully you have found them to contain the candid information, insights, streetsmart tips, helpful advice and pitfalls to avoid that you were seeking.

We have covered everything from the initial steps, self-assessment, getting information and the pros and cons of home options to getting advice, financing strategies and how to determine your home value. In addition, we discussed various legal, tax and negotiating issues as well as house hunting. Finally, we dealt with the moving experience and then how to take care of your home. Along with the sources of information section and glossary, you have all the necessary tools to be a well informed and prudent home buyer.

As in any new experience, there is the fear of the unknown. You don't want to make a mistake when there is so much at stake.

However, with the new knowledge that you have acquired, the unknown is now the known, and you can proceed with the next stage of your search with the self-confidence that you have done your "homework" thoroughly and you are extremely well-prepared.

I wish you every success in your home purchase and many years of enjoyable and warm memories.

Appendix

SOURCES OF FURTHER INFORMATION

Canada Mortgage and Housing Corporation
Federal Government Income Tax and GST Departments
Provincial Home Builders' Associations
Provincial New Home Warranty Programs
Provincial Government Publication Departments
Provincial Government Consumer Protection Departments

CANADA MORTGAGE AND HOUSING CORPORATION

This is a federal government Crown corporation. Contact the CMHC office in your region for a free catalogue of publications relating to condominiums, new construction, renovations, CMHC foreclosure and other CMHC properties for sale, real estate financing, high-ratio mortgage insurance, and real estate market data and analysis. There are provincial offices as well as local branch offices of CMHC in approximately 40 Canadian communities. Check in the Blue Pages of your telephone directory under "Government of Canada." The contact address for CMHC market analysis publications is Market Analysis Centre, Canada Mortgage and Housing, 682 Montreal Road, Ottawa, Ontario, K1A 0P7. Telephone (613) 748-2469. Fax (613) 745-1741.

FEDERAL GOVERNMENT INCOME TAX AND GST DEPARTMENTS

Revenue Canada, Customs and Excise

This government department is responsible for administering the legislation dealing with GST, among other duties. Contact them if you have any questions relating to applying for a GST registration number, how to comply with GST requirements, how to collect and remit GST, and GST exemptions and rebates. You can reach the closest GST office by looking in the Blue Pages of your phone book under "Government of Canada" and then under "Revenue Canada, Customs and Excise."

Revenue Canada, Income Tax

You are already well aware of what this government department does. You can obtain information relating to the tax aspects affecting various real estate matters, including depreciation schedules, income tax guides, circulars and bulletins, by contacting your local office. Look in the Blue Pages of your phone book under "Government of Canada" and then under "Revenue Canada, Taxation." Some of the frequently requested information material is as follows. Additions and amendments are, of course, an ongoing process.

PROVINCIAL HOME BUILDERS' ASSOCIATIONS

For publications or further information on renovating, selecting a contractor, and other material, contact your provincial or local home builders' association. Check in the Yellow Pages under "Associations." The following are the provincial associations:

- Canadian Home Builders' Association of British Columbia
- Alberta Home Builders' Association
- Saskatchewan Home Builders' Association
- Manitoba Home Builders' Association
- Ontario Home Builders' Association
- Association provinciale des constructeurs d'habitations de Quebec Inc.
- Nova Scotia Home Builders' Association
- New Brunswick Home Builders' Association
- Construction Association of Prince Edward Island
- Newfoundland & Labrador Home Builders' Association Ltd.

PROVINCIAL NEW HOME WARRANTY PROGRAMS

For new home warranty program information in your province or region relating to approved builders, warranty protection, and other matters, contact the office below:

- New Home Warranty Program of British Columbia & The Yukon
  760-1441 Creekside Drive, Vancouver, B.C., V6B 3R9
- New Home Warranty Program of Alberta
  201-208-57th Avenue S.W., Calgary, Alberta, T2H 2K8
- New Home Warranty Program of Saskatchewan Inc.
  3012 Louise Street, Saskatoon, Saskatchewan, S7J 3L8
- New Home Warranty Program of Manitoba Inc.
  220-1120 Grant Avenue, Winnipeg, Manitoba, R3M 2A6
- Ontario New Home Warranty Program
  5160 Yonge Street, Sixth Floor, North York, Ontario, M2N 6L9
- La garantie des maisons neuves de l'APCHQ
  5930 boul. Louis-H. Lafontaine Ville d'Anjou, Quebec, H1M 1S7
- Atlantic New Home Warranty Corporation
  P.O. Box 411, Halifax, Nova Scotia, B3J 2P8

PROVINCIAL GOVERNMENT PUBLICATION DEPARTMENTS

To obtain copies of statutes and regulations relating to real estate, condominiums, and landlord/tenant relations, contact the provincial government office below:

- Queen's Printer
  Province of British Columbia
  Parliament Buildings, Victoria, B.C., V8V 1X4
  (205) 952-4460
- Alberta Publication Services
  Public Affairs Bureau, Province of Alberta
  11510 Kingsway Avenue, Edmonton, Alberta, T5G 2Y5
  (403) 427-4387
- Acts & Publications
  Saskatchewan Property Management Corp.
  1st Floor East, 3475 Albert Street, Regina, Sask., S4S 6X6
  (306) 787-6894
- Office of the Queen's Printer
  Province of Manitoba, Statutory Publications
  200 Vaughan Street, Winnipeg, Manitoba, R3C 1T5
  (204) 945-3103
- Ontario Government Bookstore
  Province of Ontario
  Main Floor, 880 Bay Street, Toronto, Ontario, M7A 1N8
  (416) 326-5324

- Ministere des communications
Direction generale des publications gouvernementales
11e etage, 1279 boul. Charest ouest, Quebec, Quebec, G1N 4K7
(418) 643-9810
- Queen's Printer
Province of New Brunswick
P.O. Box 6000, Fredericton, New Brunswick, E3B 5H1
(506) 453-2520
- Government Bookstore
Province of Nova Scotia
P.O. Box 637, Halifax, Nova Scotia, V3J 2T3
(902) 424-7580
- Queen's Printer
Province of Prince Edward Island
P.O. Box 2000, Charlottetown, P.E.I., C1A 7N8
(902) 368-5190
- Queen's Printer
Province of Newfoundland
P.O. Box 4750, St. John's, Newfoundland, A1C 5T7
(709) 729-3649

PROVINCIAL GOVERNMENT CONSUMER PROTECTION DEPARTMENTS

Many provinces have free brochures relating to consumers' rights and cautions when buying homes or condominiums, or when renovating. Contact your provincial department for further information.

- Ministry of Labour & Consumer Services
Province of British Columbia, Parliament Buildings
1019 Wharf Street, Victoria, B.C., V8N 1X4 (604) 387-3194
- Consumer & Corporate Affairs
Province of Alberta
2nd Floor, 10025 Jasper Avenue, P.O. Box 161 Edmonton,
Alberta, T5J 2N9 (403) 427-4095
- Consumer & Commercial Affairs
Province of Saskatchewan
1871 Smith Street, Regina, Saskatchewan, S4P 3V7
(306) 787-5550

- Consumers' Bureau
  Province of Manitoba
  114 Garry Street, Winnipeg, Manitoba, R3C 1G1 (204) 956-2040
- Consumer Advisory Services Branch
  Ministry of Consumer & Commercial Relations, Province of Ontario
  8th Floor, 555 Yonge Street, Toronto, Ontario, M4A 2H6
  (416) 963-0321
- Office de la protection du consommateur
  400 boul. Jean-Lesage, bur. 450, Quebec, Quebec, G1K 8W4
  (418) 643-1484
- Consumer Affairs Branch, Province of New Brunswick
  Consumer Affairs Division, Department of Justice
  P.O. Box 6000, Fredericton, New Brunswick, E3B 5H1
  (506) 453-2659
- Consumer Services Division
  Department of Consumer Affairs, Province of Nova Scotia
  P.O. Box 998, 5151 Terminal Road, Halifax, N.S., B3J 2X3
  (902) 424-4690
- Consumer Services Division
  Province of Prince Edward Island
  P.O. Box 2000, Charlottetown, P.E.I., C1A 7N8 (902) 368-4580
- Consumer Affairs Division, Province of Newfoundland
  Department of Consumer Affairs & Communications
  P.O. Box 4750, Elizabeth Towers
  St. John's, Newfoundland, A1C 5T7 (709) 576-2591

GLOSSARY

To know how the real estate market operates and to function within that market successfully, you have to use and understand the language of real estate. People who buy and sell property, who borrow or make loans, all communicate with a common set of terms and concepts. Review this glossary and become familiar with the terms. In many cases, these terms are discussed in more depth in various chapters of this book.

Acceleration clause. Usually written into a mortgage allowing the lender to accelerate or call the entire principal balance of the mortgage, plus accrued interest, when the payments become delinquent. Only permitted in certain provinces.

Adjustment date. The date on which adjustments for such items as taxes, utilities, oil, etc. are made.

Agreement for sale. This agreement between the seller and the purchaser is an alternative to a mortgage for financing the purchase of real property. Under this type of arrangement the seller of the property finances the purchase rather than a lending institution. Once the agreement is made the purchaser can possess the property but legal title to the property remains with the seller until the purchaser completes making all payments to the seller.

Agreement of purchase and sale. A written agreement between the owner and a purchaser for the purchase of real estate on a pre-determined price and terms.

Amenities. Generally, those parts of the condominium or apartment building that are intended to beautify the premises and that are for the enjoyment of occupants rather than for utility; e.g., swimming pool, exercise room and tennis courts.

Amortization period. The actual number of years it will take to repay a mortgage loan in full. This can be well in excess of the loan's term. For example, mortgages often have five-year terms but 25-year amortization periods.

Amortization table. A table that shows the amount of monthly payment required to repay a loan, given a specific rate of interest, a loan amount, and the number of years in the term.

Anniversary. One year from the interest adjustment date (IAD), which is the date less than one month before the first payment. The anniversary date is the same date each year during the term.

Appraised value. An estimate of the value of the property offered as security for a mortgage loan. This appraisal is done for mortgage lending purposes and may not reflect the market value of the property.

Appreciation. Increased market value of real property.

Arrears. The amount of monthly payments due under a mortgage plus interest on these payments. A person said to be "in arrears" is behind with his or her payments.

Assessment fee. Also referred to as *maintenance fee*. A monthly fee that condominium owners must pay, usually including management fess, costs of common property upkeep, heating costs, garbage removal costs, the owner's contribution to the contingency reserve fund, and so on. In the case of timeshares, the fee is normally levied annually.

Assumed mortgage. Where the liability of the existing mortgage is assumed by the new purchaser of the property and a new mortgage is not necessary.

Balance sheet. A financial statement that indicates the financial status of a condominium corporation or apartment building, or other revenue property, at a specific point in time by listing its assets and liabilities.

Basis point. This is equal to 1/100 of 1%.

Blended payments. Equal payments consisting of both a principal and an interest component, paid each month during the term of the mortgage. The principal portion increases each month, while the interest portion decreases, but the total monthly payment does not change.

Broker. A person who legally trades in real estate for another, for compensation.

Budget. An annual estimate of a condominium corporation or apartment building's expenses and revenues needed to balance those expenses. There are *operating* budgets and *capital* budgets. (See also *capital budget*.)

Builder's lien. A lien which can be registered against the title of property as security for the payment of a contractor's bill for work done on that particular property.

Buy-down mortgage. A mortgage in which the borrower buys a home from a developer and is allowed to pay below-market interest for a limited number of years. This type of mortgage may be necessary in order to qualify for financing with a specific lender. After the stated period expires, the interest rate rises to a predetermined level or converts to an adjustable rate. The developer may compensate the lender for its lost revenues from the buy-down agreement and offsets that expense by increasing the price of the home.

Canadian Real Estate Association (CREA). An association of members of the real estate industry, principally real estate agents and brokers.

Cap. A limitation on the interest or payment the lender may charge in a variable rate mortgage. A rate cap limits the interest rate increase for the duration of the term. The less desirable "payment cap" limits the amount of monthly payment the borrower will be required to make, regardless of the effective interest rate. When the maximum payment is not adequate to cover a month's interest, the loan balance will increase rather than decrease, a condition known as negative amortization, as the unpaid monthly interest is added to the principal outstanding and interest is charged on it.

Capital budget. An estimate of costs to cover replacements and improvements, and the corresponding revenues needed to balance them, usually for a 12-month period. Different from an *operating budget.*

Capital gain. That profit on the sale of an asset that is subject to taxation.

Certificate of estoppel. (also known as "estoppel certificate") A written statement of a condominium unit's current financial and legal status. This is the phraseology used in Ontario. In other provinces, different phraseology may be used.

Chattels. Moveable possessions, such as furniture, personal possessions, etc. A furnace, before it is installed, is a moveable possession. Once installed, it is not.

Closed mortgage. A mortgage agreement which does not provide for prepayment prior to maturity. A lender may permit prepayment under certain circumstances but will levy a prepayment charge for doing so.

Closing costs. The expenses over and above the purchase price of buying and selling real estate.

Closing date. The date on which the sale of the property becomes final and the new owner takes possession; at that time all costs and charges to close the deal are payable.

CMHC. Canada Mortgage and Housing Corporation is a federal government Crown corporation which administers the National Housing Act (NHA), and provides for the insuring of mortgages made by an approved lender under a variety of programs. CMHC normally insures "high-ratio" loans; that is, loans where the ratio of debt (financing) to equity (downpayment) is over 75%.

Collateral mortgage. A loan backed by a promissory note and the security of a mortgage on a property. The money borrowed may be used for the purchase of the property itself or for another purpose, such as home renovations or a vacation.

Commitment letter. A contract issued to the borrower by a lender, reciting the basic terms of an offer to mortgage. In order to be binding on all parties, the borrower must sign the commitment to the lender.

Common area. The area in a condominium project that is shared by all of the condominium owners, such as elevators, hallways and parking lots.

Condition. This is a requirement that is fundamental to the very existance of the offer. A breach of condition or inability to meet the condition, allows the buyer to get out of the contract. In this case, the full amount of the deposit would be paid back. An inability to meet the condition set by a vendor permits the vendor to get out of the contract. The term condition is sometimes referred to as a "subject clause." In other words, subject to the condition being met.

Condominium. A form of ownership in which the owner has title to a housing unit and also owns a share in the common elements (such as elevators and hallways, and perhaps the land).

Condominium corporation. The condominium association of unit owners incorporated under some Condominium Acts automatically at the time of registration of the project. Under each of the provincial statutes, it will differ from an ordinary corporation in many respects. The condominium corporation, unlike a private business corporation, usually does not enjoy limited liability, and any judgement against the corporation for the payment of money is usually a judgement against each owner. The objects of the corporation are to manage the property and any assets of the corporation, and its duties include effecting compliance by the owners with the requirements of the Act, the declaration, the by-laws, and the rules.

Condominium council. The governing body of the condominium corporation, elected at the annual general meeting of the corporation and comprised of condo owners.

Consideration. Something of value for compensation.

Conventional mortgage. A mortgage loan which does not exceed 75% of the appraised value or purchase price of the property, whichever is the lesser of the two. Mortgages that exceed this limit must be insured by CMHC or GE.

Conversion. The changing of a structure from some other use, such as a rental apartment to a condominium apartment.

Conveyancing. The transfer of property, or title to property, from one party to another.

Counter-offer. A typical real estate transaction may involve a series of offers and counter-offers between a buyer and seller until either there is a meeting of the minds or the negotiations are broken off. A counter-offer rejects or modifies the latest offer made by the other bargaining party. There usually is a time limit attached to an offer or a counter-offer after which is automatically withdrawn and becomes null and void.

Debt service. Cost of paying interest for use of mortgage money.

Deed. This document conveys the title of the property to the purchaser. Different terminology may be used in different provincial jurisdictions.

Default. Failure to repay as agreed. To fail to pay an outstanding debt.

Deficiency notice. This means that the municipality has required work to be done on your home to meet municipal regulations, but that the work has not been done to the satisfaction of the municipality. The notice formally advises you of the problem and generally a deadline is given to rectify it.

Deposit. Money or other consideration of value given as pledge for fulfilment of a contract or agreement.

Depreciation. Reduction in market value of a building.

Discharge. A document executed by the mortgagee (lender) and given to the mortgagor (borrower) when the loan is repaid in full. This is a legal document confirming full repayment of the mortgage.

Down payment. The amount of money (in the form of cash) put forward by the purchaser. Usually, it represents the difference between the purchase price and the amount of the mortgage loan.

Easement. A right which allows one person to use the property of another.

Encroachment. Undue or unlawful trespass on another's property, usually caused by a building, or part of a building, or obstruction.

Encumbrance. A legal claim registered against a property. The claim does not necessarily prevent the property from being transferred but may affect the property's value. Examples of encumbrances are liens, judgements, rights of way, easements, leases and restrictive covenants. Mortgages are also considered to be encumbrances.

Equity. A borrower's equity in a property, if the value of the property, when sold, is more than the value of all mortgage debts or encumbrances. The amount of the equity is the difference between the value of the property and the value of the debts. If the value of the debts is more than the value of the property, then it is said that the owner has no equity in the property.

Escrow. The holding of a deed or contract by a third party until fulfilment of certain stipulated conditions between the contracting parties. Sometimes referred to as being held "in trust."

Estoppel certificate. (also known as "certificate of estoppel") A written statement of a condominium unit's current financial and legal status. This is the phraseology used in Ontario. In other provinces, different phraseology may be used.

Fair market value. The value established on real property that is determined by what a buyer is willing to pay and what a seller is willing to sell for.

Fee simple. See "freehold."

Financial statements. Documents that show the financial status of the condominium corporation at a given point in time. Generally includes income and expense statement and balance sheet.

First mortgage. The mortgage document which has first claim on the asset in the event of default.

Fixed-rate mortgage. A mortgage loan for which the rate of interest is fixed for a specific period of time (the term). If the borrower pays off the mortgage in part or full earlier than the term, there is usually a penalty. This type of mortgage is usually offered at a lower rate than an open mortgage.

Fixture. Permanent improvements to property that remain with it.

Floating-rate mortgage. Another term for *variable-rate mortgage.*

Foreclosure. Court action taken by the lender to take possession of your home. This action can start when you have failed to make a single payment. However, most lenders will grant a period of time for you to catch up on the payments owing before taking action, providing you have not purposely avoided your commitment.

Once foreclosure is completed, it is the lender's right to resell the home. From the proceeds of the sale, the lender can recover the outstanding balance of the mortgage and other costs associated with the foreclosure and resale. Any equity that you may have had in the property could be lost.

Freehold. This type of ownership of land entitles the owner to use the land for an indefinite period of time and to deal with the land in any way desired, subject to legislation, contractual obligations, and any changes that affect the title of the property. Another term for freehold is "fee simple".

Frontage. Property line facing street.

GE Capital Mortgage Insurance (GE). The only private mortgage insurance carrier in Canada. It provides, along with other services and products, insurance for high-ratio mortgages, e.g. mortgages over 75% of home purchase price.

Gross debt service ratio (GDS). The percentage of gross annual income required to cover payments associated with housing (mortgage principal and interest, depending on the lender, may also include taxes, heating, and 50% of condominium maintenance fees). Most lenders prefer that the GDS be no more than 30% but there are many exceptions.

High-ratio mortgage. This is a mortgage which finances between 75% to 95% of the purchase price or appraised value of the home, whichever is lower. Must be insured by CMHC or GE. In the event that there is not sufficient value in the property to pay off the mortgage, the lender is insured and therefore paid for the shortfall.

Interest averaging. The method of determining the overall average interest rate being paid where more than one mortgage is involved.

Interim financing. The temporary financing by a lender during the construction of real property for resale, or while other funds are due in.

Joint tenancy. An estate which arises by the purchase of land by two or more persons. This type of tenancy includes the right of survivorship which means that when one owner dies, his or her share passes automatically to the other joint tenant. A joint tenant cannot pass on his or her interest by means of a will.

Lease. An agreement which gives rise to the relationship of landlord and tenant.

Leasehold. Property held by lease.

Leasehold mortgage. A mortgage loan for the purchase of a home or improvements to a home where the building is on land which is leased.

Legal description. Identification of a property that is recognized by law, that identifies that property from all others.

Lessee. The tenant. One who pays rent.

Lessor. The person granting use of property to another.

Liabilities. What you owe.

Liquidity. A condition of cash availability. In a savings account or money market fund, for example, investors can retrieve their funds with little or no advance notice. In comparison, investing in a home equity is relatively illiquid, as funds can be taken out only by refinancing or committing to an additional mortgage.

Lis pendens. A notice which can be registered on the title of a piece of property and which shows that the property is subject to a forthcoming lawsuit. The property cannot be transferred to another owner while the lis pendens is on title.

Listings, exclusive agency. A signed agreement by a seller in which he or she agrees to cooperate with one broker. All other brokers must go through the listing broker.

Listings, multiple. (Also see *Multiple listing system.*) A system of agency/sub-agency relationships. If broker "A" lists the property for sale, "A" is the vendor's agent. If broker "B" sees the MLS listing and offers it for sale, "B" is the vendor's sub-agent.

Listings, open. A listing permitting any real estate broker to try and sell the property.

Loan-to-value ratio. The ratio of the loan to the appraised value or purchase price of the property, whichever is less, expressed as a percentage.

Market value. The highest price a buyer, willing, but not compelled to buy, would pay, and lowest price a seller, willing, but not compelled to sell, would accept.

Maturity date. The date on which the term of the mortgage expires; the mortgage must be either paid out in full or renegotiated for another term. When applying for another term, you are generally required to pay a renewal fee.

MLS. See *Multiple Listing System.*

Mortgage. The security you give a company or person for the money loaned to you, usually to buy a home. It is a registered charge on your property and should be removed when the loan has been completly repaid.

Mortgagee. An individual or institutional lender that holds a mortgage on property as security for a loan.

Mortgagor. A person who offers a mortgage on property in exchange for cash consideration.

Multiple listing system (MLS). A system licensed to member real estate boards by CREA. Used to compile and disseminate information by publication and computer concerning a given property to a large number of agents and brokers.

National Housing Act (NHA) loan. A mortgage loan which is backed by (insured by) CMHC to certain maximums.

Negative amortization. A condition that may arise in a variable rate mortgage with a payment cap. When the maximum monthly payment is lower than the amount of interest due, the loan's balance will rise as payments are made.

Nominal interest rate. The quoted interest rate for a mortgage loan.

Offer to purchase. A formal, legal agreement which offers a certain price for a specified real property. The offer may be firm (no conditions attached) or conditional (certain conditions must be fulfilled). Once the offer is accepted it becomes an "agreement of purchase and sale."

Open mortgage. A mortgage agreement which allows the borrower to repay the debt more quickly than specified and usually without prepayment charges.

Operating budget. An estimate of costs to operate a building or condominium complex and corresponding revenues needs to balance them, usually for a 12-month period. Different from a *capital budget.*

Order of sale. Term used in the mortgage document to refer to the mort-gagee's (lender's) right to sell the home, in many cases without court approval, in order to recover the full principal and interest outstanding. Generally used in the case of default of payment by the owner. If there is any money left after the property is sold, and after the lender has recovered its principal, interest and costs, the borrower would receive the balance.

Payment cap. A provision in some adjustable-rate mortgages stating that the borrower will never be required to pay more per month than a stated maximum. However, the interest rate is not subject to cap; thus, interest costs could exceed the maximum monthly payment.

PI. Principal and interest due on a mortgage.

PIT. Principal, interest and taxes.

PITH. Principal, interest, taxes and heating.

Portable mortgage. This option allows the transfer of the loan balance, interest rate and remaining term of the old mortgage to the new home. If additional money is lent, the result will be a new mortgage with a blended interest rate.

Possession date. The date that you actually get possession of the real estate purchase.

Postponement clause. The agreement of the second or subsequent lender to allow the borrower the right to renew or replace a first mortgage which becomes due before the second or subsequent mortgage.

Prepayment clause. An agreement which allows the mortgagor to make payments over and above the regular agreed-upon payments; for example, reducing the principal amount of the mortgage by up to 20% annually.

Prepayment penalty. A fee charged by the lender when the borrower prepays all or a portion of a mortgage loan more quickly than provided for in the mortgage agreement.

Principal. The amount of money actually borrowed for a new mort-gage or now owing on an existing one.

Purchase and sale agreement. See *Agreement of purchase and sale.*

Quit claim. A full release of a right to property from one person to another.

Real property. Sometimes called realty. This includes land and items attached to land such as buildings, fences, etc.

Realtor. Certification mark being the property of the Canadian Real Estate Association. Designates broker member of association.

Realty. Real property.

Redeem. To buy back or pay off what is owing on a debt. The redemp-tion period is the time you are given to redeem.

Refinance. To pay off (discharge) a mortgage and any other registered encumbrances and arrange for a new mortgage with the same lender or with a different lender.

Registered encumbrances. Legal claims against real property. Debt for which the property was pledged as security.

Renegotiate. To change the terms and conditions of a mortgage agreement prior to maturity. Renegotiation occurs with the lender who presently holds the mortgage.

Renew. To extend a mortgage agreement with the same lender for another term. The length of the term and the conditions (such as the rate of interest) may be changed.

Reserve fund. A fund set up by a condominium corporation for major repair and replacement of such things as roofs, plumbing, heating systems, etc. Sometimes referred to as a contingency fund.

Right of way. A form of easement, usually to allow public passage over private land or to allow municipalities and power companies the right to lay down and maintain sewers, gas lines, etc.

Second mortgage. A mortgage loan granted when there is already one other mortgage registered against the property. In case of default, the first mortgage is paid before the second mortgage from the proceeds of the sale of the property.

Security. Property offered as backing for a loan. In the case of mortgages, the property being purchased with the loan usually forms the security for the loan.

Semi-annual compounding. A compounding method in which one-half of the stated annual rate is assessed against the outstanding balance of a loan. This is a common form of interest calculation for mortgages.

Subject clauses. This is a term to describe a condition. Refer to the word "condition" in the glossary. In other words, the purchase of the home is subject to a condition that you have set being met.

Survey. A document that illustrates the exact quantity of land, the position of major structures on that property, any registered or visible easements or rights-of-way on the property, any building set-back requirements or zoning compliances or any encroachments.

Tenancy in common. Joint ownership of land in which each person's interest can be sold or transferred by means of a will.

Term. The length of time which a mortgage agreement covers. Payments made may not fully repay the outstanding principal by the end of the term because the amortization period is longer. The term is usually from six months to ten years.

Title search. Research of records in registry or land titles office to determine history and sequence of ownership of property.

Total debt service ratio (TDS). The percentage of gross annual income required to cover payments associated with housing *and* all other debts and obligations, such as payments on a car loan. Most lenders prefer the TDS not to exceed 40%.

Trust account. The separate account in which a lawyer or real estate broker holds funds until the real estate closing takes place.

Trust funds. Funds held in trust, either held as a deposit for the purchase of real property or to pay taxes and insurance.

Unit. Normally refers to part of a condominium owned and occupied or rented by the owner.

Usury. An unconscionable and exorbitant rate of interest.

Variable rate mortgage. A mortgage loan for which the rate of interest changes as money market conditions change, usually not more than once a month. The regular payment stays the same for a specified period. However, the amount applied towards the principal changes according to the change (if any) in the rate of interest. A *capped variable rate mortgage* means that the amount of interest that you will pay has a ceiling or cap, regardless of how high interest rates go.

Vendor take back. Where the seller (vendor) of a property provides some or all of the mortgage financing in order to sell the property. Also referred to as "vendor financing."

Warranty. This is a minor promise that does not go to the heart of the contract. If there is a breach of warranty, the purchaser cannot cancel but must complete the contract and sue for damages, that, is financial losses that can be shown.

Zoning. Specified limitation on the use of land and construction and use of building in a defined area of a municipality. For example, you cannot build a duplex on an area zoned for single-family dwellings.

ABOUT THE AUTHOR

Douglas Gray, B.A., LL.B., a lawyer by training, has extensive experience in all aspects of real estate and mortgage financing. He has acted on behalf of buyers, sellers, developers, investors, lenders, borrowers, tenants, and landlords. He also has wide experience as a personal investor in real estate, as well as being a landlord.

He is Canada's most prolific author/co-author of bestselling real estate and business books. He has written a total of 15 books on real estate, small business, personal finance and retirement planning. Please refer to the front of the book for a complete list under "Bestselling Books and Software Programs by Douglas Gray."

Mr. Gray gives seminars on real estate throughout Canada to the public and for professional development programs for the real estate industry. President of the National Real Estate Institute Inc., and the Canadian Enterprise Institute Inc., he is a recognized expert on real estate, small business, personal finance and retirement planning and is frequently quoted by the media as an authority. In addition, he has been a nationally syndicated weekly newspaper real estate columnist (*Streetsmarts*), and a regular guest expert on CBC-TV Newsworld. He is currently a columnist for over 12 national publications and has periodically contributed to the *Globe and Mail* and *Maclean's*.

He is a member of the following professional organizations: Canadian Bar Association, Canadian Association of Professional Speakers, National Speakers Association and the Periodical Writers Association of Canada.

Mr. Gray resides in Vancouver, B.C.

READER FEEDBACK AND EDUCATIONAL RESOURCES

Your candid feedback and constructive suggestions for improvement for future editions of this book is welcomed. Please write with your comments to the address below. In addition, if you would like information about customized educational seminars, consulting, and other educational services relating to real estate in Canada, please contact:

NATIONAL REAL ESTATE INSTITUTE INC.
#300-3665 Kingsway
Vancouver, B.C. V5R 5W2
Tel: (604) 436-3337
Fax: (604) 436-9155

ORDERING INFORMATION FOR OTHER BESTSELLING BOOKS AND SOFTWARE PROGRAMS
by Douglas Gray

Small Business Titles

The Complete Canadian Franchise Guide (with Norm Friend)
ISBN 0-07-551797-3

The Complete Canadian Small Business Guide (2nd edition)
(with Diana Gray)
ISBN 0-07-551661-6

Home Inc.: The Canadian Home-Based Business Guide (2nd edition)
(with Diana Gray)
ISBN 0-07-551558-X

Raising Money: The Canadian Guide to Successful Business Financing
(with Brian Nattrass)
ISBN 0-07-551490-2

Real Estate Titles

Making Money in Real Estate: The Canadian Residential Investment Guide
ISBN 0-07-549596-1

Canadian Home Buying Made Easy: A Streetsmart Guide for First-Time Home Buyers
ISBN 0-07-552900-9

Mortgages Made Easy: The Canadian Guide to Home Financing
ISBN 0-07-551344-7

Condo Buying Made Easy: The Canadian Guide to Apartment and Townhouse Condos, Co-ops and Timeshares (2nd edition)
ISBN 0-07-551791-4

Mortgage Payment Tables Made Easy: The Canadian Guide to Calculating Mortgage or Loan Interest
ISBN 0-07-551722-1

Personal Finance/Retirement Planning Titles

The Canadian Snowbird Guide: Everything You Need to Know About Living Part-time in the U.S.A. and Mexico
ISBN 0-07-560027-7

Software Programs (Disc/Manual/Book Albums)

Making Money in Real Estate (Jointly developed by Douglas Gray, Phoenix Accrual Corporation and McGraw-Hill Ryerson Limited)
ISBN 0-07-551856-2

Available at your local bookstore or by contacting:
McGraw-Hill Ryerson Limited, Trade & Professional Books Division
300 Water Street, Whitby, Ontario L1N 9B6
Phone: 1-800-565-5758/Fax: 1-800-463-5885 (orders only)
Visit our Website at http://www.mcgrawhill.ca

INDEX